WAYS OF KNOWING IN SCIENCE SERIES
Richard Duschl, Series Editor

ADVISORY BOARD: Charles W. Anderson,
Nancy Brickhouse, Rosalind Driver,
Eleanor Duckworth, Peter Fensham,
William Kyle, Roy Pea, Edward Silver, Russell Yeany

Reforming Science Education:
Social Perspectives and Personal Reflections
Rodger W. Bybee

D0061167

REFORMING SCIENCE EDUCATION

■ ■ ■ ■ ■ ■ ■

Social
Perspectives
and
Personal
Reflections

Rodger W. Bybee

with a Foreword by
Paul DeHart Hurd

TEACHERS COLLEGE PRESS
Teachers College, Columbia University
New York and London

Published by Teachers College Press, 1234 Amsterdam Avenue,
New York, NY 10027

Figure 2.1 is adapted from a sigmoid curve appearing in *The Survival of the Wisest,*
by Jonas Salk. Copyright © 1973 by Jonas Salk. Reprinted by permission of Harper
Collins Publishers.

Portions of Chapters 1, 2, 3, 6, and 9 are adapted from articles by Rodger Bybee first
appearing in *Science Education,* Vol. 61 (1) (1977), Vol. 63 (2) (1979) , Vol. 71 (5)
(1987), and *Journal of Research in Science Teaching,* 23 (7) (1986). Copyright © by
John Wiley & Sons, Inc.

"The Leader", by Roger McGough, from the Book *Sky in the Pie,* published by
Penguin Books, is reprinted by permission of the Peters Fraser & Dunlop
Group, Ltd.

Library of Congress Cataloging-in-Publication Data

Bybee, Rodger, W.
    Reforming science education: social perspectives and personal
reflections / Rodger W. Bybee.
       p.   cm.—(Ways of knowing in science series ; 1)
    Includes bibliographical references and index.
    ISBN 0-8077-3261-3 (alk. paper)—
    ISBN 0-8077-3260-5 (pbk. : alk. paper)
    1. Science—Study and teaching—United States.   2. Curriculum
change.   I. Title.   II. Series.
Q183.3.A1B93   1993
507.1'073—dc20   93-17231

ISBN 0-8077-3261-3
ISBN 0-8077-3260-5 (pbk.)

Printed on acid-free paper

Manufactured in the United States of America

98 97 96 95 94 93   8 7 6 5 4 3 2 1

For Patricia Ann

CONTENTS

FOREWORD

Since the early 1970s, there have been widespread efforts to change drastically the purposes for which science is taught. For the most part, reform has remained an illusion; the traditional mold has not been broken. A broad review of the factors that have caused the public to believe that schools are failing to respond to social changes will provide a background for the author's perspectives on the issues.

As a nation, we are leaving one era in our history and entering a new one. The change is as dramatic as the shift from agricultural to industrial societies. In the early 1970s, there was an array of publications by scholars portraying changes in our society and economy, in the ethos of modern science and technology, and in how people will live and work in future years. Kenneth E. Boulding describes the sum of the changes as a "cultural mutation."

Science and technology are recognized as lying at the center of the current shifts in our society. Education in the sciences and technology essential for living and adapting in the next century will require new goals, curricula, and instructional procedures. There is a consensus that the traditional programs of science education, which have endured for the past 200 years, should be reconceptualized.

Historically, the goals and subject matter of school science courses have been identified with knowing the "structure of disciplines" and engaging students in the use of the "scientific method." To achieve these goals, students have been required to memorize the technical language, symbols, and theoretical underpinnings of each discipline. The preferred instructional style has been a procedure that emphasized the "processes" of science in the context of a scientific inquiry. Unlike other subjects in the school curriculum, science is taught as career preparation for all students taking a science course.

In the midst of current social and cultural shifts, science has also changed. Modern science differs in a number of ways from that of past centuries. Since the turn of this century, the old boundaries that had separated the study of biology, chemistry, physics, geology, and astronomy have faded away. These disciplines and others have become fragmented into thousands upon thousands of research fields. No one knows how many research fields there are. We do know that more than 70,000 specialized journals exist to report research findings—29,000 of them founded since 1979.

Furthermore, traditional disciplines have been hybridized and renamed; for example, biochemistry, biophysics, astrophysics, biotechnology, biogeochemistry, and genetic engineering. Although *science* is a singular noun, it represents a wide range of research fields, each of which has its own language, conceptual base, and investigating procedures. The long-held notion of a value-free "scientific method" for doing science is now considered to be nothing more than a myth.

Research in modern science tends to be more holistic and integrative across fields than in past centuries. Today most research is done by teams consisting of theorists, technicians, and that very important member, the computer. Computers record and organize observations in various ways and propose interpretive models. Parallel computers are capable of relating observations to theory, providing an image of "actual reality." Whatever is learned from an experiment or investigation is seen as being forever tentative, in contrast to the notion of "basics" in traditional science.

One other feature of modern science is that research is more socially driven than theory-driven; witness the volume of research on controlling the AIDS pandemic, improving agriculture and the natural environment, gene therapy, extending human life, and (in the cognitive sciences) the learning and retention of knowledge.

Since midcentury, research in the life sciences has taken on new dimensions. The main thrust has been toward the study of the human species, the neurosciences, genetics, and human ecology. Investigations in the life sciences center in the hybrid fields of biochemistry and biophysics.

Advances in nearly all fields of science today are influenced by the marriage between science and technology. Today, science and technology operate as an integrated system for extending the production of new knowledge. The tunneling scanning microscope makes it possible to observe chemical bonding in living cells, and a new ultrafast laser is capable of breaking specific chemical bonds, enabling one to watch chemistry happen as it happens. Immediate applications include new studies of vision, photosynthesis, oxygen and hemoglobin, and protein structures.

There has been a revolution not only in the research processes of science but also in how science impacts on our society, our economy, and our lives. Achievements in science and technology have led to a global economy that is rapidly giving rise to a world community. The competitive position of any country today rests primarily upon its ability to produce and make use of the knowledge generated in the sciences and technology. The primary assets of a nation are no longer natural resources and brawn, but rather the production and utilization of knowledge. This trend has resulted in concepts of developing "human capital" and "human resources" as purposes of education.

These unparalleled changes in our society, in science, and in the economy have implications for precollege education in the sciences. With the publication of *A Nation at Risk* in 1983, the National Commission on Excellence in Education identified what these changes should mean for transforming science teaching.

The movement to reform education got off to a false start. What happened in schools following the publication of *A Nation at Risk* was a variety of uncoordinated efforts to correct problems related to schooling generally. Nationwide, close to 1,000 mandates were legislated, such as requiring more science and mathematics courses for high school graduation, making science courses more rigorous, demanding more training for teachers, lengthening the school day and year, increasing the testing of students and teachers, and redefining the authority and responsibilities of school administrators. Mostly these actions simply support the status quo of science education and neglect the basic issues in need of reform.

Since 1983, nearly 400 national reports have been published by panels, committees, and commissions representing public pressure to transform schooling in some meaningful way. A third of these reports have come from business and industry groups identifying the attitudes, intellectual skills, and knowledge required to meet the demands of a modern work force. They have made it clear that future workers will need to work smarter than in previous generations, whatever their job or career. Furthermore, the rate at which new knowledge and technology are being generated, as well as shifting societal and economic factors, will likely cause one's occupational qualifications to become outmoded four or five times during one's working life. This reality has resulted in making "learning to learn" a primary goal of science instruction. UNESCO reports that "learning to learn" is the one educational goal common to all of the 141 countries in the process of developing new science curricula. *America 2000: An Educational Strategy* describes this goal in terms of transforming the United States into "a learning society" and a "nation of learners."

Since the science curriculum reform of the 1960s, the cognitive sciences have provided new insights into human learning. Some of these are

1. New learning is influenced by what the student already knows.
2. What is to be learned by the student is limited by the extent to which it makes sense or is perceived to have personal relevance.
3. Not all students learn in the same way.

4. What is to be learned is influenced by the instructional environment of the class.
5. The extent to which much of what is remembered is limited by the degree to which it is generalizable, particularly to personal and social affairs.

Traditionally, what is learned in science courses, mostly vocabulary, is soon forgotten. Too much of teaching serves to frustrate learning; students need opportunities to invest in their own learning. These learning insights have implications for instruction as well as for the curriculum. Although an overall theory of human learning has yet to evolve, enough has been learned to make much of the prevailing subject matter in science curricula and styles of instruction outmoded.

When the national debate on new perspectives for science education began in the early 1970s, Rodger Bybee began his personal reflections on issues related to science teaching. These reflections were carried on within the framework of the influence of science and technology on modern society and its meaning for science teaching. In this book, Bybee uses a new form of scholarship that combines experience and expertise to evolve new perspectives for science teaching. These reflections extend over more than a decade. Each phase of his thinking is described, thus providing a stimulus for all of us to ponder and discuss as we refocus our thoughts on transforming precollege education in the sciences.

The past history of efforts to reform science teaching in the United States is briefly reviewed in the context of social changes. This approach provides an avenue for avoiding practices that the past shows were faulted.

The national science education reform movement began to take shape in the late 1970s, giving rise to two new reform themes: the concept of scientific literacy and a science–technology–society context for science teaching. The author points out the connections between these two themes in terms of the individual and society. These attributes are central to Bybee's concept of an ecological society as a meaningful framework for modern science curricula. Throughout the whole of the reform movement, there has been a lack of vision in describing what an education in science should mean. Nearly all professional science education societies have published lists of resolutions, position statements, standards, guidelines, policies, or requirements related to modernizing education in the sciences. While many lists contain visionary statements, a coherent rationale that binds them together to provide a map for reform has not emerged.

Bybee emphasizes that any effective transformation of science teaching rests with the teacher. Here the first step is helping each teacher to understand and internalize the new purposes of science teaching. Teachers teach what they believe in. The next step is to transform one's beliefs into teaching models that are consistent with the latest findings about learning. This approach to science education reform is in contrast to that of the 1960s, when it was assumed that if teachers simply knew more science, the reform would be assured. History has demonstrated otherwise.

Bybee then points out that the implementation of a reform requires the support of the school's administration as well as appropriate instructional resources, such as budget, equipment, and textbooks. He cautions that even under the best of conditions, curriculum changes take place slowly.

The history of curriculum reforms in precollege sciences is a history of failure. There is hope that perhaps the current reform movement will be successful, but 20 years have now passed since the reform began. Historians of education have observed that a typical educational reform effort lasts about 4 years before it fades away. The current reform movement is different. The crisis is seen as extending beyond students as individuals to the nation as a whole. The 1983 report of the National Committee on Excellence made it clear that the prevailing school science curricula were placing the *nation* at risk.

Failure of professional educators to perceive the national educational reform led President Bush to call a summit meeting in 1989, the first ever for education and only the third in our nation's history. Summit meetings are held only when the future of the country is viewed as threatened. All 50 state governors were invited to attend the meeting, one outcome of which was the formation of a national council to establish a national educational goals panel to identify new directions for precollege education in the United States. Their report was sent to Congress for debate and released to the public in 1991 as *America 2000: An Educational Strategy*.

Within the first year, half of the state governors, as well as more than 2,000 local communities, agreed to support proposals made in *America 2000*. It describes the task ahead for curriculum reform as one that "sets aside traditional conceptions" and creates a "new generation of schools" with "far-reaching changes" that are "bold, complex, and long range." This is also the tone of the more than 400 national reports on education proposed by public interest groups.

Bybee concludes his book with a discussion of the kind of leadership essential for effecting a reform of science education. After examining the issues in different educational contexts, he proposes a model for educational leadership. Yet to be determined is the influence of the federal government in setting national goals and standards for science teaching, then establishing assessment criteria and developing national tests.

However we approach the task of reform in science teaching, the venture will not be easy, much as noted in 1513 by Machiavelli in *The Prince:* "There is nothing more difficult to carry out and more doubtful of success, nor more dangerous to handle than to initiate a new order of things."

Paul DeHart Hurd
Professor Emeritus
Stanford University

PREFACE

I wrote the essays in *Reforming Science Education: Social Perspectives and Personal Reflections* over two decades. The title presents the general theme of reforming science education and my specific interest in the personal and social goals of science teaching.

In Part I, written in the mid-to-late 1970s, I predict that science education is in the early stages of a transformation and provide a historical perspective on changes in goals and curricula. In this section, I also suggest identifiable phases of reform. The second chapter describes a social perspective that should influence the transformation. The final chapter in Part I elaborates aims and goals of science education in a personal and social context.

In the early 1980s, science educators used the phrase *scientific literacy* to represent the goals of science education. In Part II, I use the myth of Sisyphus and the question "What should the scientifically and technologically literate person know, value, and do as a citizen?" to help focus and clarify discussions of scientific literacy. The 1980s also witnessed the emergence of science–technology–society (STS) as a new theme in science education. The chapters in Part II explore the connections between scientific literacy and the STS theme.

Part III consists of three articles united by the contemporary challenges of reform and the lack of change in various aspects of science education. The first chapter uses evolution as a metaphor for the process of change in teachers and teaching. The second chapter addresses the contemporary global crisis and the fact that science educators have not responded in any significant way. The final chapter is a critical analysis of STS.

Part IV consists of one chapter on leadership, responsibility, and the reform of science education. I wrote the chapter as an answer to the persistent question about what we have to do to bring about reform in science education. My answer places responsibility on the shoulders of ALL those within the community of science education and investigates the possibility of distributed leadership among science educators.

Each part of the book has an introductory statement that establishes a context for the section and discusses my thinking at the time the articles were written and published. The sections conclude with my reflections on the chapters. The reflection on the articles in each part of the book provides an opportunity to answer the questions "What is different now?" and "What would I say now?" There are some things I would change in the chapters, and issues I would give a different emphasis. Rather than making major changes in the essays, I added this final reflection on each section. I express my personal and social perspectives in the introductions and reflections.

I used several criteria to select the articles for this book. I wrote all the essays without co-authors, and the articles were published in refereed volumes. After determining the major parts of the book, I limited myself to three essays per part; I did this because there were instances in which I planned and wrote the articles in sets of three and also because three articles is probably a sufficient statement on most topics. Finally, the articles were edited only for language, style, and clarity. I did not make any substantive changes. There is some similarity among articles because I consistently appeal for a personal and social perspective and develop themes related to this perspective. However, I tried to select essays that minimize repetition.

Upon reading these articles, I realized that I owe a professional debt and personal acknowledgment to some individuals who contributed in various ways to the development of my ideas. For 25 years, I have benefited from the intellectual leadership of Paul DeHart Hurd. In recent years, I have enjoyed his friendship and was honored when he agreed to write the Foreword for this book. F. James Rutherford's advice and counsel on my doctoral dissertation established the foundation for many of the ideas I later developed and subsequently present in this volume. While at Carleton College, I had the privilege to teach with Ian G. Barbour, whose ideas and writing about theology and the environment contributed to the formulation of ideas I develop in the first chapters in this book. Likewise, my discussions with Ed Buchwald clarified many of the scientific and environmental concepts.

In the late 1970s, I had the opportunity to work on Project Synthesis and collaborated with Paul DeHart Hurd of Stanford University, Jane Butler Kahle of Miami University of Ohio, and Robert Yager of the University of Iowa to review biology education. Work on Project Synthesis and interactions with these individuals provided valuable insights and ideas that eventually found their way into my essays.

In recent years, I have profited from insightful reviews and criticisms by Audrey Champagne of the State University of New York at Albany, stimulating and challenging discussions with Joseph McInerney of the Biological Sciences Curriculum Study (BSCS), and supportive and constructive conversations with Paul Kuerbis of Colorado College.

This book began with an initial suggestion and subsequent encouragement from Richard Duschl of the University of Pittsburgh and editor for the series. Brian Ellerbeck of Teachers College Press continually expressed confidence in the project. I also wish to acknowledge the contributions of Cathy McClure, Karen Osborne, and Neil Stillman. They had the difficult task of editing the manuscript and smoothing differences in style and pointing out inconsistencies attributable to the use of articles over a 25-year period and not originally intended as chapters for a book.

For seven years, C. Yvonne Wise has been my executive assistant. I recognize her extraordinary word-processing skills, her talent as an editor, and her attention to detail; but more importantly, I acknowledge her continued understanding, support, and friendship.

I also wish to acknowledge my colleagues at BSCS, many of whom read or heard me discuss a number of ideas I present in this book. I especially appreciate the support BSCS provided for the early development of several chapters.

Finally, I dedicate this book to my wife, Patricia. Over the years, she has supported my writing and contributed in countless ways to each chapter in this book.

Part I

■ ■ ■ ■ ■ ■ ■ ■ ■

PERSPECTIVES ON SCIENCE EDUCATION

In the closing years of the twentieth century and the opening years of the twenty-first century, science education will witness significant reform. As I write this statement in 1992, it is more an observation than a prediction because everywhere one looks, from national to local levels, there is evidence of reform. The essays and articles in this part date from the mid-to-late 1970s, the time when I first began discussing the reform of science education.

The essays in this book have several themes. To begin with, we should reexamine the goals of science education because they are critically important to any science curriculum as well as to effective teaching. We must also consider the interaction between society and science education, since these interactions result in different priorities for the goals of science education. Social issues such as population growth, resource use, and environmental degradation are important, and I believe they should receive greater attention in science education programs. Finally, I present a theme of transformation or reform. Science education has always been in a process of change, but sometimes there are significant periods of transformation. I predict that the late twentieth century will mark the greatest such reform in our history.

In 1975 I completed my dissertation, *Implications of the Philosophy and Psychology of Abraham H. Maslow for Science Education in the United States*. In order to describe the implications of Maslow's ideas, I had to develop a perspective on science education that included the histories and philosophies of science and education. My major advisor, F. James Rutherford, encouraged me to develop an insightful history of science education, one based on goals. As a result, I applied the ideas of structuralism to an analysis of the history of science education in the United States.

The underlying structures of science education are goals, but these goals change over time. In the dissertation, I described how particular goals, such as teaching scientific knowledge, can be redefined over time. This is one type of change. A second type of change involves differences in priorities for goals. Finally, a third type of change involves the long-term waxing or waning of a goal in the structure of science education. As an example of the first type of change, I characterized the goal of scientific knowledge as changing from facts and information in the 1800s to conceptual schemes and major unifying themes in the late 1900s. An example of the second type of change is demonstrated by the priority of a goal such as personal development during the nature study movement at the turn of the century and its relatively low priority, especially at the secondary level, in the 1960s reform movement. The third type of change is exemplified by a goal, such as understanding and using scientific methods, gaining priority in science education policies and programs but not necessarily in classroom practices.

In the mid-1970s, many science educators realized that the major reform of the 1960s was over. Society was no longer focusing attention on space and beating the Russians to the moon. Domestic problems, the war in Vietnam, and environmental problems ranked high on the national agenda. In education, we also had a different agenda. What had been a period of enthusiasm and support for science education during the 1960s became an era of crisis and criticism in the 1970s.

I planned and developed the three articles in Part I as a set. In the first chapter, I use historical examples as a way of analyzing the dynamic qualities of goals in science education. In the latter part of the chapter, I propose different phases of transformation or reform in science education. In the second chapter, I emphasize the social forces influencing contemporary reform. Finally, in the third chapter, I present a contemporary discussion of goals. The following paragraphs present more detailed introductions to the chapters in this section.

Chapter 1, "The New Transformation of Science Education," was written in the mid-1970s and is largely based on the historical analysis from my dissertation. The themes of goals for science education and the interaction of society and science education are the significant ideas in this essay.

During this same period, I taught a course on "Sustainable Society" at Carleton College with Ian Barbour. Chapter 2, "Science Education and the Emerging Ecological Society," developed from my synthesis of the readings on social change and the environment I did for the course. At this time, I was convinced that we needed to name the new social order that was evolving. Some authors described it as a *postindustrial society,* but this term is merely a chronological indication of something that came after industrial society. I preferred *ecological society* because it helped orient public policies in general and the goals of science education in particular.

After my excursion into social change, I returned immediately to science education in Chapter 3, "Science Education Policies for an Ecological Society: Aims and Goals," in which I discuss the importance of translating purposes into policies, programs, and practices. I have found the idea of translating purposes to practices valuable in analyzing various aspects of the contemporary reform. An essential point that I began here and develop in later chapters is the continuity of translations from purpose to policy to programs to practices. Because I have found it helpful, I return to it in later chapters in this book.

Chapter 1

■ ■ ■ ■ ■ ■ ■ ■

THE NEW TRANSFORMATION OF SCIENCE EDUCATION

Throughout American history, changes in society have evoked calls for reform in education, and many today think a reform of American education is in order (Passow, 1975). Science education is no exception; and contemporary social issues are eliciting a transformation of science education. In the past, major changes in science education occurred in response to historical and social circumstances. Likewise, the current transformation in science education reflects some aspects of historical changes. In this chapter, I set forth a basic structure of science education and describe various historical models of science curriculum derived from these basic structural elements. I also present sequential steps of transformation in the models of science teaching and, finally, suggest issues that are presently influencing the reform of science education. In so doing, I demonstrate that science education has undergone transformations in the past and that it is presently in a period of transformation concerning its fundamental aims and hence the models of science curriculum and teaching.

STRUCTURE OF SCIENCE EDUCATION

Many conceive the structure of science education in terms of five major aims that underlie the organization of curriculum and instruction:

1. Empirical *knowledge* of physical and biological systems
2. Scientific *methods* of investigation
3. *Personal development* of the student
4. *Social development,* or achieving the aspirations of society (often referred to as citizenship)
5. *Career awareness*

This chapter is adapted from an article originally published as "The New Transformation of Science Education," *Science Education, 61*(1), 85–97, 1977.

After clarification of these aims I return to the organization of curriculum and instruction. I use models of curriculum and instruction to express the structure and emphasis of the aims in science education programs.

The Aims of Science Education

The first aim of science education is to provide students with the range of accumulated observation and systematic information about the universe. The facts, concepts, generalizations, and conceptual schemes generated by scientists are a part of this aim. Also included are the abstract ways knowledge may be organized (the structure of a discipline) and the functional applications of knowledge (technology). The knowledge taught is usually associated with a specific subject, for example, chemistry or geology. When constructing curricula or planning instruction, science educators consider this aim in answering the question: "What do scientists know in a specific discipline or disciplines?"

The second aim encompasses the techniques of investigation, the required skills of inquiry, the processes scientists use to produce new knowledge, and the personal attitudes important for scientific inquiry. Scientific skills and activities (such as observation, collection of data, formulation of hypotheses, and experimentation) as well as scientific attitudes (such as openness, recognition of error, and honesty) are among the various aspects of this second aim. In general, this aim exists in all sciences, and the role of methods in science education is most accurately portrayed as both content and process (Rutherford, 1964). With respect to curriculum or instruction, science educators consider this aim in answering the questions: "What do scientists do?" and "How is knowledge generated by scientists?"

In planning curriculum and instruction, educators must also consider the development of students, including the intellectual, emotional, physical, and social requisites of the students for assimilating the knowledge and methods of science. The aim incorporates all areas of education and is defined by each student or group of students in a classroom. As used in this chapter, development is not necessarily aligned with a specific theory, for example, that of Piaget or Skinner; it is used in a general sense. This aim influences the way educators answer the question: "What can the student or students know and do at a particular age or grade level?"

That science education should prepare citizens to make responsible decisions concerning science-related social issues is the fourth aim. This aim informs the answer that educators give to the question: "How will students contribute to the maintenance and aspirations of society?"

The fifth goal of science education is career awareness. Although important, the aim has never achieved major importance in curriculum and instruction; thus it is not prominent in this chapter.

Models of Curriculum and Instruction

The organization of curriculum and instruction in science reflects the way in which the aims are structured. Different aims and different arrangements of the aims account for the range of approaches to classroom science teaching. in order to clarify what is meant by the organization of science curriculum and instruction, an example from the performing arts may help. Three underlying elements in the performing arts are story, gesture, and music. But the priority given these basic elements results in three entirely different art forms. Drama emphasizes the story, followed by gesture and music; in ballet, gesture is the primary element, then music and story; opera grants primacy to music over story and gesture. Although these arts include all three elements in some form, they are very different because of the ways they emphasize, modify, and vary these elements. The same is true for science curriculum and instruction. For example, if a science teacher has decided that knowledge of conceptual schemes is *the* important aim of instruction, then the teacher would include some emphasis on method, social issues, and personal development in designing the science program. Science concepts would dominate the selection of topics and design of curriculum. However, the curriculum and instruction with personal development as the primary aim would be very different. In this case, topics and experiences that focus on students' interests and motivations would have priority over concepts. Science teachers would introduce concepts that complemented student experiences.

Examination and organization of these aims is a useful way of describing historical changes, present differences, and contemporary trends in science curriculum and instruction. Several examples from the history of science education in the United States should help clarify the structure of science education and the role of societal influence in forming and reforming this structure.

HISTORICAL MODELS OF SCIENCE TEACHING

In this section, I use three historical examples to demonstrate different models of science teaching and to show how societal pressures affect the aims and structure of science education. One is from the elementary level at the turn of the century; one is from the secondary level in the

1930s; and the last is from the curriculum reform movements of the 1960s and 1970s. Obviously, this section is not intended as a comprehensive history of science education.

Elementary School Science, Circa 1900

In the late 1800s, the combination of industrial expansion and migrations from rural areas to urban centers led to two models of science teaching at the elementary level. One was a knowledge-oriented model referred to as "elementary science"; the other was nature study and had personal development as its primary aim.

Changes in society resulting from a developing technology created a popular interest in science and gave impetus to elementary science. "The chief emphasis during this period [about 1880] was in terms of giving a wider knowledge and understanding of the rapidly increasing science and technology" (Underhill, 1941, p. 111). There were several educational leaders who contributed to this model of elementary science, namely, Francis Parker, Wilbur Jackman, William T. Harris, and E. G. Howe.

Francis Parker's model used a unifying theme for the elementary school. He wanted students to understand the universe and to use scientific techniques as a means of solving problems (Underhill, 1941). Wilbur Jackman worked with him at the Cook County Normal School, with his support developing an elementary science program that had scientific generalizations as the major organizational aims and the use of observation and experimentation as methodological goals (Jackman, 1891). Jackman's model had scientific knowledge as the primary aim and scientific methods as a secondary aim. It is interesting to note that Jackman gave the title "nature study" to his elementary science program, and his book (Jackman, 1891) gives considerable attention to scientific methodology. In fact, his methodological ideas were later of considerable influence on the nature study movement.

William T. Harris often receives credit for formulating the first substantial elementary science program (Underhill, 1941). The Harris model accented the relationship of ideas and used science, as opposed to other disciplines, as an organizational framework. E. G. Howe (1894) later changed the Harris science curriculum into a program entitled *Systematic Science Teaching*. Howe's program was conceptually similar to the Harris model, but as a curriculum, it was more elaborate. The common factor among these models during the period from 1870 to 1900 was the dominance of scientific knowledge as their aim. My thesis is that these models were substantially influenced by the transition of this country from an agrarian to an industrial–technological society.

Nature study was designed as a countervailing force to slow or stop the emigration of people from rural agricultural communities to urban industrial centers. Many people who had migrated from rural to urban environments found themselves unemployed and swelling relief rolls in the cities. Science education programs were seen by some as the remedy to this social problem. In 1895, the Committee for the Promotion of Agriculture in New York State and the New York Association for Improving the Condition of the Poor (Underhill, 1941) called a joint conference. The conference examined the causes and possible remedies for the agricultural depression; many individuals turned to nature study as a possible solution. The nature study idea had originated in 1893 as the vision of Liberty Hyde Bailey; in the context of the aforementioned needs of society, the idea gained prominence in education. Nature study was supported as a way of interesting children in farming, thereby slowing emigration to cities. "Nature study was the great remedy for the alienation of man from the land and from his neighbor" (Cremin, 1964, p. 77).

Liberty Hyde Bailey directed the nature study program at Cornell University. Over the years, Bailey and his associates were instrumental in developing and disseminating materials representing this second model of science teaching at the elementary level. Bailey (1903) contrasted nature study with elementary science in his book *The Nature Study Idea*:

> Nature study is a revolt from the teaching of mere science in the elementary grades. In teaching practice, the work and the methods of the two [elementary science and nature study] integrate . . . and as the high school and college are approached, nature study passes into science teaching, or gives way to it; but the ideals are distinct—they should be contrasted rather than compared. Nature study is not science. [It is not facts.] It is concerned with the child's outlook on the world. (p. 4)

Bailey continued, making the distinction between nature study and elementary science clear:

> Nature may be studied with either of two objects: to discover new truths for the purpose of increasing the sum of human knowledge; or to put the pupil in a sympathetic attitude toward nature for the purpose of increasing his joy of living. The first object, whether pursued in a technical or elementary way, is a science-teaching movement, and its professed purpose is to make investigators and specialists. The second object is a nature study movement, and its purpose is to enable everyone to live a richer life, whatever his business or profession may be. (pp. 4–5).

These quotations clearly outline the differences between the knowledge and the development models of science curriculum. The social conditions supported both curriculum models. The combination of an emerging industrial–technological society and the need to maintain a substantial agricultural base for society as well as reduce the unemployed in the large cities influenced the development of different curriculum models. Thus a nature study model, which stressed personal development and appreciation of nature, and an elementary science model, which stressed scientific knowledge and methods, were both implemented by science educators.

Secondary School Science, Circa 1930

Historically, at the secondary level, the knowledge model of science teaching has been the most popular one. High school teachers made their position quite clear concerning the nature study model:

> High school teachers of science must protest against a mass of so-called nature study, more or less sentimental and worthless . . . and must not be content simply with treating lightly this farcical science teaching, or passing it by with silent contempt. (Brownell, 1903, p. 253)

Scientific knowledge continued to be the dominant goal of secondary science teaching. In 1932, the federal Office of Education conducted a national survey of secondary education that included a review of science teaching guides, courses of study, and syllabi. The results were published in a monograph entitled *Instruction in Science* (U.S. Department of the Interior, 1932). A review of the objectives indicates that knowledge was the primary aim of science instruction, followed by an emphasis on scientific methods. The methodological aim, as I described earlier, is concerned with exploration (or orientation to science), abilities, attitudes, ideals, habits, and interests.

Another 1932 study compared the objectives of secondary science teachers and members of the National Association of Research in Science Teaching (NARST) (Hunter & Knapp, 1932). In 1938, NARST replicated the 1932 survey of secondary science teachers (*Report of the Committee on Secondary School Science,* 1938) and reported:

> By far, the greatest emphasis is placed by both groups (junior and senior high school science teachers) on the acquisition of useful general information and practical understandings which come from contacts with science. (p. 224)

These three reports indicate the dominant influence of scientific knowledge as the aim of secondary science teaching during the 1930s.

The aim of introducing students to the methods and experiences of scientific investigation had been discussed in the literature of science education for some time, and during the early part of the twentieth century the aim received new support. John Dewey (1938) strongly criticized the knowledge model of education. His pragmatic philosophy reaffirmed the thesis that education should be functional, center on the student, and reflect the realities of the time—which included solving many social problems. One of Dewey's significant contributions to science education was his contention that the methods of science were as important as the knowledge of science. As early as 1916, Dewey had strongly advocated an experimental model of science teaching. For Dewey, the psychological link between experience and knowledge was the effective solution of problems through the "scientific method." He stated the goal of teaching as: "The end of science teaching is to make us aware of what constitutes the more effective use of mind, of intelligence" (1938, p. 120). Dewey later stated:

> What is desired of the pupil is that starting from the ordinary unclassed material of experience he shall acquire command of the points of view, the ideas and methods, which make it physical or chemical or whatever . . . the dynamic point of view is the really scientific one, or the understanding of *process* as the heart of the scientific attitude. (1938, p. 122; emphasis)

In the context of the science curriculum, Dewey's aim of reflective thinking became the presentation of a *problem,* formation of a *hypothesis, experimentation, collection of data,* and finally, reaching a *conclusion.*

The conviction that teaching the scientific method was an important aim of science education received support from other individuals during this period. Hurd (1961) reports:

> Many scientists in this time [1920–1930] expressed the opinion that the central purpose of education in science should be the development of an understanding of the nature of science, its methods, attitudes, and cultural impact. As a result, much educational research in the succeeding years was directed toward identifying the elements of the scientific method and scientific attitudes. (p. 51).

The aim of teaching the scientific method had further support in other journals (e.g., *On the Place of Science in Education,* 1928) and books (e.g., National Society for the Study of Education, 1932; Progressive Education Association, 1938).

During the period from 1920 to 1940, the knowledge model of secondary science continued to dominate science curriculum, although an increasing emphasis was also placed on scientific methods as an important focus of that curriculum. The knowledge model reflected a back-to-basics posture often associated with times of economic austerity. I believe the emphasis on scientific methods was an educational manifestation of the need to solve the many social problems of the time. School systems changed their fundamental aims in response to the Great Depression. Similar changes had also occurred during the earlier depressions of the 1830s, 1850s, and 1870s. Education today is again experiencing pressures because of economic austerity, and we can expect the acceleration of normal evolutionary change (Ravitch, 1976).

Curriculum Reform, Circa 1960

My last example is from the curriculum reform movement of the 1960s. A perceived science manpower shortage in America triggered the curriculum reform movement that has subsequently been symbolized in the *Sputnik*-spurred space race with the Soviet Union. Whether Soviet superiority was real or imagined, in the late 1950s and early 1960s this country responded as though it was real and moved the new frontier to space. Although there are some who doubt the importance of *Sputnik I* as an incentive for change because reform was already in progress prior to the launch (National Science Foundation, NSF, 1965), without the symbol created by *Sputnik,* curriculum reform probably would have been much less.

Curriculum reform in the early 1960s adopted a model of science education described by Jerome Bruner (1960) in *The Process of Education.* Scientific knowledge was the dominant aim, and scientific method was the means to achieve this aim. In Bruner's model, knowledge consisted of science concepts forming the structure of a discipline. Bruner states his aim: "The curriculum of a subject should be determined by the most fundamental understanding that can be achieved of the underlying principles that give structure to that subject" (p. 31).

By 1964, scientific knowledge and methods were firmly established as the important aims in science education. The National Science Teachers Association (NSTA) publication *Theory into Action* (NSTA, 1964) made this point clear. The aims were now called "the conceptual schemes of science" and "the process of science." At the elementary level, these aims were later used as the primary orientation for a Conceptually Oriented Program in Elementary Science (COPES) (Barnard, 1971) and Science—A Process Approach (S-APA) (Gagne, 1967), two excellent examples illustrating different curriculum models and basic structures of science education.

There were three significant structural changes during the early 1960s: (1) The importance of the aims emphasizing personal and social development declined, particularly at the secondary level (Hurd, 1969); (2) the knowledge aim was revised, updated, and made the primary aim, particularly in the secondary level; and (3) scientific methods were implemented as the means to achieve the goal of knowledge. Although the aims of personal and social development were virtually eliminated at the secondary level, they remained intact at the elementary level, primarily due to the influence of Piaget's theory of cognitive development (Piaget, 1973).

A 1962 essay by Ralph Tyler, "Forces Redirecting Science Teaching," makes clear the influence of society on the changes in science education during this major period of transformation. Tyler cited the major forces redirecting science education as the technological revolution and the decreasing number of students entering careers associated with science and technology. He also pointed out the vast difference between the science programs that existed and the needs of those who were entering careers aligned with science. Finally, he listed the relationship between scientists and science teachers, the knowledge explosion, and the variety of student needs as other forces redirecting science education.

As a brief digression, I would point out that a stated objective of the curriculum reform in the 1960s was to increase the number of individuals pursuing careers in science and engineering. Yet this goal was to be achieved through a curriculum model dominated by the goal of scientific knowledge and lacking in materials that explicitly focused on career awareness. Early editions of programs such as PSSC physics, BSCS biology, and CBA and CHEM-study chemistry make little or no mention of careers related to these science disciplines, not to mention engineering and technology.

Criticisms of Bruner's model (Cremin, 1965; Hurd, 1970) and new social issues brought about another transformation, beginning in the mid-1960s. Urban problems arising from massive population migrations to the cities gained the attention of science educators. Many of these problems were associated with the neglected developmental aim, for example, self-concept, identify, and alienation. Human needs were not met by the ever-increasing technological morass; there was a "revolt of the diminished man" (MacLeish, 1965), and the existing image of man was stressed to the breaking point (Matson, 1966). During this time, such environmental problems as overpopulation and pollution also became common social themes. Again, society turned to science education for solutions. By 1970, influential science educators of the early 1960s, such as Jerome Bruner and Paul DeHart Hurd, were reemphasizing the developmental aim (Bruner, 1971; Hurd, 1970). Concern for the developmental aim was also shown by renewed interest in Piaget's theory (1973), discussions of humanistic psychology (Bybee & Welch, 1972), and humanistic approaches to science teaching (Bybee, 1974; Rutherford, 1972). When compared to the publications of the early 1960s, the 1971 NSTA publication *School*

Science Education for the 70s gives a more balanced recognition of scientific knowledge, methods, and personal/social development through the expressed goal of scientific literacy. There were also new science programs that gave considerable emphasis to developmental aims, for example, *Human Sciences Project, Environmental Studies,* and *Human Behavior Curriculum Project.*

TRANSFORMATION IN SCIENCE EDUCATION

Although questions concerning the transformation in science education are complex and do not lend themselves to easy answers, there are some lessons we can learn from the history of science education—lessons from the underlying characteristics of the process of change, not just from the observable results of change. In this section, I adapt a model of transformation from the writings of George Leonard (1973, 1974) and apply it to the history of science education. There are five basic steps to reforming science education:

1. New perceptions of science teaching
2. The establishment of the new perceptions through publications by significant people
3. The elaboration of theoretical constructs of the new model
4. New curriculum materials
5. Implementation of new programs

New Perceptions

Prior to the reform movement of the 1960s, science curricula and instruction simply had not kept up with the changes in science and technology. The textbooks, for example, had undergone limited reforms for some 30 years, but they were largely outmoded by the advances of scientific–technological–industrial society (Hurd, 1970; NSTA, 1964). The disparity between what was taught and the *Zeitgeist* forced new perceptions of science teaching, and these new perceptions came largely from the scientists and science educators who directed curriculum projects and developed new materials. The new perceptions led to emphasis on the old but now-accepted inquiry approach, fundamental changes in content, and large-scale classroom testing of materials before publishing. As pointed out earlier, two important changes in the goals of science education were modifications of the knowledge aim and inclusion of the methods aim in the science curriculum. By 1960, these two aims were prominent in the massive rethinking of science education (NSSE, 1960). So, the limited nature of the old materials became evident in the 1950s when juxtaposed with societal demands and the spirit of the times. From such an encounter, the synthesis of new perceptions of science teaching can arise.

Publications by Leaders

Close behind the new perceptions comes the second step in the development of the new vision. The thoughts and concepts related to the new perceptions shape a guide to action. For example, Gerald Craig's 1927 dissertation became a guide for elementary science materials in the 1930s and Jerome Bruner's *The Process of Education* (1960) and "The Act of Discovery" (1961) were guides for many elementary and secondary projects in the 1960s. These individuals' publications influenced the direction of other literature, research, and curriculum development as well. The person becomes identified with the changes, and constructive direction becomes aligned with the new vision. If this second step does not occur, the new perceptions are ineffectual in the face of older models of science teaching. But when there is a guide such as Bruner's, the new perceptions are then disseminated by the energy of those associated with the new vision.

Policies for Curriculum

The third step is the development of specific frameworks in science curricula and instruction. Bruner's claim that knowledge aligns with the structure of a discipline required translation by the physicists, chemists, biologists, or earth scientists. Perhaps the clearest example of the third and fourth steps is seen in the NSTA publication *Theory in Action* (1964). In the first section, Hurd discusses a theory of science education consistent with modern science. Among other important points, Hurd indicates that science teaching should lead to an understanding of the conceptual structure of science and the modes of scientific inquiry. Later, the publication presents conceptual schemes and processes of science. The third step provides comprehensive policies, frameworks, and a sense of direction for the needed changes in science education. In education, however, policies and blueprints are not enough; specific curriculum materials must be developed.

New Curriculum Materials

Development of curriculum materials is the fourth step. Theory was translated into curricula in numerous ways during the reform movement, informed by the perceptions, vision, policies, and models described above.

At the secondary level, for example, PSSC physics, CBA, CHEM-study chemistry, BSCS biology, and ESCP earth science, all have knowledge of the particular discipline as the major aim and methods of inquiry as the secondary aim. At the elementary level, COPES and S-APA reflect these same aims, but with a different emphasis for the respective programs. (I would note that the Elementary Science Study [ESS] materials emphasized the aim of personal development.)

Implementation of New Programs

The fifth step is the difficult task of implementation, which involves changing the old perceptions of science teachers (Rutherford, 1971). In the recent transformation of science education, *inquiry* and *discovery* have been key words describing the processes of science. These two words have subsequently been used as adjectives to describe the science materials, textbooks, articles, research studies, and numerous other sources for science teaching, all contributing to the slow change in the values and biases of individuals in the science education community. If the perceptions of science teachers continue to change until a critical mass has accepted the new model, it is safe to say that the transformation is complete. The model then stands, undergoing limited reform, until societal needs again clamor for recognition and a new transformation in the structure of science education is called for.

At the beginning of this chapter, I claimed that science education is in a period of transformation. The next section explores the question: "Which societal factors are influencing the transformation in science education?"

CONTEMPORARY SOCIETY AND SCIENCE EDUCATION

There are at least five factors that are presently influencing science education: economic, environmental, ethical, societal, and global. I have organized the discussion of these factors from the most to the least concrete and from those of immediate importance to those of long-range significance. As will be seen, however, they are all related.

Economic Factors

The first set of conditions influencing science education is economic. Little has to be said about inflation, the recession, and the ever-present possibility of a depression. Economic conditions have resulted in demands from many citizens, for a safe and secure education that translates into emphasizing functional knowledge, vocations, and careers, all in an attempt to increase employment opportunities. The knowledge and methods aims of science teaching have been given new support in such trends as the call for accountability and a "return to the basics" in science instruction.

Environmental Factors

Very closely related to economic issues are the energy crisis and environmental problems. The people of this country are aware of massive energy consumption, the depletion of natural resources, and environmental pollution. The age of energy and its technology as we now know it is rapidly coming to an end. This change has already resulted in new topics for the science teachers: the use and conservation of energy, the limited supply of natural resources, and the many controversies over hydroelectric, nuclear, and solar energy are a few examples.

Ethical Factors

The third factor influencing science education is ethics. Urban problems and the law-and-order issue in *all* classes of society have caused troubled feelings in many concerning morals and values. The ethical issue was brought to a climax by the political opportunism of the Watergate affair, which demonstrated all the evils of a contemporary Machiavellianism. There is little question that Watergate provided the fire and ashes for a new moral phoenix. A part of the burden for developing stronger democratic ideals is placed on education. Perhaps it is time to re-ask George S. Counts's probing question of the 1930s: "Dare the school build a new social order?" Counts (1932) left little doubt about his answer; it was "yes." The potential development of Counts's ideas were overshadowed by Franklin D. Roosevelt's New Deal. The resurgence of moral education (Kohlberg & Turiel, 1971) and value-clarification techniques (Simon, Howe, & Kirschenbaum, 1972) are two examples of educational ideas already being used in science teaching that can be expected to gain prominence due to the ethical issue (Fishe, 1975a, 1975b).

Societal Factors

The fourth factor influencing science education is the transition to a post-industrial society. Daniel Bell has discussed his conception of the idea in *The Coming of Post-industrial Society* (Bell, 1972), and an NSTA Damon Lecture (Bell, 1974). The characteristics of the post-industrial society have five components (Bell, 1972):

1. Economic sector: the change from a goods-producing to a service economy.
2. Occupational distribution: the preeminence of the professional and technical class.
3. Axial principle: the centrality of theoretical knowledge as the source of innovation and of policy formation for the society.
4. Future orientation: the control of technology and technological assessments.
5. Decision making: the creation of new "intellectual technology."

Bell's thesis generally represents a model of technological solution for many contemporary societal issues. A publication from the Stanford Research Institute, *Changing Images of Man* (Markley, 1974), represents a contrasting view, that of cultural evolution. The thesis of this publication is that a new image of humankind is evolving and is replacing present social perceptions and economic images that are servants to technological and industrial metaphors. The new image of humankind would:

- Convey a *holistic sense* of perspective or understanding of life;
- entail an *ecological ethic,* emphasizing the total community of life in nature and the oneness of the human race;
- entail a *self-realization ethic,* placing the highest value on development of self-hood and declaring that an appropriate function of all social institutions is the fostering of human development;
- be *multileveled, multifaceted,* and *integrative,* accommodating various culture and personality types;
- involve *balancing* and *coordination of satisfactions* along many dimensions rather than the maximizing of concerns along one narrowly defined dimension (for example, economic); and
- be *experimental, open-ended,* and *evolutionary.*

My point is not to debate which thesis—technological solutions or cultural evolution—is correct but to indicate that society is in a time of transition, as it was at the turn of the century, and that this transition entails important implications for science education.

Global Factors

By far the most abstract and potentially the most profound condition influencing science education has been discussed in literature such as *The Limits to Growth* (Meadows, Meadows, Randers, & Behrens, 1972), *Mankind at the Turning Point* (Mesarovic & Pestel, 1974), *An Inquiry into the Human Prospect* (Heilbroner, 1974); and a possible response to the global problems has been suggested by Jonas Salk (1973) in *The Survival of the Wisest*. Salk's proposition is that given proper conditions, the growth of all populations in a closed system will approximate a sigmoid curve. The key issues in Salk's argument are the changes that must occur when the growth of the human population reaches the point of inflection in the S-curve. We have perhaps reached a point where we must slow population growth, and a comprehensive reevaluation of goals, values, and behavior patterns must occur. There will, of necessity, be tremendous changes within society, and, as the title of Salk's book suggests, it will take acceptance of the fact of change, courage to change the things we must, and wisdom to make the proper decisions.

CONCLUSION

At the turn of this century (1880–1920), the United States was in a period of social transition, the greatest it had undergone up to that time. The industrial–technologic complex was emerging, and social values were changing. Now society appears to be undergoing another transition that will be more profound and far-reaching. Multiple interacting systems are influencing this change: economic, environmental, ethical, societal, and global. In my opinion, the new frontiers are here, within ourselves and our earth systems.

The idea of change in the structure of science education caused by social pressure has been discussed throughout our history. I have suggested that an analysis of historical trends indicates two features of transformation of science education: (1) There is a correlation between specific types of social changes and recognizable changes in science curriculum and instruction, and (2) the stages of transformation are recognizable. With information such as that discussed in this essay, science educators can be more conscious of their direction and development of curriculum materials and instructional techniques. All the evidence indicates that science education will change owing to the new societal demands; some will seek to reform the old, while others will seek to build anew. Whichever is the case, the consequences of not changing are too severe to abdicate our responsibility to facilitate a new transformation of science education.

Chapter 2

■ ■ ■ ■ ■ ■ ■ ■ ■

SCIENCE EDUCATION AND THE EMERGING ECOLOGICAL SOCIETY

In the last chapter, I suggested that science education was approaching a new transformation. I pointed out historical changes in the aims of science teaching and presented factors that I believe will cause science educators to reevaluate their aims. This chapter extends and elaborates those ideas: I examine the origins of our contemporary crises and describe the role of personal values and cultural paradigms in social change; I discuss the various limits to present growth and then return briefly to the theme of values as one important way humankind must respond to its myriad problems; I argue for growth toward an ecological society; and finally, I present ideas concerning the role of science education in the emerging ecological society. This chapter is primarily concerned with social issues outside of science education, although those issues directly affect policies, curricula, and instruction in science.

ORIGINS OF CONTEMPORARY CRISES

Lynn White (1967) found that the "The Historical Roots of Our Ecological Crises" are within the Judeo-Christian tradition, which has informed us that humans are apart from and dominant over nature. This anthropocentric view has resulted in perceptions and values that have profound negative impacts on the natural environment. For White, the solution is not within science and technology because

> Our science and technology have grown out of Christian attitudes towards man's relation to nature which are almost universally held not only by Christians and neo-Christians but also by those who fondly regard themselves as post-Christians. (p. 1206)

This chapter is adapted from an article originally published as "Science Education and the Emerging Ecological Society," *Science Education, 63*(1), 95–109, 1979.

White ends by proposing St. Francis of Assisi as the patron for ecologists because of his belief in the virtue of humility toward all species. "He [St. Francis] tried to substitute the idea of the equality of all creatures, including man, for the idea of man's limitless rule of creation" (p. 1206).

In *The God Within,* Rene Dubos (1972) details the facts of ecological mismanagement, which in many cases preceded Judeo-Christian writings and certainly preceded modern science and technology. Dubos nominates St. Benedict of Nursia as the patron of environmentalists because of his belief that nature must be both protected and developed through a harmonious relationship with humans.

Both White and Dubos have made several points concerning religious traditions and the origins of our contemporary crises. It may be important to suggest that our religious traditions have contributed to present problems and perhaps even to nominate as patron saints individuals whose teachings could influence cultural development in different directions. Religious traditions and patron saints help organize an individual's values and thus sway decisions, since values generally represent the worth, merit, or desirability placed on various aspects of the world we experience. Values exist in reference to some object, idea, or person, and they are seen in the judgments, claims, or preferences made concerning these objects, ideas, or persons; for example, values become evident when an individual judges that seat belts are desirable, a certain energy policy is good, or a particular presidential candidate ought to be supported because of his position on pollution control. If current lifestyles and cultural progress are to continue, wise choices are required concerning the use, reuse, neglect, or abuse of natural systems that are important to our existence. I suggest that it is in the realm of human and cultural value systems that we find the underlying origins and potential solutions of our present problems.

PERSONAL VALUES AND CULTURAL PARADIGMS

Let us begin with a formal definition of value and value systems.

A "value" is an enduring belief that a specific mode of conduct or end-state of existence is personally or socially preferable to an opposite or converse mode of conduct or end-state of existence. A "value system" is an enduring organization of beliefs concerning preferable modes of conduct or end-states of existence along a continuum of relative importance. (Rokesch, 1973, p. 5)

Stated simply, each person has a set of values that act as decision-making criteria. Some personal values are expressions of basic human needs, while others reflect culturally weighted preferences (Maslow, 1959; Pugh, 1977). The interaction between one's needs and cultural preferences probably defines one's value system.

Values that are common throughout a culture are important for the maintenance of social order; conversely, a diversity of personal and cultural values is important for social change and development. Within cultures, stories, narratives, and ideas give individuals a worldview, organize experiences, provide expectations, and represent a prevailing moral wisdom that influences their decisions. These are the myths, models, and paradigms of societies (Campbell, 1968; Jantsch, 1975; Laszlo, 1972a).

Paradigms

Thomas Kuhn's (1970) concepts of scientific paradigms and revolutions have often been applied to disciplines outside the history and philosophy of science. Of particular interest here is the application of his ideas to cultural change. To review briefly, Kuhn's thesis is that science does not develop through the slow and steady accumulation of data that continually modify theory. Rather, Kuhn argues, there are paradigms of normal science, formed by scientific revolutions, during which time new paradigms replace the old and in turn become the "new" normal scientific models. Normal scientific work is informed within the prevailing paradigm, which includes "recognized scientific achievements that for a time provide model problems and solutions to a community of practitioners" (p. viii). The normal scientist's task is to resolve ambiguities and contradictions, derive ideas implicit in the logic of the paradigm in order to solve problems, and verify predictions from the paradigm. With time, anomalies come to light that cannot be solved through application of the normal scientific paradigm. The accumulation of anomalies eventually leads to a scientific revolution and replacement of the old paradigm with a new one. The theories of Copernicus and Einstein were revolutions according to Kuhn's theory. In the social sciences, Keynesian economics and behaviorist psychology are major paradigms.

A 1956 publication by the anthropologist A. F. C. Wallace brings us closer to the theme of this chapter. In it, he discussed types of cultural change that are "deliberate, organized, and conscious efforts by members of a society to construct a more satisfying culture" (p. 265). Wallace termed these cultural changes *revitalization movements*. In a 1972 paper, published after Kuhn's *The Structure of Scientific Revolutions,* Wallace used Kuhnian concepts to further elucidate the process of cultural change. He stated that the first step in paradigmatic cultural change is innovation. The development of agriculture and industrial technology are historical examples. These changes were so important that they affected the whole culture's value structure and thus ways of organizing and thinking about the world. Clearly, not all innovations are in conflict with extant cultural paradigms, nor are they all paradigm-forming:

> To qualify as paradigm-forming, an innovation need not be a complete and adequate theory or model; rather, it is an event which solves a limited problem but does so in a way which opens up a whole new line of development. It is a major "breakthrough." Furthermore, the paradigmatic innovation has a symbolic and charismatic quality. It is often associated with the name of a cultural hero (human or divine) and it can be simply represented by some visual image or phrase or manual procedure. (Wallace, 1972, p. 469)

Ecology: A New Social and Personal Paradigm

This quotation brings us to a key point of this chapter. I contend that the major breakthrough, the event that solved a limited problem and yet opened a whole new line of social thought and cultural development, was sending men to the moon. The visual image representing this innovation is certainly the picture of the earth as seen from the moon, and the phrase "whole earth" has steadily gained social acceptance. All this has served to bring about a greater understanding of ecological relationships on the earth. My claim is that ecology is the underlying foundation of the cultural innovation and personal values for which the "whole earth" is the symbolic representation. Ecology presents an innovative paradigm that will gradually influence our social and personal value systems. I do not mean that individuals or societies will operate with overt ecological perspectives; rather, there will be a continuous development of perceptions, values, and policies that incorporate a worldview that one could identify as ecological. (I elaborate this position in the next sections.)

According to Wallace, the next step after innovation is paradigmatic core development. Here the ideas that are integral to the new paradigm are elaborated and implemented. I further contend that science educators will have a central position in developing the new cultural paradigm because of their association with science and technology as well as with the social institution of education. Below I enumerate some of the specific details of the change to an ecological society.

Social Paradigms

In *Ark II,* Dennis Pirages and Paul Ehrlich (1974) discussed paradigmatic change in the context of our contemporary social problems. Pirages and Ehrlich coined the phrase "dominant social paradigm" to describe the values and ideas that form the worldview most commonly held within a culture. A dominant social paradigm (DSP) is defined as

> a mental image of social reality that guides expectations in a society. A DSP is the socially relevant part of a total culture. Different societies have different DSPs. A social paradigm is important to society because it helps make sense of an otherwise incomprehensible universe and to make organized activity possible. It is an essential part of the cultural information that is passed from generation to generation as it guides the behavior and expectations of those born into it. (p. 43)

The primary aims of the DSP presently pervading industrial societies is progress and profit, and it rests on a value system of unlimitedness. Progress is translated into goals such as continued consumption of material goods for a maximum profit. This growth ethic has tacitly maintained the attitude that the natural environment has unlimited resources and an unlimited capacity to receive and degrade wastes.

Cultural evolution can be thought of as a shift in dominant social paradigms. With time, a DSP increasingly fails to provide solutions for local and global problems. Social support for the extant paradigm is understandably very strong. Initially any inconsistencies are explained away; with time, the inconsistencies become very clear and attempts to reconcile differences become futile. Gradually, a new DSP arises. The characteristics of a period of major social change are developing in Western society. The values that have been most successful for the industrial society are now creating more problems than solutions, and ecological concepts, which were given little attention 30 years ago, are becoming the new patterns of social development.

The salient values of the industrial society have shaped our expectations, our intentions, and our behaviors and have influenced our development until we reached the limits to growth. We are now challenged with recognizing the consequences of not questioning the old values that require a full use of energy and resources to maintain technological and economic growth, of disregarding objections about environmental devastation, of ignoring protests concerning the validity of nuclear development, and of neglecting criticisms by consumers of the goods and services received. The death of an old paradigm is occurring, and many specific social issues center on the challenges just listed. In a later section, I discuss further some of the changes in values associated with a new paradigm. Now, there must be an answer to the question other authors have not discussed: "How will a new social paradigm emerge?"

When I asked the questions "Where do new social values come from?" or "Which values are now important?" I used the biological metaphor of biodiversity and evolution and concluded that the new values were not going to emerge from a void, so they must exist in a pool of values already held within society. Here I present a variation on the original idea of Pirages and Ehrlich (1974). I propose that these new values are in a subordinate position and in fact form what I term *subordinate social paradigms*. A subordinate social paradigm is defined as a worldview held by a *minority* of individuals within a culture. In other words, the value alternatives for the solution of cultural problems already exist in society, although the values are latent, suppressed, or not widely supported (Kluckhohn & Strodtbeck, 1961; Rokesch, 1973). Subordinate social paradigms are important because they can become dominant as a selective response to cultural challenges. In Western cultures, there always have been a few who supported a subordinate social paradigm concerning the environment and the consequences of continued growth; Thomas Malthus and Rachel Carson are two examples. Although their warnings were heard, the replies of those representing the dominant value system reduced the impact of their pleas for control and conservation. A significant point supporting my proposition is that the warnings of these and other individuals, some of whom are discussed later, have gained strength over the last few decades. This is the process of cultural evolution writ large in our age. In the next section, I present some challenges that result from maintaining the old social paradigm.

LIMITS TO GROWTH

Tragedy of the Commons

Many of our cultural values have been derived from the utilitarianism of John Stuart Mill and can be summarized in Jeremy Bentham's phrase "the greatest good for the greatest number." One of the most perceptive analyses of this value system and the projected results of its continued influence is Garrett Hardin's (1968) classic paper, "The Tragedy of the Commons." In his summary, he stated:

> The tragedy of the commons develops this way. Picture a pasture open to all. It is expected that each herdsman will try to keep as many cattle as possible on the commons. Such an arrangement may work reasonably satisfactorily for centuries because tribal wars, poaching, and disease keep the numbers of both men and beast well below the carrying capacity of the land. Finally, however, comes the day of reckoning, that is, the day when the long desired goal of social stability becomes a reality. At this point, the inherent logic of the commons remorselessly generates tragedy.

As a rational being, each herdsman seeks to maximize his gain. Explicitly or implicitly, more or less consciously, he asks, "What is the utility to me of adding one more animal to my herd?" (p. 1244)

Each herdsman must make a choice concerning the use of the commons. In the short term, the herdsman receives all the benefits from an increment of one animal while any negative effects such as overgrazing are shared by all the herdsmen. The herdsman believes that he can theoretically increase his herd without limit. This is fundamentally a "me-now" ethic in contrast to an "I-thou-future" ethic, and it is prevalent in our society. Failure to see the long-term results of exceeding the carrying capacity of the land, which is limited, ends in tragedy for all.

Social Tragedies

Tragedies develop slowly. First, there are small and apparently unrelated problems; with time, the problems become more intense and, upon closer examination, it becomes clear that they are interrelated. Some examples relate directly to the theme of this chapter. The value of progress and development informed us (through the DSP) that quantitative growth was the desirable goal of both developed and developing countries; that is, the quality of life will be improved through greater production and consumption of goods. How did we then evaluate the degree to which this goal was being achieved? The indicator of progress was a high rate of growth in the per capita gross national product (GNP). With increasing clarity, we see that the goal and the evaluation are somehow inadequate. The facts show the following:

1. In spite of an average 5% per year growth in GNP during the 1950s and 1960s, there are more poor people (by any measure) in developing countries than there were in the early 1950s, and even developed countries have increased poverty, underemployment, and unemployment.
2. The problems related to the environment are perceived as a consequence of unevaluated economic growth. These problems include damage to the physical environment (pollution, strip-mining, depletion of the ozone layer), the potential dangers of people-managed processes (nuclear power plants, weather modification, genetic engineering), and the use of nonrenewable resources (forests, wildlife).
3. There is a crisis of community in developed countries (urban decay, economic uncertainties, and dissatisfaction with government).

In 1976, the world spent $350 billion on armaments to reduce insecurity, but this has, if anything, only increased tensions and insecurity (Cleveland, 1977). The anomalies and deficiencies of present patterns of growth can be summarized in four categories: (1) basic human needs, (2) basic environmental quality, (3) basic resource conservation, and (4) basic community needs.

The tragic problems outlined in the above paragraph are all related to the present goals of social growth. In the past few years, there have been a number of reports on the limits to growth. These reports describe the critical anomalies in the dominant social paradigm. The accumulated force of the reports points out the inadequacies of our present policies and encourages the emergence of a new paradigm. The inadequacies are evident in public policy. Policies are the operational statements of the social paradigm. Generally, the values of the paradigm assume a latent form in the society. They are visible in the policies, however. Failure of old policies and discussion of new policies, both of which are occurring presently, are related to the larger cultural change I am discussing. In the 1970s, the Club of Rome analyzed the world dynamics of the present increases of population, pollution, industrial output, food consumption, and use of nonrenewable resources. Its conclusion was that there are limits to growth (Forrester, 1973; Meadows et al., 1972). Major problems associated with continuing the present patterns of growth may occur in 50 years or in 200 years, but if we continue to grow at the present rate and in the same direction, there will be catastrophes varying in their impact according to the unique needs of different regions on the earth (Mesarovic & Pestel, 1974). Although the early Club of Rome reports have been criticized (Starr & Rudman, 1973), their basic premises have not been substantially refuted.

Social Limits to Growth

The debate about limits to growth has focused on the use of physical resources and the carrying capacity of the earth. Recently, however, Fred Hirsh (1976) has stated that there are *Social Limits to Growth* that have been neglected in the debate, and we are just beginning to understand them. Hirsh presents the origin of the problem:

> The source is to be found in the nature of economic growth in advanced societies. The heart of the problem lies in the complexity and partial ambiguity of the concept of economic growth once the mass of the population has satisfied its main biological needs for life-sustaining food, shelter, and clothing. (p. 1)

Stating Hirsh's long and detailed ideas another way, an economics of affluence does not satisfy all human needs, and we are at the limits where higher levels of human needs (Maslow, 1970) must be recognized as important by our social sciences, primarily economics. The debate is not whether there are limits to growth, but rather which limits, physical or social, will be encountered first and have the greatest effect on society.

Daniel Bell (1976) has pointed out another variety of our social problems. Bell shows that three realms of our society—the economy, the polity, and the culture—are governed by contrary goals. For the economy, the aim is efficiency, which means production at the lowest cost and greatest profit. For a democratic polity, the underlying principle is equality. For the culture, individual development or self-fulfillment is the goal. The contradictions are that there cannot be unlimited production, consumption, and profit controlled by a few at the top of private hierarchies and public bureaucracies and at the same time equality for all. A further contradiction is that full development of each person as an individual is impossible. To put it briefly, a society cannot maintain value systems of equality for all, personal development for all, and efficient production of all goods. Eventually, we have to reconcile the contradictions and express preferences. It is precisely because of our progress and past achievements that we now see the inherent problems in our society. We have successfully developed each of the three segments of society Bell describes, and now we are at the limits of the successful growth.

In *To Have or To Be,* Erich Fromm (1976) has presented one of the most apposite and poignant analyses of our present situation. Fromm has incorporated most of the key issues discussed thus far. In the introduction, he states:

> The Great Promise of Unlimited Progress—the promise of domination of nature, of material abundance, of the greatest happiness for the greatest number, and of unimpeded personal freedom—has sustained the hopes and faith of the generations since the beginning of the industrial age. (p. 1)

The dominant value system of unlimitedness has directed our social growth. Our perceptions concerning the production and consumption of goods and the use of the environment and resources are based on the idea that we do not have to worry about or make judgments as though there are limits. If, for example, a person or society views resources as limited, then there is also a concern for making decisions as though they will someday end. The fundamental mode of existence was to have materials, goods, and services satisfying our basic needs and induced wants. The *having* mode of existence expressed by Fromm accentuates material possessions, acquisitiveness, and consumption. Individuals in the *having* mode expend their time and energy saving and accumulating money and material. The great symbol of the having mode in our age was perhaps Howard Hughes, an individual who could have anything money could buy. However, by all reports, he ended an unhappy, addicted recluse: His personal being was a void.

According to Fromm, cultural evolution has taken us to a time and place where the basic struggle is between the values of having and the values of *being*. The being mode is based on a better quality of life and environment, personal growth and interactions based on cooperation, and meaningful human activity.

Returning to the theme of tragedy, it seems that a form of ironic tragedy is developing wherein many individuals realize the incongruities between the actual situation and the political speeches, television commercials, and newspaper advertisements. Meanwhile, the main characters in the drama remain unaware of the inconsistencies and struggle to maintain the old paradigm. Not seeing that progress has been our greatness and will be our downfall is the essence of the tragedy.

There is an interlocking and interrelated system of limits. The limits to growth are physical, social, and cultural. The rate and direction of present growth are limited, and there must be a change. How humankind will change is the subject of the next section.

HUMANKIND AND THE GROWTH CRISES

The Choices

The growth crises leave us with three critical choices: to do nothing, to allow a leader to make the decisions, or to take some responsibility as individuals. The first and least desirable decision is to "decide not to decide" and let things work themselves out. Any decision not to take action could end in the catastrophes projected by the Club of Rome. A second solution is enforced restriction of all sectors of growth and unnecessary consumption by a "friendly fascist" or "benevolent dictator." Society would be like that envisioned in the dystopian novels *Brave New World* (Huxley, 1932) and *1984* (Orwell, 1949).

Jonas Salk (1973) provides a third solution in *The Survival of the Wisest*. Salk constructed a self-regulative growth model based on his experiences with growing biological systems. The growth of many organisms frequently approximates a sigmoid curve, or S-curve, as seen in Figure 2.1. In the early period, growth is quite rapid. Then, at the point of inflection, the limits of the system are sensed by the organisms and

FIGURE 2.1 Sigmoid Curve

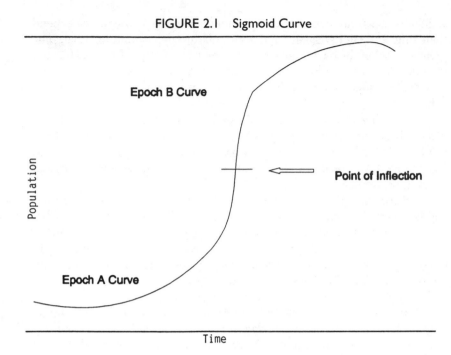

population growth slows to a sustainable level. The crucial question is: "What happens at this point?" For some organisms, the response to signals concerning systematic limits is instinctual. The knowledge required is genetic, and the response is automatic. In the case of human society, though, the situation is very different. To foresee how humans will change, we must look to ethics and values.

Ethics and Values

As the late Theodosius Dobzhansky (1956) pointed out in *The Biological Basis of Human Freedom,* evolution has resulted in a uniqueness known only in one species, and that special quality is self-awareness. Along with self-awareness come the corollaries of individual freedom and personal choice. At the same time that humans gained freedom as a result of the immense evolutionary journey, the species simultaneously developed the capacity for ethical thought. Dobzhansky states:

> The ability of man to choose freely between ideas and acts is one of the fundamental characteristics of human evolution. Perhaps freedom is even the most important of all specifically human attributes. . . . Ethics emanate from freedom and are unthinkable without freedom. . . . Ethics

are, consequently, a human responsibility. We cannot rely on genes or on natural selection to guarantee that man will always choose the right direction of his evolution. (p. 34)

Women and men are moral agents. Individuals do not make ethical choices in vacuums. As discussed earlier, personal choices are mediated by cultural values that will help protect and preserve the species societies. So, in answering the questions posited above—"How will humankind change?"—I am led to conclude that human values will play an important role in responding to the sensed limits of present growth; indeed, there must be a transformation of values if humankind is to continue to grow in the smooth form of a sigmoid curve. In *The Ascent of Man,* Jacob Bronowski (1973) summarized the role of values:

> Our actions as adults, as decision makers, as human beings, are mediated by values, which I interpret as general strategies in which we balance opposing impulses. It is not true that we run our lives by any computer scheme of problem solving. The problems of life are insoluble in this sense. Instead, we shape our conduct by finding principles to guide it. We devise ethical strategies or systems of values to ensure that what is attractive in the short term is weighed in the balance of the ultimate, long-term satisfactions. (p. 436)

This statement by a great scientist and humanist eloquently presents the human role between the opposing forces of growth. The real crises have their origins in human ideas and values. These are the underlying factors that influence our environmental, economic, and social decisions. If we are to find solutions, it will be in the realm of ideas and values. In the next section, I discuss new ideas and values that will assume dominance in our society.

GROWTH AND VALUES FOR AN ECOLOGICAL SOCIETY

As we begin our third century, American society is in a period of major transition, the second in our history (Anderson, W., 1976; Markley, 1974; Platt, 1974). Agriculture was the central factor of early American society, with an estimated 90% of the population involved in the development of foods at the time of the American Revolution (1775–1783). Agriculture remained the dominant support system until the Industrial Revolution in the late 1800s when, slowly, the primary social system shifted to include the industrial production of goods. Agriculture still provides the necessary foods, but by the 1970s less than 10% of the population was employed in this sector of society.

Ecological Society

The Coming of Post-Industrial Society by Daniel Bell (1972) suggests that we are evolving into a service-oriented economy. Growth will be in professional and technical services, such as health, education, research, and government. These changes represent the attempts of a society to meet basic human needs above the biological level, as discussed earlier by Hirsh. Bell summarizes the statistics of transition: "Today [1972] about 60 percent of the United States labor force is engaged in services; by 1980, the figure will have risen to 70 percent" (p. 15).

Postindustrial society has a preeminent professional, intellectual, and technical class. Theoretical knowledge is the source of innovation, policies, and solving problems. On the whole, discussions of postindustrial society usually put much more emphasis on technology than I intend to do in this chapter, where I stress cultural evolution. This should not be interpreted as an antitechnology bias. Technology will be important in any future society. However, it will not be important for itself; rather, it will be important as a means to other ends. The phrase *postindustrial society* indicates only that there is something beyond industrial society. Exactly what that something is is not discernible. To be sure, other authors have discussed various aspects of the transition and new society (Boulding, 1964). It seems we are presently searching for the conceptual successor to industrial society—and I suggest it is the ecological society. Ecological scientists study the ways that organisms and populations interact with one another and with the various environmental support systems. Any conception of future growth must take into account individual needs, the physical environment, and the needs of communities. We must consider the interdependent relationships among living and nonliving systems, the concept of ecosystem. By broadening the concept of ecosystem to include human relationships, we produce the idea of the ecological society. The ecological society could be the conceptual synthesis Ervin Laszlo (1974) outlined in *A Strategy for the Future* and the foundation for a new social paradigm.

During a social transformation, the dominant social paradigms that influence individual human values change. Although this seems clear and sounds logical, there is a problem when shifting to a new set of social values. The problem is psychological. During a period of major value shifts, large numbers of individuals must, of necessity, undergo a time when they lack the security of past images and values; terms such as *anomie, alienation,* and *anxiety* are used to discuss this phenomenon. These terms also describe some of the present widespread personal disorganization in contemporary society. This period has even been characterized as an "age of anxiety" (May, 1977) and the "age of uncertainty" (Galbraith, 1977).

A MODEL FOR NEW SOCIAL VALUES

As we look to the future, it is important to establish the new values in the policies of social institutions, and this would include science education. Which are the important values? Values for the new ecological society are identified by (1) predicted values based on growth models and (2) values gaining social prominence.

The first way of identifying important values for a new social paradigm is through predictions based on the most reasonable model of growth—that of organic or differentiated growth as described by Salk (1973). This model is graphically represented as a sigmoid curve, or S-curve (Figure 2.1). Several important points can be made based on this model. First, early growth (epoch A) is primarily a multiplication, while later growth (epoch B) is differentiation. This suggests, for example, a change in emphasis from quantity to quality. Second, the B section of the curve is the *inverse* of the A curve, thus suggesting that many of the dominant positive values in the future would have had a negative (subordinate) value in the past, and those values that were important for early social growth will have reduced importance in the future. For example, in the future, the values of cooperation, equality, harmony, quality, and being will have far greater emphasis than competition, inequality, domination, quantity, and having. Third, the point of the curve's inflection is equidistant from the parameters of the model; that is, the level of extinction (bottom) and the carrying capacity or limits to growth (top). These parameters can be thought of as the origins of signals, or a feedback system, regulating growth in social systems. The strength of the signals for and against continued patterns of growth will exactly offset each other at the point of inflection. Stated another way, the weight of values for growth as we have had in the past will be equal to the weight of values for different forms of growth; and, if all values have equal weight, this can cause a phenomenon of valuelessness and thus be perceived as an age of anxiety. The power of this model is to help identify some values that would take us beyond the present stage of apparent valuelessness, uncertainty, indecision, and anxiety. In the following, I present evidence supporting the changes predicted by the S-curve growth model.

Emerging Values

Between 1968 and 1971, Milton Rokesch (1974) surveyed the change and stability of American value systems. Although the values of most Americans remained stable, he did find that certain values had changed markedly.

Significantly more important in the American value hierarch in 1971 compared with 1968 were a world at peace, a world of beauty, equality, mature love, being logical and loving; significantly less important were a comfortable life, a sense of accomplishment, family security, social recognition, and being clean. (p. 227)

The values reported as important probably grew out of specific social issues with which the majority of Americans were confronted, for example, Vietnam, racism, sexism, and ecological problems. On the other hand, it is also reasonable to expect some values to become less important if problems associated with them have been ameliorated. There are several ways to interpret these results. The values rated as significantly less important are generally correlated with lower levels of Abraham Maslow's (1970) hierarchy of motivational needs, while those values that gained in importance reflect higher-level motivational needs. This change is also related to the changing social limits to growth presented earlier (Hirsh, 1976). Another general difference between the two sets of values is suggested by Erich Fromm's 1976 thesis that the values perceived as more important are concerned with *being* while those losing significance are associated with *having*.

Data from 1975 Harris polls provide further, and somewhat stronger, support for a change in American values toward those predicted for an ecological society. Harris and associates confronted respondents with the statistics that America comprises 6% of the world's population (now 5%) but consumes 40% of the world's production of energy and raw materials. The majority response concerning this level of consumption indicated it was not right. Some specific responses were the following:

- This uses our own natural resources (74%);
- this would turn the rest of the world against us (51%);
- this hurts the rest of the world's well-being (55%);
- this is morally wrong (61%);
- this requires a cutback on consumption and waste (90%); and
- this requires a change in lifestyle (77%).

How would individuals be willing to change? Harris asked the American public for specific ways in which they would be willing to change their rate of consumption. Responses indicated the public would be willing to have one meatless day a week (90%), stop feeding all-beef products to pets (78%), do away with yearly fashion changes (90%), wear clothes until they wore out (73%), eliminate annual model changes in automobiles (92%), and reduce advertising that encourages consumption (82%) (Laszlo, 1977).

I believe these data indicate that the values of the American public have changed over the last decade. The changes indicate a continued loss of confidence in the policies based on the values of industrial society and the emergence of values predicted by the S-curve model. The debate about limits to growth is, I think, symptomatic of the conflict between an old social paradigm that is now deficient and an emerging paradigm. Almost daily the values underlying the industrial society are shown to be deficient in solving contemporary problems. The goals of industrial progress have been largely attained. Some of the values that guided industrial progress include technological development based on the principle that if it can be, it must be and the beliefs that industry should be capital-intensive, more is better, material gain is essential, natural resources are unlimited, the GNP can increase indefinitely, and man will dominate nature.

To summarize, when it was necessary to subsist on the products of the land and the survival of children was low, we had to have "dominion over nature" and to "be fruitful and multiply." The challenge was to survive, and humans adapted their value systems accordingly. The next challenge was the development of technology to meet human and social needs. The result has been the highest level of affluence in human history. The concomitants of this affluence—resource depletion and pollution in all its forms—have reached an historical peak, and now these unintentional consequences must be remedied. The confluence of contemporary crises signals the end of a great era in American history, that of the industrial society. A new frontier is visible, and a new ecological society is emerging. The concerns have turned from the need to conquer the natural world in the first case, and the need to master the designed world of technology in the second case, to the need to understand ourselves and our earth systems today.

Historically, we have named our societies after that which is the prevailing means of support and development, for example, agriculture and industry. Our future support and growth will be based on ecology, which is a set of biological and psychological principles, and will become a social metaphor that will guide the formation of policy. In the short period of 20 years, *ecology* has become a household word. Ecology will increasingly influence our ideas, values, and growth as we continue the transformation from a mechanistic–industrial–technical paradigm to an organismic–environmental–community paradigm.

SCIENCE EDUCATION AND ECOLOGICAL SOCIETY

The ecological society will have science at its core. The new paradigm must be constructed on a foundation of knowledge, and this leads to the realm of science. Some have blamed science and technology for our problems, while others sought scientific and technological solutions. Both positions are partially correct and partially incorrect. I have tried to show that it is not science and technology per se that have caused the problems; rather, it is human ideas and values about scientific development and technological adaptation that have contributed to both our progress and our problems. To think that science and technology will be replaced in the next few decades is folly; to change the development and application toward important human problems is feasible.

Education will certainly be one of (if not *the*) important nonmaterial sources for the development of a new social order. As Lawrence Cremin (1976) has pointed out in *Public Education,* it will be approached with a much broader understanding; that is, education is more than school—it includes the variety of social institutions that contribute to the development of individuals, the environment, and communities.

Science education will be extremely important in the transition to an ecological society because it, by definition, is associated with both science and education. Many contemporary challenges have been discussed. How will science education respond? Responses are not passive reactions, for humans have the capacity to imagine and consciously plan for the future. The responses are often policies actively designed and administered to establish and maintain a social order. In science education, we can contribute to a new sense of purpose through policies that support slower rates and different directions of growth. Concrete suggestions for policies in science education are outlined in the next chapter. Here I suggest that the policies should take into account four basic factors.

1. *Development of the individual* places emphasis on the fulfillment of basic human needs and discovering means of nurturing continued healthy personal growth.
2. *Development of environmental quality* includes the protection, conservation, or improvement of all the factors—for example, air, water, noise, and stress—that affect individual and community development.
3. *Development of resources* means deciding what natural resources are to be used and the degree to which they are used, recycled, and conserved.
4. *Development of the community* entails greater recognition that there are groups of humans at local, regional, national, and international levels who are dependent on one another for the basic requirements of individual development and that we must cooperate in the elimination of racism, sexism, and war.

CONCLUSION

There are two kinds of evolution that are important to science educators: biological and cultural. The former is a concept integral to many curriculum programs. Cultural evolution is of concern because it redefines and redirects the aims, goals, and policies of science education. The late Arnold Toynbee left us with "challenge and response" as his formulation of history. Our cultural challenges are clear and daily they become clearer. We have reached the limits of present growth. Unlike biological evolution, cultural evolution is amenable to rational control. The recognition of limits implies choices and decisions. Information and values will help us give preference to variables and choose one alternative over other possibilities. Although my suggestions about teaching values in the science classroom do not differ greatly from those of others, I have endeavored to answer the fundamental question: "Why should values issues be incorporated into science curricula and instruction?"

The theme and conclusion of this chapter can be stated briefly: An ecological society is emerging, and science education must contribute to its evolution.

Chapter 3

■ ■ ■ ■ ■ ■ ■ ■ ■

SCIENCE EDUCATION POLICIES FOR AN ECOLOGICAL SOCIETY: AIMS AND GOALS

"Is there hope for man?" So begins Robert Heilbroner (1974) in *An Inquiry into the Human Prospect*. Asking this question instills fear and trembling because it confronts us with the possibility of hopelessness through continued disorder and potential catastrophe. After exploring the global predicaments of increasing populations, obliterative war, and environmental devastation, Heilbroner answers his question: No; the possibility for a brighter future is small. As to the question of whether worse impends, the answer is "yes." His conclusions should shake us to the core of our being. The possibility of doom exists; this is a realization that can certainly result in despair.

Heilbroner's prospect for humanity could also be a cause for action, my objective of this chapter. I think humankind has reason for hope, because hope lies in the possibility of change. As Erich Fromm (1968) points out, hope is neither passive waiting nor unrealistic forcing of the future. Rather, it is a personal state that exists prior to action. This is exactly my position. The very fact that we examine the possibilities and search for new directions indicates our intention to change. As usual, change will not be easy; it will come slowly as individuals and institutions find hope and confidence in the future.

The restoration of confidence began when the astronauts first transmitted a picture of our small planet back to earth. We were then left with a concrete image of an abstract concept. Viewing our earth from space made tangible the idea that we live in a finite system. Simultaneously with this new symbol of our age, economic, environmental, and energy crises were reported in increasing number, magnitude, and complexity. For the first time in history, we became aware of global scarcities; resources imag-

---

This chapter is adapted from an article originally published as "Science Education Policies for an Ecological Society: Aims and Goals," *Science Education, 63*(2), 245–255, 1979.

ined to be limitless were in fact limited. A food crisis existed in developing countries and an energy crisis in industrial countries. The world population continued to increase while we depleted the earth's resources and despoiled the natural environment. Although these problems are confirmed daily, there also is some evidence of a new social order espousing different patterns of growth. Two publications from the Club of Rome, *Reshaping the International Order* (Tinbergen, 1976) and *Goals for Mankind* (Laszlo, 1977), have emphasized the problems and policies for this new social order. These reports are very different from the earlier *Limits to Growth* (Meadows et al., 1972) and *Mankind at the Turning Point* (Mesarovic & Pestel, 1974), which signaled the negative prospects of our present growth policies.

Science and technology undoubtedly will have an important role in any future society. Presently, however, many see the scientific enterprise as a tyrant inflicting problems on the world. Along with a new naturalism, there is a new nervousness about the role of science and technology in our society. Science has been a great force in contemporary civilization, and now this power is being questioned. This can be seen in the reduction of government money, congressional criticism of research projects, and the *Man: A Course of Study* (MACOS) affair in science education. (MACOS, NISF-supported curriculum project that emphasized human differences across cultures, came in for sharp criticism and eventually was dismantled after congressional hearings, never having been implemented.) A common response to such criticism is that the public is ill informed; it is not scientifically literate. Although this is basically true, we cannot deny the perceptions and actions of the public concerning science and technology, even if they are erroneously or inadequately informed. For many, "scientific literacy" consists of perceptions resulting from inappropriate information, such as that the good life is largely achievable through scientific advances and technological fixes. However, their direct and indirect experience is that they do *not* have a good life. In turn, science and technology are, at least partially, blamed for their malaise. I would estimate that the scale of positive and negative perceptions of science is about balanced. Science has contributed equally to a better life and to our many problems. Rather than debating the efficacy of scientific achievements, a case can be made for rethinking the policies of science education, since much of the above discussion is related to the public's *perception* of science and technology as opposed to what in fact science and technology have or have not done. And the public's perceptions of science and technology are largely a result of science education.

The nature and origin of contemporary problems lead me to conclude, for two principal reasons, that the burden for change will fall heavily on science education. First, many problems of contemporary society are related to science and technology; second, many aspects of needed social changes can be gained from public education, specifically science education. If, after an inventory of the global situation, people are to avoid despair, the limits and possibilities of science and technology must be understood by all citizens. Certainly, a part of the restoration of accurate perceptions of science and technology will be up to science educators.

I firmly believe that science educators must contribute to our next step in cultural development. In Chapter 1, I discussed the process of change in science education and contemporary problems affecting science education (Bybee, 1977a). In Chapter 2, I clarified the relationship between science education and an emerging ecological society (Bybee, 1979a). These themes lead to this chapter, where I examine the purpose and functions of policies and then discuss new aims and goals for science education.

PURPOSE, POLICY, PROGRAMS, AND PRACTICE IN SCIENCE EDUCATION

Human beings need purpose, and society provides goals that contribute to the individual's sense of purpose. Every culture has stories, narratives, and ideas that give individuals a worldview, organize their experiences in meaningful ways, provide expectations, and convey beliefs, attitudes, and values that represent a dominant social purpose (Pirages, 1977a and b). These are the myths, models, and paradigms of societies. They lend unity, form, and order to a society because they organize individual's perceptions and influence their decisions through shared ideas, values, and behavioral norms. The different goals associated with hunting-and-gathering societies, as opposed to agricultural and industrial societies, are specific examples of what I am stating generally.

Social Purpose

In the last quarter of the twentieth century, the rapid economic growth associated with the industrial society will slowly change. In *The End of Progress,* Edward Renshaw (1976) outlined some of the reasons for the end of growth as we have known it; for example, environmental constraints, diminishing efficiency from economies of scale, and limits to the application of technology. The title of Renshaw's book also serves another function. Our society has shared in a common purpose—the pursuit of progress. The end of this great American dream apparently will leave many individuals without purpose. Purposelessness emerges because new goals are yet to be clearly articulated and recognized. In his April 1977 speech on energy, President Jimmy Carter used William James's phrase "a moral equivalent of war" with reference to the need for an energy policy. War is a good example of the unity that can be gained from the shared purpose of a society. In the case of war, the purpose is survival. There also is common agreement on a visible enemy, and victory is usually perceived to be in the near future.

The new social purpose is not clear; what is clear is that there can no longer be progress as we have known it in the past. The connection between "a moral equivalent of war" and energy policies, or larger ecological issues, is more than coincidence. However, the analogy is less than complete, since there is not common agreement on the problem. Further, ecological problems will probably not be resolved in the near future. So, although the analogy between a common social purpose in war and our present situation is less than clear, it does clarify the ambiguity of social problems and the need for new social purpose. The report of a March 1978 Gallup poll indicating that after a year there had been virtually no change in the public's attitude toward energy supports the point I am making. Only four out of ten Americans think there is an energy crisis. We do not yet have a coherent and forceful national energy policy.

As the industrial society changes, a new purpose will emerge. Therefore, part of my reason for writing this chapter is to state new aims and goals for science education, based on what I perceive to be a reasonable direction of social change. First, the relationship between cultural purpose, institutional policy, curriculum programs, and teaching practices should be clarified. Within the cultural paradigms are the most abstract, ultimate goals; these are the ideas to be pursued even if they are not susceptible to complete fulfillment. Their function is to give direction and purpose to society. At this highest level, the culturally universal goals apply to all individuals all the time simply because they are members of the culture. They are the goals about which we are most certain. However, because they are universal, they are also the least practical. For example, the ideas of a new society are too general to elicit specific suggestions for an individual science teacher. The lack of specificity suggests the need for a restatement of the goals at an intermediate level, between the individual and the cultural. A logical place to formulate these intermediate goals is in formal and informal social institutions. Together the social institutions can maintain the ultimate goals of the culture or bring about cultural change through the pursuit of new goals. At the same time, the many social institutions directly influence individual lives through the policies they hold to be important. This twofold function of social policies helps to elucidate the purpose of science education, which is to contribute to the maintenance and change of the culture as well as contribute to the development of individuals in ways unique to the institution, such as imparting an understanding of scientific knowledge and methods and an awareness of careers in science and engineering.

Policy

We can paraphrase a definition of policy given by Erich Jantsch (1975) in *Design for Evolution.* A policy is a set of guiding principles designed for the purpose of regulating simultaneously and viably a multiplicity of individuals interacting within a community (p. 6). Policies, then, are governing principles that provide a plan or course of action. Defined as such, policies may reflect either the status quo or a planned change to an emerging social order. Policies represent the unique concerns, needs, and strengths of a particular community or subgroup within a community. They are a more specific application of the culturally universal goals. Developed at an intermediate level, policies have some certainty, although less than do the culturally universal goals, and they are more practical than the social goals. But it is precisely because policies take into account a specific group and complex historical conditions that they must remain somewhat inexact and uncertain. Still, policies are indispensable, for they bridge the gap between the larger cultural goals and the particular, unique needs of the individual teacher. In science education, policies exist in a variety of forms, including yearbooks, committee reports, articles, convention papers, and methods textbooks. The critical distinction between the levels of policy and individual application is also of interest to the historian of science education. We are fairly certain about changes in policy and programs, but we are much less certain about the degree to which certain policies were implemented in classrooms. This distinction also points out a persistent problem likely to be encountered by individuals who give papers at conventions. Professional papers often aim at policy, while the individual science teachers are more interested in their particular problems. The result is the frequent request for situation-specific application of policies.

Programs

Science programs, including textbooks, laboratory equipment, instructional methods, and assessment strategies, represent the more concrete application of purposes. Derived from policies, science programs should represent the content and pedagogy specific to science disciplines, grade levels, and student populations implied by the more abstract policies and purposes. Science programs representing the new paradigm inevitably experience difficulties with acceptance and implementation. Numerous factors, such as marketing by publishers, facilities and equipment, and costs, contribute to the success of innovative programs that represent new paradigms. But the factor that probably contributes most to acceptance and implementation of innovation rests with science teachers. They must eventually assume responsibility for the new practices implicit in the policies and programs that are based on larger social purposes.

If science teachers do not implement programs and practices representing the innovations, the entire process falters and eventually fails. This sounds like a harsh judgment, but it states a responsibility of science teachers and a reality of any educational reform.

Teaching Practices

At the individual level, there must be a translation of policies into practical applications of science teaching. This is the case for the classroom science teacher who must choose a course of action in a particular situation. Individual decisions concerning the teaching of science, for example, are the most uncertain. Individual decisions are neither directly culturally universal nor policy-specific. In the final analysis, they are absolutely singular, applicable in one case and one case only. The weight of classroom decisions falls most heavily on the individual science teacher. The teacher may seek direction and counsel, consider circumstances, and balance alternatives, but only one person finally decides what happens in the course of a lesson, unit, and year. This moment-to-moment effort should be informed by policies and directed toward a goal of providing an education in science that is good for the students and for the society.

The foregoing ideas are important for locating my discussion of policies in science education. My contention is that we are evolving toward an ecological society (see Chapter 2) and that within the conceptual synthesis of an ecological society, the ultimate social goals are identifiable. There is not room here for an extended discussion of these goals. Included, however, would be such ideas as interdependence, sustainable growth, conservation of resources, population control, and global harmony. To these ends, the policies outlined in the next sections are designed to contribute to a new social order, not to maintain the present state of public policies or social conditions.

Policies for Science Education

The policies I describe are applicable to the broadest and most encompassing community of science educators. I use the phrase *community aims,* as opposed to *subject-specific* (for example, physics, biology, geology) or *grade-level specific* (for example, elementary, secondary, higher education) to ensure the broadest possible application of these policies. A decision to discuss community aims means a sacrifice of some exactitude and practicality, since the combinations of subject, grade, and individual goals will vary widely. Still, these aims and goals are a first step; other more specific policies can certainly be formulated by various subgroups within the science education community.

In the next decade, policies for science education programs and practices should include the appropriate cognitive, affective, psychomotor, and social objectives to

- Fulfill basic human needs and facilitate personal development;
- maintain and improve the physical and human environment;
- conserve and efficiently use our natural resources; and
- develop greater community at the local, regional, national, and global levels.

Science education for an ecological society is concerned with individual, environmental, and social changes. Indeed, there is an interrelationship and interdependence among all of these. I will point out later that there is a parallel between these stated aims and the science of ecology. Science education is more than what happens in school. As Lawrence Cremin (1976) suggests in *Public Education,* education in science occurs in homes, churches, synagogues, museums, libraries, factories, corporations, and the media. Each of these institutions has its own, usually informal, science curriculum. This simple fact should not be overlooked as we think about the new aim of science education.

Ecology is generally defined as the science of the interrelations between organisms (including human) and their environment. Eugene P. Odum (1959) defined ecology as "the study of the structure and function of nature (it being understood that mankind is a part of nature)" (p. 4). Organisms, populations, communities, ecosystems, and the biosphere are the organizational levels of greatest concern to the ecologist. *Organism* means an individual living thing, either plant or animal. *Population* is a group of any one kind of organism living and reproducing in a particular area. *Community* includes all the populations in a given area that are dependent on one another for basic living requirements. The community and the nonliving environment interacting together is the *ecosystem.* *Biosphere* is the portion of the earth in which the ecosystems function. These ecological units of study are incorporated (in fact, basic) to the new aim for science education. Ecologists recognize individual needs (autoecology) as well as group needs (synecology): a concern for the physical environment as well as living beings.

Implicit, too, is the fact that individual organisms, groups of organisms, and the environment are closely interrelated and dependent on one another for survival, subsistence, and continued development. This is an often-overlooked fact that must not be neglected. Many social organizations are associated with one of the three levels, their primary concerns being the individual, the environment, or the community. The policies and actions of these groups often reveal a neglect for the concerns of other units. For example, it is easy to demand that a mining operation cease because it is harmful to the environment. Such a proposal seldom includes a recommendation of what should be done for the community of people associated with the mine. Other examples include those who wish to guard the environment but forget the people, those who wish to develop individual potential but neglect the importance of fresh air and clean water, and those interested in community development at the cost of depersonalization. Omissions such as these may never be completely remedied. The stated aim of science education would certainly contribute to an understanding of the interrelationships and interdependence of those living in an ecological society.

The aforementioned aim could not be pursued for very long without confronting disciplines outside the sciences, such as ethics, politics, and economics. We may seem to be interested in the scientific facts and evidence relating to present global issues, but science educators also must incorporate the human issues that are now so prevalent in society. We are clearly concerned with problems of lifetime (conception, abortion, birth control, death with dignity), lifespace (pollution, crowding, urban decay), and lifestyle (affluence, poverty, consumption, conservation). In the next decades, our students will need the best information available concerning these problems, and they also will need to understand that they will be struggling with these not only as scientific and technological problems, but also as ethical, political, and economic issues. There is already a growing number of books dealing with environmental and ecological issues from different perspectives, such as economics (Hines, 1973), politics (Ophuls, 1977), and theology (Derr, 1975). Books with a decidedly interdisciplinary balance of these issues are also available (Meadows, 1977; Pirages, 1977b). One omission in this literature is that of education and specifically science education, although this is perhaps changing as books such as *The Global Mind* (Perelman, 1976) and curriculum materials such as the "Human Sciences Program" (Biological Sciences Curriculum Study, [BSCS], 1978) became available.

Based on the evidence of social change, there should be little doubt about the purposefulness of this aim; it is one of the most individually and socially purposeful aims in our history.

GOALS OF SCIENCE EDUCATION

This section discusses in more detail the goals derived from the new aim for science education. I justify the goals and suggest some values for consideration in the future achievement of the goals. The justifications and values are not complete; my intention here is to provide a first step for those interested in new policies.

Basic Human Needs

Science education should be directed toward fulfillment of the student's basic needs and to strengthening respect for these needs and for the fundamental rights of all humankind.

One criticism of the utilitarian ethic permeating our society is the confusion of real goods (that is, natural needs) with desired goods (that is, acquired needs). An ethic such as "the greatest good for the greatest number" does not necessarily distinguish between needs and wants. If one considers the amount of money spent each year on advertising that literally teaches many what they should *want,* then the disparity between an efficiency–profit motive and a concern for basic human needs becomes clear.

In the *Ethics,* Aristotle distinguished between desired and real goods. The former are *called* good because they are desired. The latter are *in fact* good because they are basic needs. Desired goods may or may not be really good for the individual. Let us say a child sees a television commercial for a new cereal and then asks for the cereal, claiming it is good. Is the cereal nutritionally good for the child? The possibility exists that the child says the cereal is good because the commercial promised there was a toy in the box. This view of goodness has nothing to do with the cereal being nutritionally good. The child (1) acquired a desire for the cereal because of the toy and (2) called the cereal good. There also are those things that are in fact good because they fulfill basic human needs. These are natural goods and ought to be desired but may or may not be desired. In the earlier example, the child may be hungry and need cereal with proteins and vitamins. The child may, however, not feel the need for a nutritional cereal. Still, we can say the child ought to desire cereal because of the nutritional value. Recognizing the goods that are real (that is, basic human needs) entails the moral obligation of helping to fulfill those basic needs that are really good for the individual. The major premise of this argument is that one ought to seek only the things that are really good. What, then, is really good? What are the basic human needs?

Abraham Maslow's (1970) hierarchy of motivational needs provides a relatively stable and concrete formulation of exactly what a concern for basic human needs might include. At the lowest level are physiological needs, such as food, water, and air. These are the human needs that are usually discussed relative to majorities in underdeveloped countries and minorities in developed countries. Safety, security, order, and continuity describe the next level of needs. These, too, are concerns of many in both developing and developed countries; more specifically, students' behaviors are also often influenced by these motivational needs. Next is the need to belong to groups, to be part of a community. Finally, there is a need for self-esteem and personal adequacy. Satisfaction of these needs is essential if the individual is to maintain physical and psychological health. According to Maslow's theory, there also is a need for continued growth and development. Maslow used the term *self-actualization* to describe the need for knowledge, creativity, values, and aesthetics. Fulfillment of these needs contributes to the full development of the individual. Maslow's ideas complement the work of others, such as Jean Piaget's (Piaget & Inhelder, 1969) theory of cognitive development and Lawrence Kohlberg's (1975) theory of ethical development. The theories of Maslow, Piaget, and Kohlberg clarify the philosophical and psychological nature of the goal of basic human needs.

The work of individuals such as John and Magda McHale (1977) has brought the issue of basic needs into the concrete realm of daily needs, resources, and situations of countries around the globe. Their book *Basic Human Needs: A Framework for Action* provides the synthesis of ideas and information that clarifies the goal of fulfilling basic needs. The developed world has experienced prosperity and substantial growth for a long time. We have had more than our share of goods. We must now exercise some self-restraint and share resources to meet the needs of other humans. One value that should be foremost in our achieving the goal of fulfilling basic human needs is *equity*. We should promote the equitable distribution of goods and services. Closely related to equity is another ethic, that of *beneficence* (and non-maleficence), as we will be required to give to others out of respect, kindness, and charity. And, we will be obliged not to cause harm to others.

Physical Environment and Natural Resources

Science education should be directed toward the student's understanding various aspects of the physical and human environment and the ethical decisions required in the use of natural resources.

The broad spectrum of environmental issues require, if not demand, much more attention than they have received in science curriculum and instruction. According to the results of the National Assessment of Educational Progress's (NAEP) second science assessment in 1973, students' understanding of ecological concepts declined between 1970 and 1973 (Education Commission of the States [ECS], 1976). Ironically, this period was also a time when many environmental issues were receiving attention. A conclusion easily reached is that we talk ecology and teach something else. Commenting on the NAEP result in the ECS newsletter, Paul DeHart Hurd recommended that science be taught in the context of ecological principles that have recognizable consequences for human beings. Hurd concluded:

> As science has become inextricably entwined with the economic, social, and political fabric of the nation, the social responsibility of science becomes a topic we cannot afford to ignore in the teaching of science. (Education Commission of States, 1976, p. 5)

Environmental problems require good judgment, common sense, and wise handling—all in the interest of individuals, communities, and humanity in general. Uses of the environment and resources require difficult choices. The difficult choices come because the environment and resources are in fact limited, not unlimited as we have perceived them historically. We are presently developing the new values that help mediate our decisions; our students will also be involved, and their choices as citizens will probably be critical. Environmental considerations are no longer simple. For example, prudent use of the environment means curtailing damage, nurturing preservation, and considering both individual and social demands. Decisions concerning issues such as these require the best knowledge and understanding available and socially just resolutions to the inevitable conflicts of interest. Many science teachers have appealed to Kohlberg's (1975) theory of ethical development and applied Simon et al.'s (1972) value-clarification techniques. Unfortunately, these only partially resolve the ethical dilemmas and moral debates concerning the environment. Science teachers may produce individual ethical development or clarify personal values, but they do not necessarily get the facts of the debate straight, consider the welfare of others, or incorporate the long-term worldview. I agree that science teaching should include both the understanding of environmental issues through the best, most accurate concepts and a highly developed sense of reciprocal obligation. This means broadened perceptions of self and others, short-term and long-term views, and local-to-global understanding, all of which are relevant considerations in the use of the environment. Two values that stand out in this goal are *stewardship* and *prudence*. These must eventually offset the old values of dominance over nature and careless, rash use of the environment and resources.

Community

Science education should be directed toward the student's understanding of the interdependence of individuals on one another and on their environment.

An educational goal of community is not new. John Dewey, for example, was very clear about the importance of both individualism and pluralism in a democracy. Most important, he also underscored the importance of community. In *Democracy and Education,* Dewey (1944) expressed the need for community:

> A democracy is more than a form of government, it is primarily a mode of associated living, of conjoint communicated experience. The extension in space of the number of individuals who participate in an interest so that each has to refer his own action to that of others, and to consider the action of others to give point and direction to his own, is equivalent to the breaking down of those barriers of class, race, and national territory which kept men from perceiving the full import of their activity. (p. 86)

Dewey's point is the one I am developing. If we are to reduce racism, sexism, and the possibility of total war, then we must develop a greater sense of community at the local, regional, national, and global levels.

In an article entitled "Learning Community," Joseph Schwab (1975) has argued that there should be a deliberate change in learning situations and classroom practices so that basic components of community will be contained in the educational process. Schwab's article is a variation of the basic human needs goal. He uses *privations* (needs and urgent wants that a mature and developed person cannot fulfill alone) as the central focus of his argument. He also discusses other points, such as division of labor, conquest (versus stewardship) of nature, individuality, friendship, the solving of extended (over time and space) problems, and opportunities for dialogue and dissent. Schwab's article provides a good foundation for educational policy and introduces many of the points made in this chapter on policies for science education.

For the goal of community, it seems that *cooperation* must take precedence over competition. This is not to say that competition must be eliminated; rather, cooperation must be emphasized. Inherent in the valuing of cooperation is the lesson of balancing individual rights with mutual obligation toward others. This priority of cooperation is necessary if we are to solve the important problems of our communities—be it the local or the global community.

A second essential value is an unconditional positive regard (Rogers, 1961) by the individual for the rest of humankind. This is *agape*—the far-reaching love and compassion for humanity, dependent only on the presence of other human beings. We need this type of understanding if we are to overcome the seemingly insurmountable barriers to community.

Another aspect of community involves extending an individual's perception of community from local to global, from present to future, from independent to interdependent, from the individual to group. This aspect includes, to use Martin Buber's (1922/1970) phrase, an understanding of *I and Thou*. This aspect of community relates to both cooperation and unconditional positive regard if one considers ideas such as self-reliance and self-restraint, the cooperative distribution of abundant resources to those in need, and the conservation of scarce resources by those in possession. Any one of these aspects demands as prerequisites a concentrated, *concerted* effort toward disarmament and peace.

In science classrooms, there are many opportunities to stress the goal of community. Laboratories, projects, and activities can be areas in which students experience community interdependence through collaboration, group responsibility to the class, and shared successes and failures. Inquiry-oriented experiences in science are ideal ways to develop a sense of community among students. From this first step, the expansion of the goal to local and global community can take place through new problems, projects, and discussion.

CONCLUSION

During the last decades of the twentieth century and early decades of the twenty-first century, our society will undergo substantial change. A new social order will emerge from the old. The new order could be an ecological society. If it is, growth will continue in the ecological society, goods and services will be produced and delivered. Growth will, however, be sustainable growth, not the substantial, exponential growth of the past. New values will emerge and be accepted in the ecological society. Principal among them will be equality and beneficence in the distribution of goods and services to others in our society and the world, stewardship toward the environment and prudence in the use of natural resources, cooperation and friendship among those with whom we are in community.

The evolution of a new social order will of necessity mandate a different conception of an aim such as scientific literacy. If a conceptual synthesis such as the ecological society is anywhere near accurate, then there will be the need for new aims, goals, and objectives in science education.

Science education will increasingly develop an ecological perspective in the policies that guide programs. To this end, I discussed an aim and three goals that seem warranted for the near future. The new aim and goals for science education are based on the fundamental units of ecological study: organisms, environment, populations, community, and the encompassing concept of ecosystem. Translated, these become a concern for basic human needs, the environment and natural resources, and community. Concepts and decisions about the interaction, interrelatedness, and interdependence of these three realms for survival, sustenance, and continued development of humankind must be the concern of science educators in the next decade.

The chapter began with Robert Heilbroner's pessimistic view of there being little hope for a bright future and ends with my view of reserved optimism. Hope exists in the possibility of changing present patterns of growth and achieving a global equilibrium. Social institutions will contribute to this new order by developing new policies. These changes are already occurring: The evidence is seen and heard daily in the widespread discussion about policies. Science education also should consider new directions. Science education policies for an ecological society require our students to be scientifically literate and ethically motivated, for they will be confronting the critical choices relative to fulfilling basic human needs, decreasing environmental damage, conserving natural resources, and developing peace in the global community.

■ ■ ■ ■ ■ ■ ■ ■ ■

REFLECTIONS

What would I change if I could rewrite Chapter 1, "The New Transformation of Science Education"? As I reread the article and reflected on this question, I was struck by the lack of emphasis on the goal of societal aspirations or citizenship. This lack of emphasis was probably due to the fact that I had based a significant part of the analysis in the chapter on my dissertation. In the dissertation I developed implications of Abraham Maslow's theory, which emphasizes personal development, and that orientation subsequently influenced my view. Now, I would make the social goal of citizenship much clearer and stronger.

The basic argument of the essay—that we were in a new transformation—has clearly been borne out. I did not foresee, however, how large and significant the contemporary reform would be. In the mid-1970s, I focused on science education and did not anticipate the new transformation to include a more general reform of education.

In the essay, I presented a five-step process of change:

1. New perceptions of science education
2. Publications by significant people
3. Policies for new curriculum models
4. Construction of new science programs
5. Implementation of new science programs

Although it was somewhat supported by history, I was speculative about this five-step process of change. Contemporary reform, however, is basically confirming that this process of change is occurring in science education. In the following paragraphs, I elaborate on the five-step process of change in the context of contemporary education reform.

The hundreds of contemporary reports on educational reform have clearly challenged old perceptions and elicited new ones concerning science teaching. In particular, the theme of scientific literacy as the goal of science education is a view quite different from the theme of the 1960s, when we were trying to increase the number of scientists and engineers to fill what at that time was referred to as a science manpower shortage.

A new vision also is evident. I would certainly nominate *Science for All Americans* (American Association for the Advancement of Science [AAAS], 1989) as an influential publication, for it provides a positive vision and constructive direction for science education.

As examples of the third step, I would cite policy statements such as that of the California Science Framework (1990); reports by Bybee et al. (1989a,b; 1990a,b) from the National Center for Improving Science Education on elementary, middle, and high school science programs; reports from NSTA on *Essential Changes in Secondary School Science: Scope, Sequence, and Coordination;* the National Academy of Science (1990) report *Fulfilling the Promise: Biology Education in the Nation's Schools* and reports from BSCS on *New Designs for Elementary School Science and Health* (1989) and *Developing Biological Literacy* (1993). Finally, I would add the National Science Education Standards to the preceding list of policy statements.

In the original essay, I proposed development of curriculum materials as the next phase of reform. In the late 1980s, the National Science Foundation (NSF) supported several new programs, such as the BSCS program for elementary and middle schools: *Science for Life and Living: Integrating Science, Technology, and Health* and *Science and Technology: Investigating Human Dimensions,* the Education Development Center (EDC) program *Insights,* the Technical Education Resource Center (TERC) program NGS-Kids Network, and Full-Option Science Study (FOSS) from Lawrence Hall of Science. In the early 1990s NSF also funded development of several new high school programs including the American Chemical Society (ACS) program *Chem-Conim* and the BSCS program *Biological Sciences: A Human Approach.* Local school districts are also developing programs based on national and state frameworks. There is more local development than I expected when the change model was first proposed in 1977.

Finally, there is the task of implementation, an essential step in reform and one that is usually neglected. We know more about the process of implementation because of the research of individuals such as Gene Hall, Michael Fullan, Susan Loucks-Horsley, and Shirley Hord. I now see implementation as absolutely critical and the most difficult step in the process of reforming science education.

There is more overlap among the stages of reform than I first suggested. For example, school districts often consider issues of program adoption and implementation at the same time. However, in general, I support the stages and think they are useful in an analysis of change, whether the change is at the national or local levels.

In Chapter 2, "Science Education and the Emerging Ecological Society," I would now use the term *sustainable society.* The ideas in the chapter are important, and basically I would still argue that the analysis is still appropriate for science education. The process of social change is complex, clearly involves values, and takes longer than I imagined. I still find the S-curve model and the role of personal values helpful in understanding and responding to contemporary issues such as environmental problems.

Finally, in Chapter 3, "Science Education Policies for an Ecological Society: Aims and Goals," the policy aims and goals set forth a general position that I still hold. The goals of basic human needs (personal development) and community (social aspirations) will balance the goals of scientific knowledge and scientific methods if we are to pursue the stated aim of the contemporary reform—scientific literacy for all students.

Part II

■ ■ ■ ■ ■ ■ ■ ■ ■

STS AND THE SISYPHEAN QUESTION IN SCIENCE EDUCATION

In the early 1980s, reports began emerging on the state of education in America. Education needed reform and improvement. *A Nation at Risk* (National Commission on Excellence in Education [NCEE], 1983) was the symbolic statement that propelled education into contemporary reform. Science education figured prominently in all the various reports, but especially in *A Nation at Risk*. One theme in the reports seemed quite clear: The public had lost confidence in science education because science educators had not responded to social changes; they were still basking in the glories of the reform of the 1960s, a period referred to as the Golden Age. Evidence supporting the successes of programs developed in the 1960s was scant. In fact, most of the programs developed then were no longer being used, teachers were not involving students in laboratory work, and national assessment scores were low. The Golden Age of curriculum reform was over. In the 1980s, we entered a new era.

October 1982 was the twenty-fifth anniversary of *Sputnik,* and the media made all the inevitable comparisons. On the one hand, the media recalled the science education reform, asking why it was not successful— while simultaneously implying that we did not need to change science education because we had just had a reform. Many science educators thought the same way. Nonetheless, everyone expected higher achievement. The media also thought that the NSF-supported programs had been implemented when, in fact, they had not been. But there had, however, been a significant change in science programs and teaching.

The early commissions and reports provided feedback indicating the educational system had to adjust. In this part I use the term *new purpose* as a way of saying that society has changed and that science education programs and practices should also change accordingly. Even though the term *scientific literacy* had been around for about 30 years, *scientific literacy for all students* was replacing the theme of science man-power and emerging as the major goal. The science–technology–society (STS) theme was replacing that of inquiry teaching as a way of summa-rizing a new emphasis for science curricula.

In Chapter 4, "The Restoration of Confidence in Science Educa-tion," I returned to the use of the terms *purpose, policy, programs,* and *practices* to express the continuity that should exist between the goals of science education, plans for action, science curricula, and science teach-ing. I added *policy* to the earlier list, since the contemporary reports were mostly policy statements. As I developed the theme of scientific lit-eracy, I specifically appealed to several prominent educators, such as John Goodlad, Mortimer Adler, and Lawrence Cremin, and to the Na-tional Commission on Excellence, all of whom had discussed educational goals.

While I was on sabbatical leave from Carleton College during the academic year 1984–85, I edited the 1985 NSTA yearbook and gave it the title *Science–Technology–Society.* I was also deeply impressed by Lawrence Cremin's (1976) *Public Education* and found quite helpful his question about the knowledge, skills, values, and sensibilities that educa-tors should develop. In Chapter 5,"The Sisyphean Question in Science Education," I paraphrased Cremin's question and used the myth of Sisy-phus to develop the ideas of scientific literacy that were initially stated in Chapter 4. I later strengthened the connection between scientific literacy and the STS theme. While working on the essay and NSTA Yearbook, I had several long discussions with Faith Hickman, then at the University of Colorado, and I acknowledge her contribution to the tables on STS interactions and concepts.

In the summer of 1984, I attended a conference at Exeter and had several discussions with Glen Aikenhead, who was then editor for the trends and issues section of the journal *Science Education.* Glen asked me to think about writing an article addressing the ongoing debate between Bob Yager and Ron Good and their respective colleagues. The debate centered on a definition of science education as a discipline and the place and role of science–technology–society as a curriculum emphasis. I was aware of the debate and was intrigued by the idea, since, as in most de-bates, both individuals had made some useful points and overstated oth-ers. I also thought the debate had another valuable asset—it had science educators thinking about and discussing our discipline. I completed the article while on leave in 1985. The article, included here as Chapter 6, "Science Education and the STS Theme," was presented at a symposium on "Science Education: Definitions and Implications for Research" at the 1985 Annual Meeting of the National Association for Research in Sci-ence Teaching (NARST).

Many science educators rightfully have a strong identification with science and thus appeal to scientific disciplines as they propose an emphasis for curriculum and instruction. They often downplay, or ignore, educational goals, such as personal development and social aspirations. The latter goals are the ones that I tried to develop in various ways in the three chapters in this section.

Chapter 4

■ ■ ■ ■ ■ ■ ■ ■ ■

THE RESTORATION OF CONFIDENCE IN SCIENCE EDUCATION

The burgeoning number of reports by prestigious commissions indicates the American public has lost confidence in current science education programs and practices. The loss of confidence in science and technology education is due in part to our maintenance of outdated purposes, policies, programs, and practices. We need a new vision of what science and technology education is and what it is supposed to accomplish. If we have such a vision, then there can be a basis for making judgments about new curriculum programs and classroom practices. A sense of purpose provides a grounding of one's actions, intentions, aims, and reason for teaching science, and it provides a view beyond the present circumstances.

One symptom of the loss of purpose is an overemphasis on the present; for example, "what to do on Monday." Another is an exclusive appeal to techniques; for example, "how to do it." If we continue responding only to symptoms, there will certainly be an increasing loss of confidence because science and technology education will become more disjointed and continue to lack direction. To use a medical metaphor, we can relieve the symptoms without curing the disease. Science educators need to cure the disease of maintaining old goals and not developing new purposes aligned with the needs of contemporary society. Educators are going in many directions and are apparently busy. Metaphorically, it is neurotic activity because little is actually being accomplished, like the proverbial man who jumped on his horse and rode off in all directions. Almost daily, we witness the loss of personal and professional confidence as teachers leave the profession, the public demands improvement, and commissions suggest that the time for change is at hand.

The imperative seems clear. The practical aspects of science teaching must be directed by the purposeful aims of science and technology edu-

This chapter is adapted from an article originally published as "The Restoration of Confidence in Science and Technology Education," *School Science and Mathematics, 85*(2), 95–108, 1985.

cation. We must remember that destination defines a trip, not how one travels. It is time to clarify science education's goals and purposes.

THE CRISIS IN SCIENCE AND TECHNOLOGY EDUCATION: A SOCIAL PERSPECTIVE

The word *crisis* has the power to gain the public's attention. October 4, 1982, the twenty-fifth anniversary of *Sputnik,* was an occasion for the media to ask how things were in science and technology education—and they found there was a crisis. NBC evening news had a special segment on it; there were also reports on CBS morning news (October 6) and National Public Radio (*Options in Education,* weeks of September 28, October 11), as well as in the *New York Times, Time,* and *Newsweek.* Recognition of the crisis culminated when President Reagan included the nation's science and technology education needs in the State of the Union message on January 25, 1983.

In four short months, the American public learned about what science educators had been discussing for several years—the shortages of scientists, engineers, and science and mathematics teachers; the lower achievement scores of American students as compared to those of students in other countries; and the science courses required for high school graduation in the United States compared to those in the Soviet Union, Japan, and Germany.

Environmental Concerns

In the decades since the *Sputnik*-spurred curriculum reform, we have entered a new era symbolized by several very different events: the 1962 publication of *Silent Spring,* the 1969 moon landing, the 1972 publication of *Limits to Growth,* and the oil embargo of 1973–1974.

In *Silent Spring,* Rachel Carson (1962) directed society's attention to the negative effects of pesticides. She warned that the indiscriminate use of chemicals could "still the song of birds," "the leaping of fish," and "linger in the soil." If changes were not made, society could soon experience a silent spring. The book was hotly debated. Industry attacked the book while defending its products. Some scientists criticized her supporting evidence; others were moved to act on the book's general message. The government began investigations of DDT and other pesticides. During a congressional hearing, Carson stated her basic conviction: "I deeply believe that we in this generation must come to terms with nature." Rachel Carson with *Silent Spring* had the power to gain public attention and make her views national priorities. In 1965 Congress passed the Clean Air Act and in 1969, the National Environmental Policy Act. The *Apollo* moon landing was in the same year. The greatest accomplishments and deepest concerns of science and technology stood side by side as we entered the 1970s, and neither the concerns nor accomplishments were reflected in science education.

Landing a Man on the Moon

The moon landing signaled the end of an era of significant research and development formulated by President John F. Kennedy in the early 1960s. In a special message to a joint session of Congress (*The Public Papers of the Presidents of the U.S.*, 1961), he stated:

> First, I believe that this nation should commit itself to achieving the goal, before this decade is out, of landing a man on the moon and returning him safely to the earth. (pp. 404–405)

The 1960s were also a period of marked social change. Critics of the war in Vietnam, members of the counterculture, and those involved in the environmental movement all drew connections between social problems and science and technology, and these connections were grounded in negative perceptions and values. Many people became ambivalent toward science and technology: Science and technology held both great promise and great danger.

Limits to Growth

Early in the 1970s, Meadows and colleagues (1972) warned that there are limits to growth. The oil embargo and subsequent shortage (1973–1974) made this warning a concrete experience for many Americans. Since the mid-1970s, energy has been a major national concern and priority in research and development.

Over the same 20-year period, developments in science and technology were remarkable. We became the world leader in high technology, and American scientific advances were paralleled by few other nations. The computer revolution is a central example, one that likewise is having an important impact on education. Our 1960 goals of meeting the shortage of scientists and engineers and of placing a man on the moon had been achieved. The curriculum reform and programs of the 1960s and 1970s (such as pssc physics, cba chemistry, bscs biology, and escp earth science) can be cited as contributing to these successes. Paradoxically, these successes have contributed to the present problems. Although society has changed and science and technology have progressed, science and technology education has not.

Ecological Scarcity

The environmental crisis will continue unless we change. Some projections for the next decades include ecological scarcity as a central issue. Many in society are coming to realize what ecologists have known for a long time: There are limiting factors within ecosystems, and those factors can influence the individual organisms and populations in the system. So it is with humans and their health and welfare. Ecological scarcity is a concept that includes such common ideas as environmental pollution and resource depletion. Ecological scarcity is basic to many of the economic, social, and political issues of our time—but many do not understand why and how this is the case.

Throughout history, we have witnessed personal, social, and planetwide growth that has been sustained by our natural resources—fuels, land, water, and air. We now realize, however, that our ecological systems are limited. Resources can become depleted by exhausting fuels, impoverishing land, contaminating water, and polluting air. Like people and institutions, the environment has a limited capacity, and, according to many indications, we are approaching it. A major document supporting this assertion is *The Global 2000 Report to the President* (Barney, 1980). I quote the major findings and conclusions.

> If present trends continue, the world in 2000 will be more crowded, more polluted, less stable ecologically, and more vulnerable to disruption than the world we live in now. Serious stresses involving population, resources, and environment are clearly visible ahead. Despite greater material output, the world's people will be poorer in many ways than they are today.
>
> For hundreds of millions of the desperately poor, the outlook for food and other necessities of life will be no better. For many, it will be worse. Barring revolutionary advances in technology, life for most people on earth will be more precarious in 2000 than it is now—unless the nations of the world act decisively to alter current trends. (p. 1)

The reality of ecological scarcity emerges in the midst of apparent abundance. In a moment of history, the problems of ecological scarcity also are converted to controversies surrounding personal, economical, political, and planetary systems. There are many science-related social issues that citizens do not understand; medical advances and computer technology are two examples. Yet they are asked to make decisions on issues such as toxic wastes, acid rain, and the use of life-prolonging technologies. Are science education programs preparing future citizens, including future scientists and engineers, for their social role? I think the answer is "no."

DIMENSIONS OF THE CRISIS WITHIN SCIENCE EDUCATION

There are four types of problems frequently cited by science educators to describe the crisis: practical, program, policy, and purpose.

Practical

Of all the issues confronting science educators, from kindergarten through graduate school, in public and private schools, and in formal and informal educational settings, the practical problems are the most immediate and demanding. These include budget cuts, staff reductions, declining test scores, and disruptive students. Problems such as these, which confront classroom teachers on a daily basis, are the most basic manifestation of numerous other problems in education.

Program

Program problems have several defining qualities. They are fairly concrete, but slightly more abstract than the practical problems. They entail a broader and longer-term impact on science education. They are basically intrinsic; that is, they are still largely influenced by science educators themselves. Examples include outdated curriculum materials; lack of innovative instruction; inadequate supplies, facilities, and equipment; reduction and elimination of graduate programs; and a need to revise teacher education programs.

Policy

Policy concerns are primarily extrinsic; that is, they influence the practices and programs but are initiated outside of the discipline. They, too, have a long-range impact, and they tend to be abstract but to call for concrete applications. Examples include mainstreaming (PL 94-142), accountability, the basics movement, equal opportunity initiatives, and vocational development. All of these policy initiatives require changes in curriculum materials and the overall approach of science teaching. Even better examples of policy changes are ones associated with state guidelines and school district syllabi, because these often call for new approaches to science teaching.

Purpose

Finally, problems related to the purpose of science in the schools are the most abstract and, paradoxically, also the most basic. Policies, programs, and practices are based on science education's broad aims and goals. Examples of purpose problems include discussions of the relationship of science education to science and society, scientific and technological literacy, and new directions in science teaching.

The problems associated with all aspects and levels of science teaching—practical, program, policy, purpose—have resulted in a loss of confidence among both individuals within the profession and citizens outside of science education. My point is neither that practical, programmatic, and policy issues are unimportant, nor that these problems will be automatically solved through the identification of a new purpose. All of the dimensions just described are interrelated and interdependent components of science education. The subsystems need coordination, balance, and direction. This coordination is the function of the aims and goals. Informed decisions about budgets, textbooks, or special students may have to be based on ideas and values fundamental to all of science education.

To summarize, the crisis developed because science and technology education programs have not kept up with major social changes and advances in science and technology. The need to change has become essential. The signals were first seen in a variety of small and apparently unrelated problems, such as an occasional critical article or report. The cumulative effects of outdated purposes, policies, programs, and practices make the need for change vivid to both professionals and the public. As the crisis developed, various committees and commissions began studying the situation and making recommendations on a regular and consistent basis.

BEYOND THE CRISIS: REFORMULATING THE GOALS FOR SCIENCE AND TECHNOLOGY EDUCATION

The word *crisis* is defined as a crucial situation, an unstable condition, a time when rapid change is impending, and the period prior to either improvement or deterioration. The meaning of the word comes from the Greek, *krisis,* meaning "turning point" and the Latin, *krinein,* meaning "to separate, to decide." Science and technology education is at this point. Many discussions of the crisis in science education have focused on the shortage of scientists and engineers and our ability to compete with the USSR, Japan, and Western Europe in defense, space, technology, and automobiles. If we respond only to the immediate crisis, we may provide only short-term solutions. Attention must be directed to another aspect of the crisis, toward omissions of the last curricular reform. We must include greater recognition of the personal and social dimensions of science education.

Orientation Toward Scientific Literacy

If any mistake was made in the 1960s, it was to orient science programs exclusively to the development of future scientists and engineers, those college-bound students with an aptitude for science and mathematics. Concomitantly, the curriculum programs were purged of any orientation toward a public understanding of science and technology. This occurred because exclusive emphasis was placed on science as pure (a stress on the structure of disciplines) and on science as a process (a stress on models of scientific inquiry). I have no argument about what was done or should be done to encourage and educate students to become scientists and engineers. What we did not do was to provide science education appropriate to the needs and concerns of students *as future citizens*. We should direct attention to the aim of scientific and technologic literacy for all our citizens. In order to begin reformulating our definition of literacy, it will help to examine the thoughts of other educators concerning the goals of education.

What Schools Are For

John Goodlad, in his book *What Schools Are For* (1979), points out that education is a pervasive social function and identifies two types of gap between where society is and where it might be. One is an engineering gap; the other is an educational gap. The engineering gap includes the need to increase the number of scientists. Closing this gap requires processes of social engineering and is not a primary function of education. The educational gap is measured by the distance between the most noble human visions and present human functioning. Goodlad states that there is an appropriate match between social purposes and educational goals. He stresses that all of society's needs and problems ought *not* to be perceived as an educational gap, especially when education is specifically equated with schooling. Goodlad uses the engineering shortage of the 1960s as an example of an inappropriate shift of educational goals to achieve a social purpose. In many respects, we confronted a similar situation in the mid-1980s.

> To make education into a vehicle for social engineering usually results in both disillusionment and the corruption of education. A short-term

shortage of engineers is best met by providing social inducements for young adults to enter engineering, not by shifting the balance in the whole elementary and secondary school toward science—a piece of logic we did not really see in the late 1950s and early 1960s. (Goodlad, 1979, p. 17)

Goodlad (1979) argues that there is a need for educational reconstruction in a direction that serves certain essential social purposes. He continues:

If these purposes are too many and too grandiose, schools will have no sense of symmetry. Losing sight of their educational goals, they may pursue various activities hyperactively, but the education they provide probably will grow worse. (p. 32)

I think we have misperceived the more fundamental purposes of science education for the more immediate problems described earlier in the categories of policies, programs, and practices. Solving the problems of programs and practice can become *apparent* purposes. The revealing symptoms—that is, Goodlad's hyperactivity and my examples of "what to do on Monday" and "how to do it"—support the contention that there has indeed been a misplaced sense of purpose.

The Paideia Proposal

In *The Paideia Proposal: An Educational Manifesto,* Mortimer Adler (1982) addresses the issue of the objectives of schooling: personal growth, or self-improvement of mental, moral, and spiritual dimensions; citizenship; and career preparation. Adler is concerned with life-long education, as he makes clear by pointing to the fact that these objectives are really to be achieved in adult life. He summarizes:

Here then are the three common callings to which all our children are destined: to earn a living in an intelligent and responsible fashion, to function as intelligent and responsible citizens, and to make both of these things serve the purpose of leading intelligent and responsible lives—to enjoy as fully as possible all the goods that make a human life as good as it can be. (p. 18)

A Nation at Risk

In 1983, the National Commission on Excellence in Education (NCEE) called for a reform of education in its provocatively titled report, *A Nation at Risk: The Imperative for Educational Reform.* The first section of the report reviewed the familiar litany of factors indicating we were a nation at risk: levels of functional illiteracy, low achievement scores, decline in SAT figures, and low levels of science achievement. The theme of science and technology was prominent in this influential report. It warned of a generation of scientifically and technologically illiterate Americans and a growing chasm between a small scientific and technological elite and a citizenry both ill informed and uninformed in scientific matters. The following quotation from content recommendations in A Nation at Risk (NCEE, 1983) supports the orientation I am arguing:

> The teaching of science in high school should provide graduates with an introduction to (a) the concepts, laws, and processes of the physical and biological sciences; (b) the methods of scientific inquiry and reasoning; (c) the application of scientific knowledge to everyday life; and (d) the social and environmental implications of scientific and technological development. Science courses must be revised and updated for both the college bound and those not intending to go to college. (p. 25)

Points a and b are longstanding goals of science education, but c and d represent a new purpose for science programs. There is a need to develop goals for science programs that present basic scientific and technologic concepts and processes in the context of personal and social applications and issues. In review, it seems there is rather close agreement among educators, such as Goodlad and Adler, and reports on educational goals. Science educators should direct attention toward both the individual's personal development and the individual as a citizen.

RESTORING CONFIDENCE: A NEW DEFINITION OF SCIENTIFIC AND TECHNOLOGICAL LITERACY

Science and technology education is a social institution, and as such its purpose should be directed toward meeting the needs of both society and individuals in ways unique to the institution. In our society, the most immediate way citizens learn about the products, processes, and effects of science and technology is through formal and informal science instruction. This defines the uniqueness of our discipline. It should come as no surprise to science educators that our fundamental purpose remains essentially the same—to maintain and enhance the scientific and technologic literacy of individuals in society. What has changed in the past 25 years is a definition of scientific and technologic literacy. A first step in reformulating our purpose could be a discussion based on a question posed by Lawrence Cremin in Public Education (1976): "What knowledge, values, skills, and sensibilities relative to science and technology are important for citizens in the last decades of the twentieth century?"

Implications of the Question

Several assumptions underlie this question. First, the question is being asked in the mid-1980s. The answer must reflect the current context of social and scientific needs and the projected problems and goals for the future. Second, the question includes both science and technology. In the past, we have underscored science and ignored technology in educational programs. Yet citizens actually encounter more technology in their lives. Third, the question is concerned with knowledge, values, skills, and processes. In the past, science programs have emphasized the concepts and facts of science and generally ignored the values that underlie it. The skills and processes of science receive attention in policies and many programs, but they are not widely implemented (Weiss, 1978). Support for research and development means more than knowing about R&D. It also means valuing scientific and technological activities that are central to the health and welfare of our society, and it includes the processes of science that became important goals in the 1960s. Fourth, the question implies that not all knowledge, processes, skills, and values are essential. Some aspects of science and technology are more important for citizens than others. Answering the question also forces us to be selective in the design of education programs. Finally, the question clearly addresses citizenship by implying that science and technology education should make a direct contribution to an important aim of public education: to create informed citizens who actively participate in the democratic process.

An Answer

My answer to the question incorporates an orientation for goals and an implied curriculum emphasis. First, *citizens should know, value, and use science and technology in their personal lives*. They should understand and appreciate the applications of science and technology in matters such as diet, energy use, communication, and problem solving. Second, *citizens should have some understanding of how science and technology relate to social issues;* for example, how to use resources, curb population growth, maintain environmental quality, and apply technology. Third, *citizens should understand and appreciate science and technology as a human endeavor,* such as in the relationship between basic and applied research, the role of technological development and social progress, and the relationship (or nonrelationship) of social problems to science and technology. Citizens need accurate conceptions of science and technology in society because they have to make many decisions that involve science and technology. In addition, this aim underscores the context of science in society; that is, citizens need to understand the history, philosophy, and sociology of science and technology. Finally, there is need for an introduction, in the context of science and technology, of ways that *citizens can participate in the democratic process*.

What knowledge is implicit in this statement of scientific literacy? All the concepts of traditional science are potentially contained in this goal. However, there are implied restrictions as to which concepts are taught and the provision that the concepts be introduced in a social context. The emphasis is on a human ecological orientation to the knowledge taught in science programs for future citizens.

What values are important? Again, all the traditional values of science could be included: reductive analysis, holistic–ecological understanding, the nonscientific value dimension, and environmental and conservation goals. Stewardship and prudence are also important.

What skills are important? All the inquiry and process skills emphasized in recent decades are still fundamental to science programs. In addition, the present social situation suggests that facility with decision making and the use of personal computers and various information-retrieval systems should be added to the skills of scientific and technologic inquiry.

What sensibilities relative to science and technology are important for future citizens? The word *sensibility* incorporates intellectual, ethical, and emotional responses to conditions and events. In this case, we are concerned with future citizens' receptivity and responsiveness to the role of science and technology as a social enterprise. In the next decade, citizens must respond intelligently and perceptively to personal, environmental, and social issues relative to science and technology. There is the obvious need for knowledge and skills related to these issues, but there is the additional need for individuals to understand something of the role and importance of science and technology in our society. The fundamental sensibilities required of citizens are an openness toward science and technology and an awareness of the limits and possibilities of science and technology in bringing about an improved quality of life and/or increased harm to life on this planet.

CONCLUSION

The restoration of confidence in science and technology education begins with the realization that we must separate our perceptions from the goals that have influenced our thinking in the last three decades. Then we will have to reformulate our purposes. A new view of scientific and technologic literacy is needed—one more congruent with perennial educational goals. We can achieve the final step by careful analysis of the goals of science education in the context of contemporary society and the education of all citizens in society.

These modifications of science education's policies, programs, and practices are possible within the constraints, capabilities, and capacities of our personal and social systems. Already there are fiscal responses at the local, state, and federal levels. No doubt there will be further financial assistance, but it probably will not be at the level we experienced in the 1960s and 1970s. I think we can expect that much more of the burden for change and updating will be placed on local school districts working cooperatively with colleges and universities. This is perhaps as it should be, since local practitioners know their schools, students, and community needs.

This chapter stands in contrast to some aspects of recent reports. Although there is little doubt about the need to upgrade mathematics, science, and technology education, I have sincere doubts about the main thrust of some recommendations. The National Science Board (1983) suggested that this country may become an "industrial dinosaur" unless a crash program is adopted. I do not believe it is entirely appropriate for schools to try to save the country from becoming an "industrial dinosaur." If the country is headed in this direction, it is not the result of our educational system, and the remedy cannot be found so exclusively within schools. Further, schools could not save the country from becoming an "industrial dinosaur" even if they wanted to do so. The problem is much more complex and intricately tied to private enterprise, economics, politics, and public policies.

If an unsatisfactory level of scientific and technologic literacy presently exists, then we need a view beyond these present circumstances—a new vision of the purposes of science education—to an imagined world with satisfactory levels of literacy. Once we have established this new view, it is within our capacity to develop policies, programs, and practices to achieve the new purposes. This process will certainly contribute to the restoration of confidence in science and technology education.

Chapter 5

■ ■ ■ ■ ■ ■ ■ ■

THE SISYPHEAN QUESTION IN SCIENCE EDUCATION

Sisyphus was doomed forever to roll a huge rock up to the top of a mountain. Each time he approached the top, however, the rock succumbed to the relentless pull of gravity. Wearily, he retrieved the rock and began his struggle again. Science educators are like Sisyphus. Every generation of educators must confront anew the fact that advances in science and technology and changes in society result in the need for educational reform. Indeed, science educators have the endless task of reformulating purposes, renewing policies, redesigning programs, and revising practices.

Myths are made to be interpreted in light of present circumstances. As Sisyphus neared the top of the mountain, his purpose was almost fulfilled. Then, there was a pause. The rock rolled down the mountain. What went through Sisyphus' mind as he returned to the plain below? That walk down must certainly have been a welcome respite from his labors, but he had also lost his sense of purpose. For a time, he had no vision of his goals, though he did have occasion to rethink them. Not recognizing the reality of the mission, not developing a new sense of purpose, asking only how to achieve the daily task—this is the tragedy, for Sisyphus and for science educators.

Science educators can be thought of as being in a pause, momentarily having lost their sense of educational purpose. The loss, however, is more apparent than real. In some cases, science educators are maintaining purposes and goals appropriate for the 1960s and 1970s but inappropriate for the 1980s and beyond. In other cases, they have begun listening to the suggestions of public officials, representatives of business and industry, scientists, and engineers whose goals are national defense, economic growth, and the promotion of scientific and engineering careers. If these

This chapter is adapted from a chapter originally published as "The Sisyphean Question in Science Education: What Should the Scientifically and Technologically Literate Person Know, Value, and Do—As a Citizen?" In R. W. Bybee (Ed.) (1986), *Science–Technology–Society 1985 NSTA Yearbook* (pp. 79–93). Washington, DC: National Science Teachers Association.

goals and the recommendations of these interested groups are all accepted as having equal importance, it becomes difficult for educators to agree on a direction for educational reform.

If we are to make sense of reforming science education, it is critical that we begin by rethinking the goals of science and technology education. The process of rethinking, and even debating, the goals of science teaching should help resolve the problem of apparent lack of unified purpose.

"What should the scientifically and technologically literate person know, value, and do—as a citizen?" is the Sisyphean question for science educators. It is a question for reflection as we descend the mountain, return to the rock, and prepare for our daily labor.

I address the question by first briefly presenting a perspective on educational goals. Science educators listened too little to one another in the reform we mounted in the 1960s and 1970s. Instead, we listened almost exclusively to scientists biased toward science and engineering as professional careers. Encouraging youth to go into scientific and engineering careers was one of the major goals of the Golden Age of science education. As a result, less emphasis was placed on developing science curricula appropriate for *all* students, and technology and social goals were all but eliminated from science education. The current trend has been toward increased association between education and private enterprise. The result has been inclusion of representatives from the private sector at meetings and in discussions of new directions for science education. We must be aware that participants in these discussions may not always understand or may have lost sight of the longstanding goals of personal development and social aspirations. It is important to review what contemporary educators have said, especially in this period of commissions, committees, panels, and reports. The following discussion provides insights and perspectives on the goals of education.

PERSPECTIVES ON CONTEMPORARY EDUCATION

Education has the complementary goals of developing individual qualities of students (intellectual, physical, ethical, spiritual) and preparing students to exercise their rights, duties, and social responsibilities. The ideas of several prominent educators on general educational approaches and priorities apply equally well to science and technology education.

Public Education

In *Public Education,* Cremin (1976) states that education occurs from exposure to a variety of formal and informal sources. He argues that we should take an ecological perspective of education, one which "views educational institutions and configurations in relation to one another and to the larger activity that sustains them and is in turn affected by them" (p. 36). He reminds us that a wide variety of institutions educate the public: schools, the family, libraries, museums, churches, television, industry, and business. We must recognize that education also occurs outside the school system. He urges that new directions for education should not be restricted to specific subsystems within the education system. He points out that educational goals and practices are developed for a variety of publics, ranging from classrooms to the Supreme Court, and proceed at a variety of levels extending from the local to the global community.

There are several points worth noting concerning an ecological view of education. One is that education should be directed to the individual's emerging needs and development. In particular, efforts should be made to help individuals develop their unique qualities. A second aspect of education is based on the Greek concept of paideia, which involves a larger sense of social, political, and ethical aspiration. Thus education should be directed to the development of both individual qualities and social aspirations.

What does Cremin recommend as a means to achieve an appropriate education for the individual and the community? He suggests a simple beginning point:

> We converse—informally in small groups and more formally through organizations via systematic political processes. The proper education of the public and indeed the proper creation of "publics" will not go forward in our society until we undertake anew a great public dialogue about education. (1976, p. 74)

Cremin's proposal has already been realized: We are now engaged in a great public dialogue at local, state, and national levels. There are hundreds of commissions, reports, and books on the status, needs, and future of public education. From the Sisyphean perspective, we have plenty to think about as we descend the mountain and approach the task of educational reform.

Cremin urges us to recognize that educational questions are among the most important that a society can raise. He poses some of his own:

> What knowledge should "we the people" hold in common? What values? What skills? What sensibilities? When we ask such questions, we are getting to the heart of the kind of society we want to live in and the kind of society we want our children to live in. We are getting to the heart of the kind of public we would like to bring into being and the quality we would like that public to display. We are getting to the heart of the kind of community we need for our many individualities to flourish. (1976, pp. 74–75)

These questions, approached in the context of science and technology education, are central to this essay—they are the Sisyphean questions in education.

The Paideia Proposal

In *The Paideia Proposal: An Educational Manifesto,* Adler (1982) gives his formulation of the goals of basic education:

> Here then are the three common callings to which our children are destined: to earn a living in an intelligent and responsible fashion, to function as intelligent and responsible citizens, and to make both of these things serve the purpose of leading intelligent lives—to enjoy as fully as possible all the goods that make a human life as good as it can be. (p. 18)

Adler points out, as Cremin did, that formal schooling is only a part of education. Adler's manifesto underscores the need for all students to have a high-quality education that develops basic knowledge, values, and skills, thus enabling them to enter adult life as productive individuals and responsible citizens. Adler's (1982) position, based on pledges from the Declaration of Independence and the Constitution that guarantee citizens the rights of liberty and the pursuit of happiness, is: "The innermost meaning of social equality is substantially *the same quality of life for all.* That calls for *the same quality of schooling for all"* (p. 6).

I believe the new goals for science and technology must be for *all* students, with the single exception of students who are extremely disabled. New goals for course materials and new instructional strategies must be applied not only to advanced-placement courses or classes for slow learners but also the core science curricula.

High School

In *High School,* Ernest Boyer (1983) takes a comprehensive and realistic approach to educational reform. One of his points is particularly relevant to this discussion:

> After visiting schools from coast to coast, we are left with the distinct impression that high schools lack a clear and vital mission. They are unable to find common purposes or establish educational priorities that are widely shared. They seem unable to put it all together. The institution is adrift. (p. 63)

Science programs in schools need not remain adrift. We need only realize that developing new goals founded on the science–technology–society theme can help provide a much-needed unity of purpose for science teachers and ultimately bring about a reform. The magnitude of the task is large, and an appropriate and accurate vision is necessary. The struggle to improve science education is continuous in a dynamic society. The labor of Sisyphus is indeed an apt metaphor.

PERSPECTIVES ON SCIENTIFIC AND TECHNOLOGICAL LITERACY

Many science educators and organizations have contributed valuable ideas to the theme of scientific and technological literacy. For example, Hurd (1970, 1972, 1984) has long argued that the inclusion of understanding the ramifications of science and technology in personal and social life is an essential aspect of scientific literacy. An entire issue of *Daedalus* ("Scientific Literacy," 1983) is devoted to the topic.

Practical, Civic, and Cultural

In his excellent essay "Science Literacy: The Public Need," Benjamin Shen (1975) writes about three distinct but related forms of scientific literacy: practical, civic, and cultural. Practical literacy is "the possession of the kind of scientific and technological knowledge that can be immediately put to use to help solve . . . the most basic human needs [of] health and survival" (p. 27). Civic literacy is the awareness of science and technology as they relate to social problems. It enables citizens and their representatives to apply their common sense to the issues. Cultural literacy is the understanding of science and technology as major human achievements. Cultural literacy does not necessarily solve practical problems or resolve civic issues, but it helps bridge the gap between "the two cultures" (p. 28).

Shen's ideas provide a good beginning for the reformulation of the goals of science education. Science educators must assure that science teaching contributes not only to the student's personal development but also to the student's development as a citizen, a person with civic duties, rights, and obligations. An aim of all public education is and should be to encourage informed and rational citizen participation in the democratic process.

In my view, scientific and technological literacy is dependent on citizens' receptivity to and appreciation of science and technology as enterprises with significant influences on their lives and on society. Citizens are called on to evaluate the uses and consequences of science and technology. They must decide to support or reject basic and applied research programs. They must decide whether to help establish public policies that enhance or protect the quality of life. Whether citizens are informed or ill informed, their attitudes affect social policies as much as their knowledge and skills do.

How can we encourage citizens' responsiveness to personal, environmental, and public policy issues involving science and technology? Certainly, students should learn basic science concepts and processes. Students also should understand the nature of science and technology. In addition, they should understand the limits and possibilities of science and technology as forces for social change.

Science–Technology–Society

Science teachers are being called on to answer a contemporary and expanded version of the question the philosopher Herbert Spencer asked in 1859: "What knowledge is of most worth?" Spencer's answer was "science." So is mine. What kind of science is most useful to the citizen today? The knowledge relevant to science—technology—society (STS) issues, for these are issues that citizens will help resolve. Essential topics include population growth, air quality and atmosphere, energy shortages, water resources, land use, world hunger and food resources, hazardous substances, human health and disease, and war technology (Bybee, 1984a, 1984b). In addition, vital issues are frequently raised in the fields of transportation, space exploration, microelectronics, and biotechnology.

Science has been a primary concern of education programs, but technology has been almost ignored. Yet citizens actually experience technology much more than science. Citizens encounter technology in numerous simple forms, such as eyeglasses, watches, and telephones, or in complex forms, such as computers, automobiles, and fax machines. To be sure, science and technology are related, but technology is a part of each citizen's direct and daily experience and generally science is not. A study of the status of STS programs found the following:

> There is little or nothing of STS in currently available textbooks. Our group reviewed a number of widely used textbooks . . . and found virtually no references to technology in general, or to our eight specific areas of concern. In fact, we found fewer references to technology than in textbooks of twenty years ago. The books have become more theoretical, more abstract with fewer practical applications. They appear to have evolved in a context where science education is considered the domain of an "elite" group of students. (Piel, 1981, p. 106)

Technology is not yet a part of most education programs. Every citizen should recognize the importance of acquiring knowledge about technology and to accept this as a major objective of science education.

A FRAMEWORK FOR SCIENTIFIC AND TECHNOLOGICAL LITERACY

My conceptual framework for scientific and technological literacy is outlined in Figure 5.1. The general goals of acquiring knowledge and developing skills and values define categories that help organize the material for presentation in class. The framework centers on three essential themes (science and technology concepts, the process of inquiry, and STS interactions) and specifies corresponding general areas of emphasis. For each of these themes, I have provided suggestions of topics for study or, where applicable, skills to develop. I have also included several unifying concepts and skills that are appropriate for introducing STS materials.

Application of this framework to the concepts, processes, and issues chosen for specific curriculum materials should be completed by science teachers, science supervisors, and curriculum developers in the context of their students, schools, and communities. Note that any program based on this framework should introduce the areas of emphasis in the order indicated within each column, thus progressing from simple to complex, concrete to abstract, and immediate to future perspectives.

The concept of STS should be presented to students in such a way

FIGURE 5.1   A Conceptual Framework for Scientific and
Technological Literacy

Goals	Acquisition of Knowledge	Development of Learning Skills	Development of Values and Ideas
Themes	Concepts of Science and Technology	Process of Scientific Inquiry and Technological Problem Solving	Interaction of Science, Technology, and Society
Areas of Emphasis and Activities	Personal Matters Civic Concerns Cultural Perspectives	Information Gathering Problem Solving Decision Making	Local Issues Public Policies Global Problems

that they will develop an understanding of the significance of the issues and be motivated to acquire knowledge and develop values and skills. Definitions of the relevant terms and discussions of the interrelationships of science, technology, and society are given in Figure 5.2.

Encouraging student acquisition of knowledge related to science and technology is a central aim of science teaching. In Figure 5.3, I present a detailed collection of general concepts that I formulated with the assistance of Faith Hickman. These concepts are meant to encourage development of the worldview essential for understanding certain aspects of contemporary life. One reason for choosing these particular concepts is that they unify and integrate the subject matter of science, technology, and society. There are other important concepts, but this collection is meant to provide an initial overview that will facilitate acquisition of the specific knowledge necessary for scientific and technological literacy.

A summary and description of the inquiry skills necessary for the study of science and technology and useful for the evaluation of social problems is presented in Figure 5.4. Skills for both scientific inquiry and technological problem solving are included in the figure. I have found it useful to separate the skills of scientific inquiry and technological problem solving. For example, students' initial curiosity and questioning about the natural world provide motivation for developing inquiry skills. Questioning and searching for information, combined with observing and organizing information, are part of the processes of informal scientific inquiry that are emphasized in elementary school science education. They set the stage for the introduction of formal inquiry in secondary school science classes. Decision-making skills are used in the study of science-related social issues.

The Goal of Acquiring Knowledge

We want science education to encourage students to respond to issues, to care enough to be informed. Unfortunately, many citizens think that science is beyond their grasp. The concepts of science and technology provide students with a background of knowledge that helps them develop the confidence and motivation to investigate and evaluate current issues.

Personal Matters. One of the most fundamental goals of education for scientific and technological literacy is the acquisition of knowledge that will help citizens deal with personal matters. The primary objective is to inform the public on matters that directly affect their lives. There are numerous areas in which access to basic information could help improve the quality of life for individuals, such as nutrition, family health needs, developmental needs of children, home energy conservation, and the effects

FIGURE 5.2   Science, Technology, and Society Interaction

Science. A systematic, objective search for understanding of the natural and human world. A body of knowledge, formed through continuous inquiry. Science is characterized by use of an empirical approach, statements of generality (laws, principles, theories) and testing to confirm, refute, or modify knowledge about natural phenomena. Science is a way of explaining the world.

Technology. The application of scientific knowledge to solve practical problems and achieve human goals. A body of knowledge, developed by a culture, that provides methods or means to control the environment, extract resources, produce goods and services, and improve the quality of life. Technology is the way humans adapt to the environment.

Society. The collective interactions of human beings at local, regional, national, and global levels. Human groups whose members are united by mutual interests, distinctive relationships, shared institutions, and a common culture. The human setting in which the scientific and technological enterprise operates.

Relationship of Science and Technology. Knowledge generated by scientists contributes to the development of new technologies. New technologies influence the scientific enterprise, often influencing research questions and the methods used to answer them. Technological developments lead to improved methods and instruments for scientific research.

Relationship of Science and Society. The scientific knowledge and the processes used by scientists influence our world view—the way we think about ourselves, others, and the natural environment. Scientific knowledge has both positive and negative social consequences. The impact of science on society is never entirely beneficial and rarely uniformly detrimental. Society's problems often inspire questions for scientific research. Research priorities are influenced by requests for proposals, grants, and funding through public and private sources. The social context affects the reception of new ideas, and social factors within findings. Science-related social controversies usually center on issues of research priorities and proprietorship of knowledge.

Relationship of Technology and Society. Technology influences the quality of life and the ways people act and interact locally, nationally, and globally. Technological change is accompanied by social, political, and economic changes that may be beneficial or detrimental to society. The impact of new technology is never entirely beneficial and rarely uniformly detrimental. Social needs, attitudes, and values influence the direction of technological development. Technologies often arise in response to cultural values and serve the needs of dominant social groups. Social control of technology is seen in demands for the development or assessment of new technologies. Technology-related social controversies usually center on issues of efficiency, equitability, cost-benefit risk, and regulation.

Relationship of Science, Technology, and Society. Science and technology have influence social development throughout history at all levels of society. The most direct interactions are between technology and society, but the technology is complemented by scientific knowledge. Although science and technology are distinct, they are so intertwined that most interactions between either and society do in fact involve all three.

FIGURE 5.3   Unifying Concepts for Science, Technology, and Society

---

Systems and Subsystems. A system is a group of related objects that form a whole, or a collection of materials isolated for the purpose of study. Subsystems are systems contained entirely within another system.

Organization and Identity. Systems have identifiable properties. There are boundaries, components, flow of resources, feedback, and open and closed aspects of the system's organization. Changes in properties may cause a change in the system's identity.

Hierarchy and Diversity. Matter, whether nonliving or living, is organized in hierarchical patterns and systems. There are hierarchical levels of organization, ranging from subatomic to cosmic. There is increasing complexity of organization within physical, biological, and social systems. Diversity can increase the stability of systems.

Interaction and Change. Components within systems interact, and systems interact with each other. There is usually evidence of the interaction. Evidence of interaction provides opportunities for identification and analysis of causal relationships. Systems change over time. The course of change may be influenced to modify properties, organization, and identity of systems.

Growth and Cycles. Linear growth occurs by a constant amount over a time interval. Exponential growth occurs by an increasing rate (at a constant percentage) over a time interval. Some systems change in cycles.

Patterns and Processes. Interactions, change, growth, and cycles often occur in observable patterns and as a result of identifiable processes.

Probability and Prediction. Some changes are more predictable than others. Statistical calculations provide some degree of accuracy (a probability) in the prediction of future events.

Conservation and Degradation. Matter and energy are neither created nor destroyed. Both may be changed to different forms. This is the First Law of Thermodynamics. Considered as a whole, any system will tend toward increasing disorder. This is the Second Law of Thermodynamics.

Adaptation and Limitation. All systems respond to environmental or cultural challenges. There are limits to environmental, organismic, and social changes. Adaptations may be biological, physical, technological, social, political, or economic.

Equilibrium and Sustainability. Equilibrium occurs when components of a system interact in ways that maintain a balance. Due to adaptation, growth, and change, all systems exist on a continuum from balanced to unbalanced. The extent of the equilibrium or disequilibrium is a function of the system's capacity to carry the load created by factors operating in and on the system. A social system is sustainable if its organization results in stability of its natural resources and environment

---

FIGURE 5.4   Skills of Scientific Inquiry and Technological Problem Solving

Questioning and Searching. Identifying meaningful questions and problems about the world and locating and discovering relevant information are basic inquiry and problem-solving skills. Questioning and searching are first steps toward problem-solving and decision-making.

Observing and Organizing. In observation, the senses are used to gather information about objects, events, or ideas. Once information is observed and gathered, it must be organized in relation to space, time, and causality.

Measuring and Classifying. Measuring and classifying most commonly involve (a) counting objects or events, establishing one-to-one correspondence, and organizing objects according to numerical properties and (b) computing the dimensions, capacity, or duration of objects, systems, and events, forming groupings based on these measurements and putting objects or events in order according to a pattern or property.

Comparing and Conserving. Comparing includes identifying similarities and differences in separate objects and systems, and noting changes in a single object or system over time. Conservation means that quantitative relationships between materials and systems remain the same even if the materials and systems have undergone perceptual alterations.

Analyzing and Synthesizing. Analysis involves reducing information to simpler elements to determine the organization and dynamics of objects, systems, events, and ideas. Analysis includes describing components, clarifying relationships among systems or subsystems, and indentifying organizational principles of systems. Synthesis involves bringing together information to form systems based on organization principles or patterns. Analysis stresses reduction and to parts and synthesis stresses construction and the whole.

Identifying and Describing. Question and problem identification and description are the first steps in formal inquiry and problem-solving. Included are identification of scientific, personal, and social problems, gathering information, and determining what is known and unknown about a problem.

Hypothesizing and Predicting. Hypothesizing and predicting are used in answering questions, tackling a problem, and designing scientific experiments or technological devices. Making reasonable guesses based on available information, making assumptions of conditionality ("If. . . then. . ."), determining possible conclusions, and predicting probable conclusions are the necessary skills. Students may use inductive (specific to general) and deductive (general to specific) reasoning and propositional thinking.

Separating and Controlling. The skill of separating and controlling variables is necessary to the design of scientific experiments and helpful for analysis of data, solution of problems, and evaluation of policies. Determining the similarities and differences of conditions or events, identifying relevant factors and combinations of factors, and controlling factors to determine how changes influence reactions are the three major steps. Students may use hierarchical thinking (such as building classification keys) and formal logic in the process.

FIGURE 5.4 (continued)

Exploring and Evaluating. Describing the decision to be made, gathering information, using information to determine the alternatives, and examining the consequences of different decisions are all preliminary activities to decision-making. Evaluating consists of determining the reliability of information and then making value judgments based on the information and external criteria such as the costs, risks, and benefits of the alternatives.

Deciding and Acting. Making a choice based on information and evaluation and being prepared to justify the decision are the final steps of decision-making. Identifying opportunities for taking action is a skill that paves the way for acting to solve personal and social problems.

of environmental problems (such as air and water pollution) on personal health and welfare.

Civic Concerns. Citizens cannot participate effectively in the democratic process unless they have an awareness and understanding of civic concerns. Half of all legislative bills in Congress are related in some way to science and technology. Students need to know what kinds of issues they will be asked to resolve as future citizens and recognize why their participation is beneficial to society. There are many topics appropriate for study, such as problems of renewable and nonrenewable resources; short-, middle-, and long-range solutions to the energy problem; the need to limit population growth; and environmental quality in the home, school, community, and world.

Cultural Perspectives. Historical, philosophical, social, and political perspectives on science and technology can contribute to students' understanding of the roles of science and technology in society. Recognizing science and technology as human endeavors and appreciating the limits and possibilities of science and technology help students develop realistic attitudes toward science. Discussion of the concept of STS interactions provides good preparation for the later exposure to difficult and controversial issues. The social effects of science and technology should be stressed: the effect of research (basic and applied) and development on social progress; the connection between technological innovation and employment; the social roles of science and technology in matters such as energy, armaments, and mining; and the role of technology in developing countries.

The Goal of Developing Skills

Skills based on the processes of scientific inquiry and technological problem solving provide necessary preparation for the study of most traditional fields of science. They are equally valuable as tools for obtaining information on social issues and evaluating and solving the problems of society.

Information Gathering. We live in an information-rich society. The goals of obtaining and using information are fundamental to science. Today this activity requires not only observing nature but also gathering information from various sources in society. Skills of scientific inquiry have tradition-ally included questioning, observing, organizing, measuring, and classi-fying. Students should develop these skills as well as research skills such as locating sources of information, extracting the information, and using information-retrieval systems.

Inquiry and Problem Solving. Problem solving is another traditional goal of science teaching. The skills used in scientific inquiry and technological problem solving (identifying questions and problems, hypothesizing, pre-dicting outcomes, and separating and controlling variables) are usually taught in the context of designing scientific experiments, but they can and should be applied to personal and social problems as well.

Decision Making. Decision making is new to the science classroom, but it is a logical extension of inquiry and problem solving in a personal and social context. After the initial inquiry and problem solving, possible al-ternatives are identified and evaluated. In decision making, choosing the "best" alternative to resolve an issue involves making value judgments on the desirability of each alternative.

The Goal of Developing Values and Ideas

Class discussion of STS issues helps students develop insight into their current values and assumptions and recognize the importance of being receptive to ideas. It motivates them to develop sound values and to be responsive to change when necessary. Learning to apply their skills to solve problems and resolve issues gives students encouragement to act, to participate as citizens.

Local Issues. Emphasizing local issues provides a good starting point for the clarification and development of general STS themes. The specific per-sonal matters and local issues will vary with schools' locations. Topics should relate to larger concerns, but student interest and motivation may be increased when topics are introduced at personal and local levels. Ex-amples of topics of local interest are energy resources, waste disposal, recycling, erosion, groundwater contamination, air and water pollution, and food production.

Public Policies. Public policy issues frequently have STS themes. These issues provide opportunities for teaching basic science concepts and a forum for encouraging civic participation. State, regional, and national problems include many of those studied in a local context. Environment, resources, and population are the major areas of concern.

Global Problems. Many problems related to science and technology are of global dimension. Surveys I conducted found that the global problems given highest priority by scientists and engineers include world hunger, population growth, air quality and atmosphere, water resources, war technology, and human health and disease (Bybee, 1984a, 1984b). There is a need for students to develop a global perspective so that as citizens they will be prepared to exert what influence they can to help solve social problems even on the global scale.

CONCLUSION

Educators at all levels, from preschool to graduate school, recognize the immense influence of our scientific advances and the significance of our social problems as we progress toward the twenty-first century. We are keenly aware of the disparity between the needs of society and the appropriateness of our programs. At the same time, education is beset with budget cuts, staff reductions, teacher burnout, increasing numbers of students, and numerous new curriculum requirements. Other unsettling issues render the daily task of teaching difficult. Reluctance to reform programs is understandable. At the same time, the reasons and responsibilities for reform are compelling. We have a choice. We can give in to the forces acting on us or, like Sisyphus, we can continue our mission. Weary and overloaded though we may be, science and technology education awaits our new initiative. Just as Sisyphus must have had courage in order to continue, we cannot afford to have a failure of will at this crucial period in history. Citizens have a genuine need to understand the impact of science and technology on our society and the social issues they must evaluate. Educators have a responsibility to meet this public need. So, again, we are at the foot of the mountain, with the challenge to find and accept a new answer to the Sisyphean question.

Chapter 6

■ ■ ■ ■ ■ ■ ■ ■ ■

SCIENCE EDUCATION AND THE STS THEME

In this chapter, I clarify the relationship between science education and the science–technology–society (STS) theme and explain why this theme is rightfully a part of our educational purpose. I first examine a debate over the definition of science education, then proceed to a historical review of science education's social purpose, and finally discuss STS in science education and some issues that might be engaged by including this theme in science education programs and practices.

DEFINITIONS OF SCIENCE EDUCATION

The literature includes several definitions and discussions of science education as a discipline (Watson, 1983; Westmeyer, 1983; Yager, 1983a). In the mid-1980s, there was a professional debate centering on defining the domain of science education, stimulated by the issue of locating STS topics within the discipline (Good, Herron, Lawson, & Renner, 1985a; Yager, 1985a&b). The following two examples serve as introduction to this debate.

Origins of the Debate

In 1982 Jack Renner made the point that "the purpose of science education . . . is to be concerned with the education in science of the students who populate the schools" (p. 709). This description of purpose, however, is neither clarifying nor helpful because the definition is essentially circular—science education is concerned with education in science. Earlier in the 1982 article, Renner had indicated that science education also had the dual purposes of improving existing and establishing new

This chapter is adapted from an article originally published as "Science Education and the Science–Technology–Society (STS) Theme," *Science Education, 71*(5), 667–683, 1987.

procedures for science teaching. For Renner, purpose—the goal of science education—seemed to be derived from learning theories, in particular those associated with his and his colleagues' research on Jean Piaget's theory. So for Renner, the goal of science teaching is cognitive development. Renner justified his position by appealing to the statement of the Educational Policies Commission (1961) on *The Central Purpose of American Education* and citing the following quotation that summarizes the central purpose of education: "The purpose which runs through and strengths all other educational purposes—the common thread of education—is the development of the ability to think" (p. 6). I certainly agree. There is no doubt about the development of reasoning as a fundamental aim of education. But even this statement must be understood in *context*. One must ask: "The ability to think *about what*?" This aim, the context of the quotation, and my question are addressed further in a later section. First, I describe the other position in this debate.

In "Defining the Discipline of Science Education," Robert Yager (1984) presents his definition of science education:

> Defining the discipline of science education to be the study of the science–society interface removes the restriction that science education is a school or collegiate program. At the same time, it does not exclude such settings as places that the interface may be effectively considered. Such a designation provides parameters for research efforts, curriculum planning, and educational programs. (p. 36)

Here Yager first indicates that science education is the discipline that studies the science–society interface, then seems to justify his definition of science education on the grounds of a broadened conception of where and who engages in science education. This position is perhaps understandable, but it neither addresses nor resolves any fundamental issues. Yager (1984) continues his discussion with another, clearer definition:

> Science education is defined, then, as the discipline concerned with the study of the interaction of science and society—i.e., the study of the impact of science upon society as well as the impact of society upon science. There interdependence becomes a reality and the interlocking concept for the discipline. Research in science education centers upon this interface. (p. 36)

The word *study* is somewhat confusing in this definition. If Yager means that which students pursue in educational programs, then there is some justification for the definition, but the definition is quite limited in scope. However, late in the quotation Yager seems to suggest that study may mean the knowledge that science educators pursue in their research.

For this position, there is little or no justification because there are individuals from other disciplines—for example, policy analysis—who also study topics within the broad framework of science and society (see, for example, journals such as *Bulletin of Science, Technology, and Society, Issues in Science and Technology,* and *Science, Technology and Human Values*).

Concerning these two views, Renner's position appropriately identifies a fundamental purpose of education, namely, the development of reasoning. His position centers primarily on the individual and gives little recognition to any social purposes of education. There is no reason for Renner to exclude the STS theme from science education, since it could facilitate the development of reasoning. Yager centers his definition almost exclusively on the social context of science education, ignoring other major goals, and then limits that position to the degree that he does not clarify or support any specific themes for study, such as STS theme.

Debate over STS Issues

Based on Yager's (1983a,b, 1984, 1985a,b) conception of science education, Hofstein and Yager (1982; Yager & Hofstein, 1984) advocated that societal issues function as central organizers for the science curriculum. The Yager–Hofstein position has served to continue debate about the definition of science education, particularly the inclusion of STS issues in school science programs.

Hofstein and Yager (1982) begin with the sentence, "Science education as a discipline is concerned with the interface between science and society" (p. 539). They continue by indicating that *concerned* means that science education must respond to social changes and that various societal issues should be reflected in school science programs. While comparing science education in the 1960s and 1980s, they make this point:

> A more central societal concern currently is teaching science for scientific enlightenment; the knowledge considered to be important is that which supposedly will be useful and relevant to the solution of societal problems. (p. 541)

Later, they provide the basis for new goals: "The goals of the 80s are derived from the interaction of science, technology, and society" (p. 541). Note that this position is different from their earlier statement that science education is the discipline concerned with the *study* of interactions between science and society, a statement that is aligned with the central thesis of my argument; namely, that the goals of science education must be reformulated to include the personal and social dimensions that have been ignored for more than three decades. However, there are other important goals of science education, such as those suggested by Renner—the development of reasoning.

The authors cite advantages of making social issues central to curriculum organization, and they provide examples of curriculum programs that include societal issues, although the examples they cite are not as issue-centered as the position they present.

Robert Kromhout and Ron Good (1983) reacted negatively to the Hofstein–Yager position. They generally supported "the use of socially relevant problems as motivation for a coherent study of fundamental science" (p. 647), but differences between the two positions can be identified in the phrase, "a coherent study of fundamental science." Later, they indicate that science education should teach "the coherent *structure* which is the heart and soul of the scientific method" (p. 648). Here is a summary of the Kromhout–Good position:

> The computer, the technology of objectives and multiple guess, modularized individual study materials, science history, sociology of science, sociological impacts of technology (although each has made valid and valuable contributions to education), and even the antiscience of creationism have displaced the efforts to teach, through direct personal experience and problem solving, an understanding of the power and scope of the problems on which science can cast significant light as well as those questions of value judgment on which science does *not* lead directly to a solution. (pp. 648–649; emphasis Kromhout & Good's)

In the Kromhout–Good position, one can see that any attempt to include socially relevant topics would distract science teachers from educating students about the structure and methods of science. Paradoxically, they justify this position by the need for citizens to understand the scientific and technologic base of our civilization. They further support their position by appealing to the need to develop the ability to reason noted in 1961 by the Educational Policies Commission.

Kromhout and Good conclude by asserting that the use of social issues in curriculum organization is dangerous because social activists will manipulate and pervert science education (p. 650). This strongly stated position is inadequately clarified and weakly supported.

Debate centering on the definition of science education and the STS theme has continued with little new or different being added to the basic positions (Good, Herron, Lawson, & Renner, 1985a; Good, Renner, Lawson, & Herron, 1985c; Yager, 1985a,b). The 1985 National Association for Research in Science Teaching (NARST) meeting included a symposium on "Science Education: Definitions and Implications for Research," for which this chapter was originally prepared. A paper by Good, Kromhout, Lawson, and Renner (1985b) served as the focal point of the symposium.

In summary, the emerging STS theme has caused us to review and, to some extent, clarify our conception of science education. Some see the STS theme as central to science education, making little mention of other goals such as the development of reasoning. Others focus almost exclusively on developing thinking and reasoning, and giving little attention to goals related to the STS theme. In their zeal, authors on both sides of this debate have overstated their positions and inadequately dealt with the nature of science education as a discipline (Westmeyer, 1983).

In this chapter, I argue that STS ought to be included in science education programs. I justify this based on an understanding of science education as a social institution, a position only partially recognized in earlier discussions. As a social institution, science programs and teachers should contribute to achieving the goals of personal development and societal aspirations. I elaborate this position in the next section.

A CONCEPTION OF SCIENCE EDUCATION

In this section, I present a conception of science education's broad purpose in order to provide a rationale for inclusion of the STS theme in school science programs. I use several historical documents to support my position.

Combining Science and Education

Science education combines the specific content and processes of science and technology with the general purposes of education. Although this may seem a statement of the obvious, science educators have tended to pay more attention to science and less to education in their definition and justification of goals. My discussion centers on *education,* an orientation that is sometimes recognized but never emphasized in professional discussions. Yet education is, or ought to be, the fundamental orientation of our profession. Science describes the type of education with which we are involved. Concentrating on education clarifies our larger purpose while maintaining the integrity of scientific and technologic content and method.

In at least two articles discussed above (Good et al., 1985a; Good, et al., 1985c), significant attention was given to the question: "What is science?" In "Science Education: Definitions and Implications for Research" (Good et al., 1985b), the authors state: "To develop an understanding of what *science education* is, the name needs to be analyzed and that analysis, we believe consists first of describing science" (p. 139). Subsequently, the authors provide several good, fundamental definitions of science about which there can be little argument. But to answer the other question—"What is education?"—the authors simply supply a dictionary definition. Such an approach to defining education is inadequate for professional science educators. In the next section, I provide a broader view of education and its purposes.

A careful answer to the first question—"What is science?"—involves several fundamental aspects of science education programs, including structuring of concepts in the curriculum and introducing the processes of science. This question should also orient one to the career awareness goals of science education curricula and instruction.

By answering the second key question—"What is education?"—one further defines science education and its purposes. Since I elaborate on this question in the next section, I will mention education here only briefly. Although definitions of science tend to differentiate science education from other subcategories (for example, art education, mathematics education), definitions of education provide broad and unifying goals for all subcategories of education. That is, examination of education provides an understanding of the larger purposes of schooling in science. I maintain that an appropriate understanding and definition of education justifies inclusion of the personal and social goals and this position directly connects to the sts theme. Further, this orientation provides the *contextual* orientation for the knowledge, process, and career goals of science teaching.

It should be clear that my contention that the content and processes of science ought to be presented in a personal and social context in no way suggests a redefinition or diminution of science (or technology). It does help define and limit the knowledge, processes, and career awareness that ought to be included in science education programs. In the following section, I review the broader purposes of education.

The Purposes of Education

Education, and hence science education, is a social institution. As such, it shares the directives common to all social institutions: (1) providing for the needs and continued development of individuals and (2) fulfilling the requirements and aspirations of a democratic society. These aims are achieved in ways unique to each social institution. In the case of science education, this means education about the knowledge, applications, skills, and values relative to science and technology. Note that education in science ought to include the personal and social goals just mentioned. Here, too, there is a connection between science education and the

STS theme. The following historical perspective serves to elucidate and support the purposes of education I just presented.

HISTORICAL PERSPECTIVE

Education in the eighteenth century had a clear purpose—to develop Christian citizens. As times changed, so did the purpose of education. In the early nineteenth century, one purpose was to educate citizens for work in factories and industry. Even though the aims changed, underlying education was the basic idea that schooling should serve individual needs and ultimately society's needs for maintenance and development.

Historically, various education reports have supported the broad purposes of personal fulfillment and social development. Establishing this concept of educational purpose and then proceeding to identify contemporary policies for science education is important. Below I briefly review some historically prominent discussions of educational purpose.

The Cardinal Principles of Secondary Education

In 1918, the Commission on the Reorganization of Secondary Education completed its work and published *The Cardinal Principles of Secondary Education*. This report called for a shift from a narrower religious indoctrination to a broader socialization of students. The seven cardinal principles proposed for the schools were health, command of fundamental processes, worthy home membership, vocational competence, effective citizenship, worthy uses of leisure, and ethical character. The individual and social themes are easily recognizable in these seven principles.

Science in General Education

In 1938, the Progressive Education Association published *Science in General Education*. In a chapter titled "The Purpose of Education in a Democracy: Implications for the Science Program," the committee made explicit their position:

> The purpose of general education is to meet the needs of individuals in the basic aspects of living in such a way as to promote the fullest possible realization of personal potentialities and the most effective participation in a democratic society. (p. 23)

The report went on to specify four basic aspects of living: (1) personal living, (2) immediate personal–social relationships, (3) social–civic relationships, and (4) economic relationships. In both the broad statement and narrower categories, the individual and social themes are again evident. The committee devoted a chapter to each of these basic aspects of living.

General Education in a Free Society

General Education in a Free Society was written by the Harvard Committee and published in 1945. Near the book's beginning, the purpose of general education is presented:

> General education, as education for informal, responsible life in our society, has chiefly to do with . . . the question of common standards and common purposes. Taken as a whole, education seeks to do two things: help young persons fulfill the unique, particular functions in life which it is in them to fulfill, and fit them so far as it can for those common spheres which, as citizens and heirs of a joint culture, they will share with others. (p. 4)

The Committee differentiated between general and specific education. As seen in the above quote, general education was viewed as that part of schooling concerned with a student's life as a responsible human being and citizen. Special education was viewed as occupational or vocational training education (not to be confused with the contemporary definition of special education). The Harvard Committee unequivocally included science education as a part of general education, stating that "below the college level, virtually all science teaching should be devoted to general education" (p. 156).

Two other points from *General Education in a Free Society* are worth noting. The first relates to "traits of mind." The traits of mind to which the Committee gave priority are "to think effectively, to communicate thought, to make relevant judgments, to discriminate among values" (p. 65). These, like the development of the ability to think emphasized by the Educational Policies Commission (1961) and discussed earlier in this chapter, are to take precedence over other aims across general education programs. The Committee also pointed out that these traits are *not separable* in practice.

The second point anticipates discussions in the next section on STS in science education. After a general discussion of science as both process and product, the Harvard Committee outlined broad characteristics of a science program:

> Science instruction in general education should be characterized mainly by broad integrative elements—the comparison and contrast of the individual sciences with one another, the relations of science with its own

past and with general human history, and of science with problems of human society. There are areas in which science can make a lasting contribution to the general education of all students. (p. 155)

In summary, *General Education in a Free Society* provides support for development of reasoning and extends that goal to include communicating, making judgments, and discriminating among values. The actual science program would have an integrative approach that presented science in a cultural context, including recognition of social issues related to science.

Educational Policies Commission

The Educational Policies Commission (1961) report on the central purpose of American education has been used by Renner (1982) and by Kromhout and Good (1983) to support their position that developing the ability to think is the primary purpose of science education. Thinking, reasoning, and critical thinking are all important education aims (Bybee & Sund, 1982), but I would add a second question: "Think *about what*?" The report does indeed answer this question and provides support for my position.

The beginning of the report dwells on the theme that education should serve the needs of individuals and society: "The American people have traditionally regarded education as a means for improving themselves and their society" (p. vi). The report continues, "The need, therefore, is for a principle which will enable the school to identify its necessary and appropriate contributions to individual development and the needs of society" (p. vii).

These positions are offered as a rationale for the development of rational powers, or the ability to think. What are the more practical areas presented once the goal is stated? Recalling the 1918 report of the Commission on the Reorganization of Secondary Education, the 1961 report gives the following aims of school: fundamental processes, health, worthy home membership, vocational competence, effective citizenship, worthy use of leisure, and ethical character.

The 1961 report provides further justification for the stated purpose by appealing to changes in the world, for example, energy use, communications, space, disease, expanding populations, and use of technology. The development of rational powers is indeed a part of the larger purpose of personal and societal development. Logically, psychologically, and pedagogically, the development of the ability to reason must occur within a context. In science education, that context is appropriately provided through inclusion of the STS theme.

THE STS THEME IN SCIENCE EDUCATION

In this section, I clarify and elaborate on the STS theme in science education, noting that use of the preposition *in* implies that the STS theme is only part of science education. This theme provides a new orientation for school programs, one very different from those of earlier goals and curriculum models or those that use specific, narrowly defined issues as the organizational focus for all of science teaching. A conceptual framework for science–education research and development sets the stage for later discussions.

A Conceptual Framework

A conceptual framework should include the primary areas in which objectives are formulated: scientific and technologic knowledge and processes as well as personal–social applications. Earlier, in Figure 5.1, these areas are represented in the three essential themes of science and technology concepts, the processes of inquiry, and science–technology–society interactions. Under each of the three main categories, areas of emphasis, participation, and study are suggested. Overall review of the conceptual framework suggests an orientation toward the personal and social purposes of science education, while examination of the separate columns identifies specific objectives in the area of knowledge and skills in STS interactions.

The conceptual framework helps translate concepts, processes, and understandings into curriculum programs and instructional practices. Progression down the columns leads from personal to cultural, from information gathering to decision making, and from local to global perspectives. Generally, the framework goes from simple to complex, concrete to abstract, and immediate to past and future perspectives. In Chapter 5 and elsewhere, I have elaborated on various components of this conceptual framework (Bybee, 1984b; 1986b).

The STS Orientation

Schooling in science ought to enhance the personal development of students and contribute to their lives as citizens. Achieving this purpose requires us to reinstate the personal and social goals that were eliminated in the curriculum reform movement of the 1960s and 1970s. On a more practical level, an STS orientation would mean research and development of curriculum and instruction to do the following:

- present science knowledge, skills, and understanding in a personal–social context;

- include knowledge, skills, and understandings relative to technology in the curriculum;
- clarify the knowledge, skills, and understandings relative to the STS theme that are appropriate to different ages and stages of development;
- identify the most effective means of incorporating STS issues into extant science programs; and
- implement STS programs into school systems.

Issues and Problems

Over the years that I have been interested in STS and science education, there have been many issues and problems raised concerning the implementation of this theme. With the help of colleagues, I completed several surveys assessing the STS theme in science education. We sampled populations of college students (Bybee & Najafi, 1986), science teachers (Bybee & Bonnstetter, 1986), an international group of science educators (Bybee & Mau, 1986), and scientists and engineers (Bybee, 1984a). My intention here is not to review this research but rather to use these studies as an information base for answering some questions concerning the STS theme.

One of the first questions critics ask is which social issues are important? Based on my review of rankings from the surveys, the problems listed below are perceived to be most important:

- air quality and atmosphere,
- world hunger and food resources,
- war technology,
- population growth,
- water resources,
- energy shortages,
- hazardous substances,
- human health and disease,
- land use,
- nuclear reactors,
- extinction of plants and animals, and
- mineral resources.

A second question is often asked: "Is there support for the STS theme?" Yes, every population sampled indicated support for the STS theme as a part of school science programs.

Another concern that runs through criticisms of STS is based on the misconception that the entire science education program will be based on these goals and exclude traditional attention to such areas as scientific knowledge and processes. First, the discussion earlier in this chapter and in Chapter 5 should have revealed this concern as based on a misconception. Second, although the amount varied among the groups sampled, the percentages below represent the minimum amount of instructional time respondents thought should be devoted to science-related social issues:

Elementary school	10%
Middle/junior high school	15%
High school	20%
College/university	25%.

Ample time would thus exist for development of other goals of science education, such as knowledge, inquiry, and career awareness. Rather than diluting these goals, there is every possibility that students would learn more about science and technology because the subject would be presented and experienced in a context that had personal and social meaning.

Another concern is that science teachers are not prepared to implement the STS theme. But they were not prepared for the reforms of the 1960s and 1970s either. They did not know how to teach the "structure of a discipline" and "modes of inquiry." As professional science educators, we should first ask whether the STS theme is an appropriate orientation for curriculum and instruction. If it is, then it is in part our professional obligation to conduct research and provide instructional materials, in-service programs, methods textbooks, and summer school classes that will prepare teachers to implement the STS theme.

Science teachers often complain that they do not know about social studies and thus cannot teach this component of the STS approach. Science teachers should concentrate on the scientific and technologic dimensions of the issues; all they are being asked to teach in the social studies area is what they should know as citizens who participate in the democratic process.

Another criticism is that teaching STS will blur the distinction between science and nonscience. Exactly the opposite is the case, as the controversy of creationism versus evolution in school biology programs demonstrates. Science teachers, administrators, school boards, and even scientists have had to review the arguments and examine their positions. Debates ranging from two individuals to courts of law have served to clarify the distinction between science and nonscience, religion in this case. In the end, we all know more about the basic tenets and goals of both science and religion. In addition, we know something of the way these issues are debated and resolved in a democracy.

Finally, there are critical comments concerning evaluation. I note here that two national assessments in science have included science, technology, and society items (Hueftle, Rakow, & Welsh, 1983; National Assessment of Educational Progress, 1978; Rakow, Welsh, Hueftle, 1984). This fact should be an indication of the importance of the STS theme. In the conclusion of their 1984 article on the national assessment in science, Rakow, Welsh, and Hueftle had this to say:

> Gains were made by 9- and 13-year-olds, and relatively small declines by 17-year-olds in science, technology, and society items. Yet, these issues do not appear to have wide coverage in the commonly used textbooks at any of these grade levels (Pratt, 1981; Hurd, 1981). While it is likely that creative teachers are supplementing the textbooks with STS topics, it is reasonable to suggest that student images of social issues related to science and technology also are a product of media coverage and out-of-school science experience (such as zoos, museums, and nature centers) rather than traditional school learning experience exclusively. (pp. 577–578)

The existence of national assessments of STS suggests that some importance is placed on this theme. The national biology test of the National Science Teachers Association and the National Association of Biology Teachers also will have STS items (McInerney, personal communication, June 1986). Yet it is fairly clear that instructional materials and classroom testing practices have lagged behind the new priorities.

CONCLUSION

Professional debate over the definition of science education and the STS theme can be characterized as a dialectic originating with Yager's (1984) original thesis and the antithesis presented by Kromhout and Good (1983) and Good and colleagues (1985a, 1985b, 1985c). In this chapter, I have reviewed, criticized, and attempted to synthesize both positions by identifying science education as a subsystem of education. A review of several significant education reports provided support for the inclusion of goals related to the fulfillment of personal and social needs and aspirations. Including these goals within education, and hence science education, provides support for the STS theme in science education.

REFLECTIONS

The early 1980s were a turning point in science education. Publication of *A Nation at Risk* in 1983 symbolized the beginning of contemporary educational reform. In science education, the results of Project Synthesis were published in 1981 by Norris Harms and Bob Yager. I would cite this project and the publication of its results as the symbol that officially ended the Golden Age and initiated the new reform of science education. Still, perceptions and programs from the Golden Age lingered, and such always presents a danger—continuing with the old when there are opportunities for change. The early 1980s were a time of crisis. Some science educators questioned use of the term *crisis* because they equated it with disaster or tragedy. I have equated it with turning point, a time of danger and possible disaster or of improvement through change.

In this period, there was a shift from satisfaction with and support for such secondary programs as PSSC physics, CBA and CHEM-study chemistry, BSCS biology, and ESCP earth science and elementary programs such as SCIS, ESS, and S-APA toward an emphasis on how-to materials—short, motivating activities that science teachers could use. There is, I think, still too much emphasis on these activities when there is a need to develop a larger perspective on science curriculum and instruction. Curriculum developers, school districts, and, ultimately, science teachers need to have a vision of science education so that the details of specific lessons can contribute to the articulated goals of scientific literacy. We have to clarify the larger purposes of science teaching before the practical problems can be resolved.

In Chapter 4, "The Restoration of Confidence in Science Education," I addressed the issue, thinking about purpose before practice. Although the crisis has abated, thinking about these issues is still essential and will ultimately broaden our perspectives of science education.

In Chapter 5, "The Sisyphean Question in Science Education," I elaborated on several subjects first discussed in "The Restoration of Confidence in Science Education." I have been intrigued by the myth of Sisyphus and Albert Camus' insight about Sisyphus walking down the mountain. I combined this myth with an adaptation of Lawrence Cremin's probing query about the goals of education and developed the Sisyphean question for science education. This essay was my attempt to make a concrete, debatable statement about scientific literacy and the STS theme. The framework for scientific and technologic literacy is a set of policies that should be debated and modified as curriculum specialists and science teachers develop new programs.

The Sisyphean question—"What should the scientifically and technologically literate person know, value, and do—as a citizen"—is, in my opinion, timeless. Science educators should be answering the question every time a curriculum is developed and a lesson is taught, even though the answers will vary across time, disciplines, grade levels, and individual teachers. I provided one answer to the question, an answer that was appropriate for the mid-1980s and discussed in the context of STS.

"Science Education and the STS theme" (Chapter 6) used a debate within science education to once again state the significance of the personal and social goals of science education. In this essay, I appealed to historical rather than contemporary statements to support my position that inclusion of STS in science education programs is appropriate and justifiable.

Part III

■ ■ ■ ■ ■ ■ ■ ■ ■

CONSIDERATIONS IN REFORMING SCIENCE EDUCATION

The chapters in this section concern the changing role of teachers and the new science curricula, the planetary crisis and the need for greater recognition of environmental issues in science programs, and the fact that the science–technology–society (STS) theme is more rhetorical than real. Although the chapters may seem diverse, they develop specific themes—implementation, the environment, STS—that were identified in earlier chapters.

In 1988, Audrey Champagne asked me to prepare an essay for the American Association for the Advancement of Science (AAAS) National Forum. The theme for that year was science teaching. I was pleased to prepare the essay, "Contemporary School Science: The Evolution of Teachers and Teaching," which has become Chapter 7, because it gave me the opportunity to present some ideas based on my participation in several projects to improve school science. The Biological Sciences Curriculum Study (BSCS) and International Business Machines (IBM) had collaborated on a design study that considered how technology might be incorporated into elementary school science. Based in part on this design study, BSCS received funds from the National Science Foundation to develop the elementary program *Science for Life and Living: Integrating Science, Technology, and Health*. I also chaired two curriculum and instructional panels for the National Center for Improving Science Education. The latter was funded by the U.S. Department of Education's Office of Education Research and Improvement (OERI). These experiences led me to two conclusions. First, that implementation—specifically the change of teachers and teaching—was the critical issue in reforming science education; and second, that science teachers could not and should not be expected to achieve the changes alone. We may have learned our lesson about "teacher proofing" programs, but we should not confuse the new phrase *teacher empowerment* with a position suggesting that science teachers can achieve changes in curriculum and instruction without the support of all of those associated with the educational system. I used evolution as an analogy in the essay because it worked and analogies often give insights that are missed in straight narrative.

"Planet Earth in Crisis" was the theme for the 1991 National Association of Biology Teachers (NABT) Convention. This theme was undoubtedly based on the emergence of new environmental problems, such as ozone depletion and global warming. My concern about the environment and ecology is longstanding. I began writing on the environmental theme in the mid-1970s. In "Planet Earth in Crisis: How Should Science Educators Respond?" (Chapter 8), I make a direct and powerful statement to science educators by asking and answering the question: "How should science educators respond to the crisis?"

Not unrelated to the "Planet Earth in Crisis" theme is the essay "The STS Theme in Science Curriculum" (Chapter 9). I noticed that there were numerous articles proclaiming the need for STS and extolling the virtues of the theme and that there were a variety of STS materials available. Science educators had developed policies supporting the implementation of STS, and they had provided curriculum. So what do we know about the implementation of STS? Is it a part of the school curriculum? What do students learn who experience STS programs?

Chapter 7

■ ■ ■ ■ ■ ■ ■ ■ ■

CONTEMPORARY SCHOOL SCIENCE: THE EVOLUTION OF TEACHERS AND TEACHING

Contemporary language about educational improvement often uses the metaphor of revolution. But I think it is more constructive to think about the reform of science education in evolutionary rather than revolutionary terms. In this essay, I consider the adaptations in the environment of the education system that are necessary to meet the demands of the new generation of science curricula, focusing in particular on teachers and teaching.

Certain parallels exist between biological evolution and educational change. Both are slow and conservative processes in which pressures act selectively on variations in extant populations. Educational change occurs in environments of considerable diversity—there are enormous differences among school districts and within a district, and there can be considerable variation among its elements. Teachers, for example, exhibit large variations in their subject-matter knowledge, pedagogical skills, and philosophy of education. Because of these, certain teachers will be more amenable than others to the changes required to implement new programs. However, successful adaptation of the system requires that all highly variable elements respond constructively to pressures on them.

EXTERNAL PRESSURE ON THE SYSTEM

Pressure for the reform of school science emanates from many sources: governors' reports, legislative mandates, increased state regula-

This chapter is adapted from a chapter originally published as "Contemporary Elementary School Science: The Evolution of Teachers and Teaching" in A. B. Champagne (1988) (Ed.), *Science teaching: Making the system work* (pp. 153–171). Washington, DC: American Association for the Advancement of Science.

tions, the declining national economy, new perspectives on science learning resulting from psychological and educational research, and advances in science and technology. Contemporary education reports call for new purposes and policies for American education (Bennett, 1986; Committee for Economic Development, 1985; National Commission on Excellence in Education, 1983; National Science Board, 1983; Task Force for Economic Growth, 1983). These reports include proposals for curriculum change aimed at the reform of science education (Brunkhorst & Yager, 1986; Bybee, 1985a, 1985b, 1987a, 1987b; Harms & Yager, 1981; Hurd, 1984, 1986; National Academy of Sciences, 1988; National Science Board, 1983; National Science Teachers Association, 1982; Yager, 1984).

At the federal level, the National Science Foundation (NSF) responded to these recommendations by initiating a program to develop innovative curriculum materials for school science, kindergarten through high school. In 1987, the NSF funded three major projects for the development of new science programs for the elementary school, with five additional awards following in 1988. In 1989, the NSF awarded grants to develop materials for science education at the middle level. Although the eight new NSF programs vary in scope, approach, and materials, all are very different from the traditional textbook-based programs that currently dominate elementary school science (Weiss, 1987). These new school science programs will create pressures on the educational system, especially on the science teachers who will be expected to teach them. Even though the new NSF programs will not be available for implementation until the early 1990s, it is time to begin considering how the system can be adapted to program demands. The experience of the curriculum reform movement of the 1960s provides a useful lesson to those of us who are responsible for implementing the new generation of science programs.

HISTORICAL BACKGROUND

During the 1960s and 1970s, a number of new science programs were developed for schools (Hurd, 1969). Examples at the elementary level include Science—A Process Approach (S-APA), Elementary School Science (ESS), and Science Curriculum Improvement Study (SCIS). There were other excellent programs, such as the Conceptually Oriented Program in Elementary Science (COPES), the School Science Curriculum Project (SSCP), and the Elementary School Science Project (ESSP). These programs had two important features in common. First, the programs were designed to give students direct experience with the objects and events of the natural world. Second, they were designed with the intention of being teacher-proof. The developers' intent was to design the programs in such a way that they would be successful without the teachers necessarily being an important factor in their success.

Today these programs are used in very few schools. Even at the time they were developed, the programs were not widely implemented, and in those instances where they were, their use was not sustained (Weiss, 1977, 1987). When implemented properly, the programs were effective in achieving their goals for student learning (Bredderman, 1983; Shymansky, Kyle, & Alport, 1982, 1983), but the assumption that teacher-proof programs could be developed—that the written materials and activities could do it all—was a false one. We know better now.

Using the evolution analogy, the program developers viewed schools and teachers as marginal environmental pressures that the program developers somehow had to accommodate. In the case of teacher-proof programs, the school environment selected against innovative variations. The evolution analogy suggests that the education community needs to change its perception of reform. Those in the educational system must view teachers as an evolving population that can accommodate environmental pressures caused by a curriculum change.

The lessons learned from previous attempts to reform school science are that two kinds of adaptations must occur: (1) Programs must be adaptable to the teachers' knowledge, skills, dispositions, and approaches, and (2) teachers must be provided with opportunities to accommodate new programs by developing new knowledge, skills, dispositions, and approaches. Efforts to enable both types of adaptation are evident in the current reform. Under NSF guidelines, program developers were required to form partnerships with publishers before beginning development. Publishers continually stress the marketability of programs. Although the programs are innovative, they are not so different that teachers' current knowledge and skills cannot accommodate them. The NSF also requires that curriculum developers attend to implementation, a process that necessitates adaptations in the school environment to accommodate the new programs.

The most significant of these adaptations involves the nature of science teaching. Programs based on new conceptions of how children learn science employ radically different teaching techniques to which science teachers must adapt. The best measure of the success of the new programs will be the degree to which teachers come to manifest the essential characteristics of science teaching that the materials embody.

A NEW GENERATION OF PROGRAMS

The direction of the change is determined by the new curricula, which presumably are responsive to societal demands as reflected in the recommendations of the national reports previously cited. The new science programs supported by the NSF reflect the spirit and substance of the call for reform. Although programs under development by the BSCS, the Education Development Center (EDC), Lawrence Hall of Science (LHS), and the Technical Education Research Centers (TERC) have many characteristics in common, they have significant differences, such as the degree to which they use technology, the articulation of curriculum and instruction, and importance placed on implementation by the developers and publishers (Bybee & Landes, 1988a,b; Bybee and Landes, 1990; Foster, Julyan, & Mokros, 1988; Sandler, Worth, & Matsumoto, 1988).

Curriculum Foundations

Several features of the new programs differentiate them from current programs and practices, which are textbook-driven and do not generally reflect contemporary goals of science education or approaches to teaching science (Burke, 1980; Gould, 1987; Jaus, 1981; Neuman, 1981; Staver & Bay, 1987; Weiss, 1977, 1987).

First, the curriculum content is different. Traditional textbook programs are usually divided into such topics as plants, animals, magnets, rocks, minerals, and dinosaurs. The primary student learns names, facts, and definitions. In contrast, several new programs are based on major conceptual schemes, such as energy, systems, evolution, and equilibrium.

Second, technology, both as content and tool, is an innovation that characterizes contemporary reform. Examples of technology as content include "Technology as a Way of Doing," which is a major theme of the BSCS program *Science for Life and Living: Integrating Science, Technology, and Health*. The EDC program *Insights: Hands-on Inquiry Science Curriculum* includes units on technology, such as "Bridges and Structures" and "Moving Things." Use of technology in the science classroom, especially computer courseware, is a significant change in this era of reform.

A good example of the use of technology as a learning tool is the TERC project *NGS-Kids Network,* which uses telecommunication as a means of study. In the *NGS-Kids Network* project, the students collect data on a local phenomenon, such as the pH of rainwater. They use telecommunications to upload their data to a national center that in turn summarizes all data from across the country and downloads that summary to local classes. The students then analyze the national data as well as their local data. The importance of information technologies in educational reform is discussed in several contemporary reports (Boyer, 1983; Linn, 1987; National Science Board, 1983). The addition of technology to the science curriculum and its use in the classroom have significant implications for the practice of science teaching (Bybee & Ellis, 1989). Teachers must be prepared to teach about technology and to use technology to teach. This increases the number of process skills that science teachers must be prepared to teach, for example, making decisions, evaluating risks, and considering benefits. Teachers must also learn to use the new technology—computers, educational courseware, laboratory interfacing—and to integrate them into their current teaching practice.

Third, "less is more" expresses the contemporary approach to curriculum content. Today fewer concepts are studied in greater depth and fewer skills are developed to greater proficiency. This feature of the new science programs contrasts markedly with textbook series, which over the years have increased the number of topics presented and the superficiality of their treatment. This new approach to the construction of science curricula is based on new views about the learner (Brook, 1986–1987; Newmann, 1988). Studying a subject in depth gives students more time to become actively involved (mentally and physically), to explore phenomena, and to construct explanations of the natural world. Teaching fewer concepts and skills requires inclusion of more unifying or encompassing concepts and skills in science programs.

Topics are selected in such a way that students learn about science and technology in a personally and socially meaningful context. For instance, topics in the TERC program are based on data students collect about acid rain, pets, and plants. BSCS materials include topics related to the student's current and future life—tools, transportation, and fitness. EDC materials, designed especially for urban children, develop science concepts in the context of urban environments—forces, chemicals, and ecosystems. Major scientific concepts and processes are developed through experiences that are naturally engaging to children. These aspects of the new science programs reflect important ideas about science learning, specifically that learning science in personal and social contexts motivates students and enhances learning.

These examples reflect a fourth difference in the new science programs, namely, that content and teaching methods are based on assumptions about students as learners. Those assumptions are as follows: Students are motivated to learn about their world; students have developmental stages that influence learning (Piaget, 1973); students have different styles of learning (Kuerbis, 1987); and students come to school with explanations, attitudes, skills, and sensibilities about their world (Carey, 1986; Champagne & Klopfer, 1984). Two characteristics of instruction in the new science programs—hands-on activities that engage students with objects and events from the natural world, and cooperative learning that encourages students to work together and help one another learn (Johnson, Johnson, & Holubec, 1986a)—are based on these assumptions.

The hands-on approach is certainly not new to science education. All science programs developed in the 1960s and 1970s used this instructional approach. The approach has been shown to be effective in producing desirable outcomes (Bredderman, 1983; Shymansky et al., 1982, 1983). There is, however, substantial evidence indicating that a hands-on approach is not widely used for teaching science in schools (Weiss, 1987). If the new science curricula with their hands-on approach are to be successful, teachers must learn to use them effectively.

Cooperative learning, however, is new to this generation of science programs. The concept is based on research in social psychology. Cooperative learning is more than students working in groups. The method requires that each student understand the learning task and group goal, each student be responsible for the others' learning, and each student be cognizant of the criteria for success. Teachers are responsible for monitoring how well groups are functioning, developing needed interpersonal skills among group members, helping groups evaluate their success, and intervening where problems emerge (Johnson & Johnson, 1987; Johnson et al., 1986a). Clearly, the success of cooperative learning requires major adaptations in the role of the teacher and the character of the classroom.

In addition to basing instruction on learning theory, the new science programs use explicit teaching models to convey the method. This use of explicit teaching models in science programs is consistent with the emergence in recent years of the use of instructional models at all grades and in all disciplines (Joyce & Showers, 1988). Madeline Hunter's and Bernice McCarthy's models are popular examples of this trend in instruction. Local reform of science programs often incorporates the Hunter, McCarthy, or other models. Each new project—BSCS, EDC, LHS, and TERC—has a systematic instructional approach. The instructional models vary, but all are integral to the science curriculum and represent an approach to science teaching that is based on the assumptions about student learners discussed above. They are designed to facilitate the students' construction of knowledge, attitudes, and skills. The success of the science programs will depend on teachers' ability to integrate the new teaching models with their current practices and with existing districtwide models without compromising the intent of the science teaching models. The use of these science teaching models will require considerable adaptation on the teachers' part.

NEW CHALLENGES FOR TEACHERS

The new science programs present formidable challenges for science teachers. The challenges are the "environmental contingencies" of successful adaptation, in the evolution analogy. Although I recognize the magnitude and difficulty of the changes required of teachers, I see no alternative. Teachers are the essential links between the curriculum and students. Teachers bear the ultimate responsibility for implementing science programs. However, teachers must be supported by other components of the educational system; administrators, supervisors, and school boards must share the responsibility (Berliner, 1984; Porter & Brophy, 1988; Shulman, 1986, 1987).

Among the challenges posed to teachers by the new science curricula are learning new content, developing a new conception of the science learner and its implications for instruction, learning how to use and incorporate instructional technology into the science classroom, and developing strategies to manage science equipment in the classroom. These are all elements of what Lee Shulman (1986) includes as part of the pedagogical knowledge that underlies teachers' classroom performance, knowledge about science, knowledge about how science is learned, and knowledge about how the objects in the classroom—textbooks, equipment, and computers—are managed. All this knowledge must be integrated into a coherent whole by each teacher. Successful implementation of the new programs requires that each teacher learn these new ideas and integrate them with his or her views of teaching and learning.

New Content

The knowledge base required to teach the new science programs is different from that currently required of teachers. It includes the conceptual schemes of science and technology as well as the procedural skills and rules by which the growth of knowledge occurs in science and problems are solved in technology. The dimensions of knowledge are deceptively simple. Consider the major conceptual schemes, such as those in the BSCS program: order, change, patterns, systems, energy, and balance. In contrast to other scientific concepts, such as the Krebs cycle and Bowen's reaction series, these concepts are immediately recognizable, understandable, and manageable in the everyday world, by teachers and students. Most important, they are fundamental concepts of science. These conceptual schemes are not discipline-specific; rather they are applicable to many domains, including technology, health, and social studies. The important quality of these conceptual schemes is their immediate utility and their contribution to the development of more sophisticated concepts.

Procedural skills and rules of science and technology are a second dimension of the knowledge base. The skills, called *processes of science,* include observation, organization, measurement, prediction, analysis, investigation, and decision making. (These examples are process skills emphasized in the BSCS program.) Like the conceptual schemes, these skills have immediate utility, are not discipline-specific, and include both general skills, such as critical thinking and reasoning, and science-specific skills, such as classification.

In addition to conceptual schemes and procedural skills, the nature of the scientific enterprise is an important element of the content. This, together with technology, is a new domain that science teachers will be expected to teach. These new topics are important for students to learn and, in addition, are highly motivational, since they relate to the student's life, have practical utility, and can be taught using interesting problems and concrete materials.

A New Conception of the Science Learner

Central to the new conception of the science learner is the constructivist view of learning (C. W. Anderson, 1987; Carey, 1986; Champagne & Hornig, 1987). Constructivism is a dynamic and interactive model of how humans learn. According to this theory, students redefine, reorganize, and elaborate their current concepts through interactions with objects, peers, and events in the environment. Students "interpret" objects and phenomena and subsequently explain their world in terms of their current conceptual understanding. Application of constructivist theory to teaching involves challenging students' current conceptions through discrepant events—experiences that conflict with students' current ideas and result in the students' realization that their current explanations are inadequate. They subsequently provide students with experiences that suggest alternative ways of thinking about the world. When a student's conceptions are challenged, a state of disequilibrium occurs. Cognitive equilibrium is reestablished through opportunities, in the form of experiences and time, for that student to construct a conception that is more adequate than the original.

In the early stages of developing the BSCS program, I recognized the need for a systematic approach to instruction (C. W. Anderson, 1987; Champagne, 1987) and developed an instructional model that incorporates the essential features of constructivism. The BSCS model is described briefly in Figure 7.1. Using this teaching model challenges teachers to understand the concepts and procedures being developed for the student and simultaneously to teach in a way that is in accord with theories of student learning as well as with the specific content to be learned. The BSCS instructional model is an illustration of these points. The new science programs incorporate learning theory into instructional models that provide guidance to the teachers on appropriate strategies for science teaching. However, it is ultimately the teachers' responsibility to apply the model and adjust it for the unique characteristics of the content being taught and for the students expected to learning.

Technology in the Science Classroom

In the 1990s, computers will be incorporated into most science programs. They will be used for instruction and telecommunications as well as for collection and organization of data from science experiments. The

---

FIGURE 7.1   The Biological Sciences Curriculum Study (BSCS) Instructional Model

---

ENGAGEMENT

This phase of the instructional model imitates the learning task. The activity should make connections between past and present learning experiences and anticipate activities and focus students' thinking on the learning outcomes of current activities. The student should become mentally engaged in the concept, process, or skill to be explored.

EXPLORATION

This phase of the teaching model provides students with a common base of experiences within which they identify and develop current concepts, processes, and skills. During this phase, students actively explore their environment or manipulate materials.

EXPLANATION

This phase of the instructional model focuses students' attention on a particular aspect of their engagement and exploration experiences and provides opportunities for them to verbalize their conceptual understanding or demonstrate their skills or behaviors. This phase also provides opportunities for teachers to introduce a formal label or definition for a concept, process, skill, or behavior.

ELABORATION

This phase of the teaching model challenges and extends students' conceptual understanding and allows further opportunity for students to practice desired skills and behaviors. Through new experiences, the students develop deeper and broader understanding, more information, and better developed skills.

EVALUATION

This phase of the teaching model encourages students to assess their understanding and abilities and provides opportunities for teachers to evaluate student progress toward achieving the educational objectives.

TERC project NGS-*Kids Network* is a pioneer effort in the integration of technology, in this case telecommunications, into school science programs. Implementing program that use computer technology will require teachers with practical knowledge of computer hardware and software. Science teachers do not need to know the intricate electronics of the hardware, nor do they need to understand the complexities of programming. However, they do need to know the appropriate classroom use of information technologies. Teachers also need to understand the relationship of courseware to systematic instructional strategies, for example, the integration of microcomputers with the cooperative learning group strategy. Johnson, Johnson, and Stanne (1986b) and Johnson and Johnson (1987) have demonstrated that this integration is effective in reducing problems of classroom management and enhancing student learning.

Materials Management

Management of materials is an additional challenge posed by the hands-on character of the new science programs. The care, set-up, storage, and ordering of materials and supplies are essential to the successful implementation of these programs. Program developers are including suggestions in guides and print materials for teachers to reduce the problem of materials management. There are some solutions to this problem, but they often require seeking the cooperation of other adults in the school system or teaching students to be responsible for their own materials.

NEW DEMANDS ON SCHOOL SYSTEMS

In 1987, the Carnegie Foundation for the Advancement of Teaching surveyed 13,500 teachers and discovered that the teachers regarded reform efforts as less than successful (Carnegie Foundation for the Advancement of Teaching, 1988):

- Fifty percent of teachers gave a grade of C to the reform movement.
- More than 30% said class sizes had increased since 1983.
- About 80% said they had the same or less time to spend with other teachers.
- About 27% said they had less time to prepare for teaching on a daily basis.
- About 30% said they had less freedom from nonteaching duties.
- Fifty-nine percent indicated that morale in 1987 was worse than in 1983.

Despite these criticisms, teachers indicated that there had been improvements. A majority of teachers cited as examples more clearly defined goals, higher expectations for students, more individualized instruction methods, improved use of technologies, improved textbooks, and more leadership from principals.

Clearly some desirable reform has occurred, but it is also evident that there is still room for improvement. That improvement ultimately centers on teachers and teaching. But teachers cannot accomplish the reform of school science programs alone—there also must be reform elsewhere within the school system. Successful reform requires taking a systems perspective, changing school structures, and instituting programs of professional development. We must prepare the environment so that it promotes desirable changes in teachers.

A Systems Perspective

Education reform is an evolutionary change in teachers and teaching that occurs within a system functioning as a whole due to the interdependence of its parts (Bertalanfy, 1986; Churchman, 1979; Laszlo, 1972b; Rapoport, 1968; Thorsheim, 1986). The school system is the environment of education reform. Although there are many components within the school system, teachers are the most critical ones. The new science programs define many components of the system, including content, equipment, assumptions about learners, and instructional approaches. Successful implementation requires that teachers adapt content and pedagogy to their teaching style, students, schools, and community (Hall & Hord, 1987; James & Hord, 1988).

Characteristics of the school and community determine in large measure the successful implementation of innovative programs. How open are the school system and community to change? How easily do resources (for example, materials, equipment, and information) flow into the school system? What are the sources of and types of feedback from the community and the school system?

Both the community and district influence program implementation, as the following illustrations from the new programs demonstrate. The TERC program NGS-*Kids network* requires computers, modems, and telephone lines to connect science classrooms with the telecommunications network. Implementation of this program requires considerable commitment of fiscal resources from the school district. Without community and district support, the program cannot be implemented.

The BSCS program illustrates the importance of community and district support of a different kind. The sixth-grade curriculum has a health unit, entitled "Self and Others," about human reproduction and sexuality. This is an example of content capable of generating community controversy. The district administrators have the responsibility for maintaining information flow between the district and the community when the potential for controversy exists. Controversy is much more likely to be constructive and reach amicable resolution when information about the program is introduced to the community in a planned way. Using the evolution analogy, it is the district administration's responsibility to develop a "selective advantage" for teachers using the new programs. A systemic approach establishes and sustains the selective advantage of innovative programs and teaching.

Structural Support for Implementation

Program implementation requires configuration of budgets, equipment, and personnel. This structural support is the responsibility of school administrators. Their support should be based on a clear understanding of the new science program, including the program philosophy, goals, content, and pedagogy. Administrators need to understand how the new program differs from current programs and why the new program should be adopted and implemented. Knowing the resource requirements for program implementation and maintenance is essential. How much do materials cost? What will the program cost annually? What are the hidden costs? There must be budgetary allowances for items beyond the purchase of the program, support for an aide to manage materials for the classroom teacher, time for planning prior to implementation, and time for professional development. For all these reasons, close communication among administrators, teachers, and science supervisors is necessary throughout the process of program implementation.

Professional Development of Teachers

The success of the education reform movement depends on teachers who have the knowledge, disposition, and skills to teach in ways that reflect the goals of the new programs. In the long term, improvement of the science knowledge and teaching skills of teachers is the single most important environmental outcome to be derived from the development and implementation of the new programs.

This will be achieved through the professional development of teachers. The evolution analogy provides an informative perspective on professional development. Several principles from biological evolution are evident:

- Evolution occurs in populations; so, one must consider the population of science teachers within the school, school district, state, or nation.
- Selection occurs at the level of individual organisms; so, individual teachers demonstrate more or less acceptance on use of innovative programs.
- Populations change over time; so, one must consider the range of innovative changes within the population of teachers and try to develop selected changes over a period of time.
- The frequency of various kinds of organisms in a population changes; so, the number of teachers who effectively and appropriately implement an innovative program will change.
- Only a few characteristics change in a population at any time; so, concentrate on a few, very important changes in staff development and let the teachers make other changes later.
- Populations are complex but stable systems of myriad interactions; so, recognize the interactions among teachers and the stable features of curriculum and instruction that must be maintained while changing other features of curriculum and instruction.
- Selection for variations in a population results in changes in a particular direction; so, make sure administrators and supervisors "select" for the variations aligned with the innovative program.

The analogy with evolution suggests that, in planning for change in the population of science teachers, we consider the teaching characteristics of a population of teachers and clearly define the desired change in terms of science teaching as it is reflected in the new science programs.

Increasing variation in science teaching strategies is a challenge. The evolution analogy is useful in thinking about how changes in the science teacher population might develop. Change in biological systems occurs when forces act from without and when accidents occur within. Changes in genetic material occur when an external force—ionizing radiation, for example—interacts with DNA to produce a change in its structure. Change of a different kind occurs in genetic material during natural processes within the system. For example, chromosomes cross over when "accidents" occur during cell division (recombination).

The process of change in social systems parallels that in biological systems. In changing a population of teachers, external forces—new science programs and professional development programs—produce changes in individual teachers. Unlike biological evolution, where changes are random and conditions in the environment determine which organisms will survive, the process of changing teachers is deliberate. The forces are chosen to produce specific changes. The choice of content and teaching procedures, for example, determines the direction of change.

Equally important to changing teacher behavior are the effects of teacher interactions. Every school system has individual teachers who are trying new approaches, some probably aligned with the directions described in this chapter. Encouraging cooperative work among teachers provides the opportunity to recombine some of their ideas and approaches. One teacher may use educational technology, and another may have a system to manage materials effectively. The recombination can result in two teachers who design ways to use technology in the management of materials. This example is simple, but it demonstrates another way to increase the variation of teaching within schools. Professional development within the school system can drive the evolution of the system toward the desirable characteristics exhibited by exemplary teachers in the system.

General characteristics, such as inclination to innovate or enthusiasm, identify those teachers whom the administration may designate as members of a leadership team for changing the science program. The intent is to increase variation within the population of teachers. Variation within a population is beneficial; it allows for favorable response to the uncertainties of environmental change. We must not, therefore, attempt to develop the same traits in all teachers, but rather to cultivate a variety of skills upon which they can draw as new and currently unrecognized challenges arise.

Sustaining innovative programs in the school system is another challenge. After the adoption of a new program, school administrators and science supervisors typically act in ways to support the implementation of new programs and teaching methods. Once the innovation is in place, however, system support is withdrawn. Then innovations flounder. Sustaining new science programs requires more than short-term support; it requires permanent changes in the larger system.

CONCLUSION

The primary goal of the new science programs is to improve scientific and technologic literacy. An equally important, although unstated, goal of these programs is to improve teachers' science teaching skills. The programs reflect contemporary national goals for science education. The content and teaching methods incorporated in the programs are based on developers' interpretations of the most up-to-date theories about how students learn and what science is most worth knowing. As teachers implement these programs, they will be learning new science content as well as new ways of teaching science. If, in addition, they come to understand why this content and these methods were chosen, they will make important progress in their professional development. Teacher empowerment is a goal of educational reform. Knowledge empowers all. Pedagogical knowledge empowers teachers.

Chapter 8

■ ■ ■ ■ ■ ■ ■ ■

PLANET EARTH IN CRISIS: HOW SHOULD SCIENCE EDUCATORS RESPOND?

The End of Nature is the alarming title of a book by Bill McKibben (1989). McKibben explains the title as follows:

> By the end of nature I do not mean the end of the world. The rain will still fall and the sun shine, though differently than before. When I say "nature," I mean a certain set of human ideas about the world and our place in it. But the death of those ideas begins with concrete changes in the reality around us—changes that scientists can measure and enumerate. More and more frequently, those changes will clash with our perceptions, until, finally, our sense of nature as eternal and separate is washed away, and we will see all too clearly what we have done. (p. 8)

There is a difference, for example, between knowing that smoking may be harmful because it stresses your cardiovascular system and having your doctor sit down, look at you with a solemn stare, and say "I have some very bad news." You may continue living, but your perception of life and living will be quite different. This is, I believe, an analogy of the message contained in McKibben's book. What McKibben argues is that humans have altered the Earth's systems to a point of crisis—nature as we generally *have thought of it* no longer exists. Science educators should pause and ask: "What does this mean? What should we do?" My answer is direct: We should educate students in ways of ameliorating the planetary crisis. The imperative to survive justifies teaching about our place in natural systems, and it obligates us to act in ways that ensure sustainable growth. If this sounds urgent, you already have one message of this chapter.

This chapter is adapted from an article originally published as "Planet Earth in Crisis: How Should Science Educators Respond," *The American Biology Teacher, 53*(3), 146–153, 1991.

The End of Nature is not the only recent book to signal the critical condition of the planet. On the same list are Stephen Schneider's (1989) *Global Warming;* the World Commission on Environment and Development (WCED) (1987) report, *Our Common Future;* a special issue of *Scientific American* on "Managing Planet Earth" (1989); and Barry Commoner's (1990) *Making Peace with the Planet.* A brief historical review of reports on the state of the environment clarifies the developing urgency of the situation and my reason for writing again on the theme of human ecology (Bybee, 1977b, 1979a, 1979b, 1984a, 1984b).

THE YELLOW LIGHT TURNS RED

In the last half of the twentieth century, environmental issues have expanded from local to global; they have evolved from minor to major; and they have extended from personal concerns to public policies. The cautions expressed in the 1950s and 1960s are now mandates to cease and desist. The yellow light is red. A brief review of several important books supports this assertion.

A Distant Early Warning

Silent Spring by Rachel Carson (1962) signaled the American public about the dangers of environmental pollution, particularly DDT. Carson announced that during this century humans acquired significant power to alter the planet's nature:

> The balance of nature is not the same today as in Pleistocene times, but it is still there: a complex, precise, and highly integrated system of relationships between living things which cannot safely be ignored any more than the law of gravity can be defied with impunity by a man perched on the edge of a cliff. The balance of nature is not a *status quo;* it is fluid, ever shifting, in a constant state of adjustment. Man, too, is part of this balance. Sometimes the balance is in his favor; sometimes— and all too often through his own activities—it is shifted to his disadvantage. (p. 218)

Later in *Silent Spring,* Carson indicates our point of decision:

> We stand now where two roads diverge. But unlike the roads in Robert Frost's familiar poem, they are not equally fair. The road we have long been traveling is deceptively easy, a smooth super highway on which we progress with great speed, but at its end lies disaster. The other fork

of the road—the one "less traveled by"—offers our last, our only chance to reach a destination that assures the preservation of our earth. (p. 244)

Silent Spring was a distant, early warning signaling the need to change human interactions with the environment. The book also symbolized the environmental movement of the 1960s, which centered on the issues presented by Carson—clean air, water, and soil, and the preservation of wildlife. Although some individuals attended to the message, society, as demonstrated by its public policies, did not take the path less traveled.

A Global Perspective

In the decades since Rachel Carson's warning, the environmental perspective has expanded from local to national to global. In the 1990s, we realize the global scale of many environmental problems. For many individuals, this expanded perspective began with publication in the early 1970s of *The Limits to Growth* (Meadows et al., 1972). Based on computer modeling, the study concluded:

> If the present growth trends in world population, industrialization, pollution, food production, and resource depletion continue unchanged, the limits to growth on this planet will be reached sometime within the next one hundred years. (p. 24)

The Limits to Growth provides insights into a number of concepts related to environmental problems. The first of those concepts is represented in the title itself—limits. Other concepts included those described by Garrett Hardin (1968) in "The Tragedy of the Commons"—exponential growth and carrying capacity. In addition, the book presented a worldview and systems modeling, both essential to an understanding of global problems then and now. With *The Limits to Growth,* the consequences of human interactions with natural systems were projected from a national to a global perspective.

In 1981, Lester Brown's book *Building a Sustainable Society* presented a vision of the road less traveled. Although reports such as *The Limits to Growth* had suggested sustainable growth as an appropriate response, Brown described the essential character of a sustainable society and outlined policies that would help achieve the needed changes. Most of the book prescribes specific policies for population, resources, environment, and many social institutions. Since 1984, Brown and colleagues have monitored the transition toward sustainable growth with a series of *State of the World* reports (1984, 1985, 1986, 1987, 1988, 1989, 1990).

Other reports acknowledging the global connections between ecology and society include *Our Common Future* (WCED, 1987), *North–South: A Program for Survival* (Brandt, 1980), *The Global 2000 Report to the President: Entering the Twenty-first Century* (Barney, 1980), *World Conservation Strategy* (International Union for the Conservation of Nature and Natural Resources/WWF/UNEP, 1980), and *Common Crisis, North-South: Cooperation for World Recovery* (Independent Commission on International Development Issues, 1983). These reports were developed through coordinated, and cooperative, efforts of nongovernment and government agencies and international organizations. Over the years, different individuals have also provided insights about the planetary dimensions of human and environmental interactions; notable among those publications are Barbara Ward and Rene Dubos' (1972) *Only One Earth*, Barbara Ward's (1979) *Progress for a Small Planet*, Rene Dubos' (1980) *The Wooing of Earth*, Paul Ehrlich's (1968) *Population Bomb*, Barry Commoner's (1974) *The Closing Circle*, and Erik Eckholm's (1982) *Down to Earth*.

Our Common Future (WCED, 1987) presents a comprehensive agenda for global action. The agenda is based on the concept of sustainable development—a concept that combines humans and ecology.

> Humanity has the ability to make development sustainable—to ensure that it meets the needs of the present without compromising the ability of future generations to meet their own needs. The concept of sustainable development does imply limits—not absolute limits but limitations imposed by the present state of technology and social organization on environmental resources and by the ability of the biosphere to absorb the effects of human activity. (p. 8)

After this definition of sustainable development, the report describes the dynamic quality of sustainable development.

> Sustainable development is not a fixed state of harmony, but rather a process of change in which the exploration of resources, the direction of investments, the orientation of technological development, and institutional changes are consistent with future as well as present needs. (p. 9)

There is a connection between sustainable development and various environmental and human reforms, including institutional changes—in this case, science education. To date, progress toward sustainable development is not impressive. As humanity approaches the twenty-first century, we are realizing the significance of our interactions within nature. Changes in the chemistry of the atmosphere, modification of climate, threats to the world's supplies of fresh water, a reduction of biodiversity, and an increase in the population leave us with a planet in crisis. Humans are changing natural systems on a global scale and in ways that are, at a minimum, detrimental and, for the most part, irreversibly destructive. Could there be more compelling reasons to teach students about global changes and introduce them to options for action? What have educators done?

HOW HAVE EDUCATORS RESPONDED TO THE PLANETARY CRISIS?

Generally, educators have responded neither appropriately nor adequately to the need for sustainable development. To the degree educators have responded, they have reacted primarily by identifying and describing contemporary problems, such as the energy crisis, acid rain, or population growth; the result has been uncoordinated, unconnected educational materials. Most of the curriculum materials, such as units on energy, resources, environmental pollution, and population growth, are peripheral to educational programs and collectively do not contribute much to a resolution of the planetary crisis. Educators' responses are inadequate for several reasons. They have, to begin with, focused their attention on singular problems by creating materials informing students about the problems; those materials have not established a global perspective or developed the concept of sustainability. In addition, many global problems are not included in the curriculum because the problems are interdisciplinary and thus not deemed appropriate for traditional disciplines, such as biology, chemistry, physics, earth science, social studies, civics, and so on. Finally, the materials typically are "units," that is, they are short in duration; there are no long-term sustained efforts to educate students about appropriate responses to the planetary crisis. There are curriculum materials that have a global perspective, introduce the concept of sustainability, and address interdisciplinary issues (American Chemical Society, 1988; Botkin, Elmandjra, & Malitza, 1979; Christensen, 1989; Perelman, 1976), and I applaud the efforts of science teachers who incorporate these materials; but it is still the case that we must take a longer and more coordinated approach to educating students about the planetary crisis. In biology, for example, there is a clear need for wider implementation of the BSCS program *Biological Science: An Ecological Approach*. This approach builds the conceptual themes of biology, for example, evolution, genetic continuity, complementarity of organisms and environment, regulation and homeostasis, and complementarity of structure and function. Several chapters in the National Research Council book *High School Biology: Today and Tomorrow* (Rosen, 1989) support themes of this chapter (see, in particular, Harte [1989], Hurd [1989], McInerney [1989]). I propose that the first step in developing this perspective is to establish and internalize the concept of sustainability.

SCIENCE EDUCATORS MUST CONSTRUCT A VISION OF SUSTAINABILITY

The Limits to Growth (Meadows et al., 1972) forced an examination of the present and projected results of exponential growth. In addition, the title brought to our attention the origins of many contemporary problems. The limits to growth are associated with ecological systems. The issues addressed in the book—population, food production, industrialization, pollution, and consumption of nonrenewable resources—are fundamentally problems originating with ecological scarcity. Contemporary problems are often reported in a biological, social, economical, or political context. Upon examination, however, they relate to the capacity of our ecological systems to meet demands for basic human needs such as food, clean air, and clean water; for natural resources such as fossil fuels; and for elimination of waste products. There is no better example of this point than the conflict in the Middle East. At root, that conflict is over a scarce resource—oil. That root conflict is unfortunately translated into international economic and political conflict—and the potential of war.

Sustainable Growth

Just as there was a change in our concept of growth as we moved from an agricultural to an industrial society, our concept of growth in our industrial society is changing due to the limits of ecological systems. Growth, however, will continue—but it must be in directions and at rates that maintain the integrity of ecological systems. The new growth must be *sustainable,* supplying the necessities of human existence without destroying the environment or depleting natural resources. The term *sustainable* applies as well to our biological and social needs. Socially, we must be able to maintain our ecological systems while providing nutritional and physical necessities to society. The spirit and inner vitality of the population must also be upheld through periods of hardship, adjustment, and transformation. Sustainable growth refers to patterns of development that maintain a long-term balance between population demands and environmental capacities. In other words, growth must be directed toward fulfilling basic human needs without depleting natural resources, damaging the physical environment, or endangering the community. Lester Brown and colleagues (1984) describe sustainability as follows:

> Sustainability is an ecological concept with economic implications. It recognizes that economic growth and human well-being depend on the natural resource base that supports all living systems. Technology has greatly expanded the Earth's human carrying capacity, most obviously with advances in agriculture. But while the human ingenuity embodied in advancing technology can raise the natural limits on human economic activity, it cannot entirely remove them. (p. 1)

They go on to define a sustainable society as "one that shapes its economic and social systems so that natural resources and life support systems are maintained" (p. 2).

The concept of sustainability is not new or unique. The idea is based on the ecological principle of carrying capacity, discussed so well by Garrett Hardin (1968) in his classic "The Tragedy of the Commons," and the concept of equilibrium as applied in both scientific and social contexts. Jonas Salk (1973) based *The Survival of the Wisest* on the implication of an S-shaped, or sigmoid, growth curve. Later, Salk and his son examined human population growth trends in *World Population and Human Values* (Salk & Salk, 1981). They used the sigmoid curve as an explanatory model for biological growth and extended that model to factors involving human choice and human values. Sustainable growth and a sustainable society have been discussed and described from other perspectives as well, including strategic policies (Ruckelshaus, 1989; Thibodeau & Field, 1984), politics (Pirages, 1977a, 1977b, 1978), economics (Daly, 1977; MacNeill, 1989), ethics (Stivers, 1976), and theology (Barbour, 1980). Sustainability is the central unifying idea society most needs at this point in human history, and science educators are in a position to help construct an understanding of the concepts and values related to this important idea.

SCIENCE EDUCATORS MUST CLARIFY POLICIES FOR CURRICULUM AND INSTRUCTION

The concept of sustainability is abstract and general. Although reports such as *State of the World* (Brown et al., 1990) and *Our Common Future* (WCED, 1987) have made specific policy recommendations and acknowledged the important role of education, few individuals or reports have discussed policies for education. The task of clarifying educational policies has rightfully been left to educators, and generally we have not responded. Following is a discussion of educational policies that are guidelines for curriculum and instruction. The policies are based on an ecological model. I first identified the fundamental divisions of ecology—organisms, environments, and populations—and then asked what it is about these divisions that is essential from a global perspective of sustainable development. My answers included both a conceptual and an ethical orientation. Here are the answers, stated as policies for curriculum and instruction. Curriculum and instruction should guide learning toward (1) understanding and fulfilling basic human needs and facilitating personal development, (2) maintaining and improving the physical environment, (3) conserving natural resources and using them wisely, and (4) developing an understanding of interdependence among people at local, national, and global levels, that is, development of a sense of community.

Basic Human Needs and Personal Development

The ideas inherent in the first policy are simple and straightforward: All humans have basic physiological needs such as clean air, clean water, and sufficient food. They also need adequate shelter and safety. At higher levels, humans need to belong to groups and to perceive themselves as adequate persons. Simply stated, individuals need sustenance, order, community, and purpose for healthy physical and psychological development. Educational programs can contribute directly to the fulfillment of basic needs of students. They can be designed to help individuals gain knowledge about fulfilling these needs, they can inform individuals about the unfulfilled needs of others, and they can present the problems and possibilities of fulfilling human needs. Note the universal nature of this policy. *All* individuals have basic needs. Food and the development of a personal identity are both needs. Individuals in developed nations often think that alleviation of hunger and freedom from disease are the only needs in developing countries. The hierarchy of needs (Maslow, 1970) makes it clear that individuals in all nations are influenced by a variety of needs, although the needs may be different from one individual to the next and from one country to the next. A principal function of any society is to fulfill the needs of its members. Directing science education toward understanding and fulfilling human needs would realign the ways needs are being met.

Science educators recognize only part of the problem, however, in presenting ideas that can help fulfill basic human needs. In *State of the World,* Brown and colleagues (1990) clarify the role of values:

> In the end, individual values are what drive social changes. Progress toward sustainability thus hinges on a collective deepening of our sense of responsibility to the earth and to future generations. Without a reevaluation of our personal aspirations and motivations, we will never achieve an environmentally sound global community. (p. 175)

To have any effect, policies must include both ideas and values, and the values must be compatible with the policy and serve to direct personal decisions toward achieving and maintaining sustainable growth. The values of justice and beneficence underlie the policy designed to fulfill basic human needs. With resource scarcity and a majority of the world's people having unfulfilled basic needs, such as food, developed countries can no longer afford unnecessary goods and overconsumption, even in the cause of economic growth; the claim that all people are living a better life relative to the past rings hollow. Achieving this aim requires beneficence toward others, a value that can restrain personal consumption and encourage greater sharing. In turn, justice encourages the fair and equitable distribution of goods and services. This policy is more than an appeal to altruism. Adoption of lifestyles that make use of appropriate goods and services in developed countries may help those in less developed countries and can contribute to fulfilling the needs of others in developed countries.

The Physical Environment

The second policy for curriculum and instruction is designed to care for and improve the natural environment. Air, water, and soil are the common heritage of humankind, and they are essential to fulfilling basic needs. Many individuals perceive the environment as a receptacle of unlimited capacity to receive and degrade waste. But environmental systems are limited, and the negative synergistic effects of pollution are becoming clear. Realizing our dependence on the environment establishes a moral obligation both to ourselves and to future generations to ensure that the environment can continue to sustain life. Education programs should enable individuals to make informed decisions and take appropriate actions, in the short and long terms, to maintain and improve the physical environment.

Resources

The third policy, which concerns the conservation and wise use of resources, is closely related both to improvement of the physical environment and to fulfillment of basic needs. Just as we once believed in the limitless capacity of the environment to degrade waste, so too we once thought that resources were unlimited. They are not. Education for sustainable growth should inform students of the need for resources, transitions to new resources, and the conservation of nonrenewable resources.

If one perceives the environment and resources as unlimited, then it is not necessary to make value judgments about their use. The aim of sustainable growth has an ecological ethic grounded in the idea of limited environmental capacities and limited depletion of resources. This view, in a word, requires prudence. Likewise, those with a vision of sustainability must think of themselves as stewards: managers and administrators of our natural environment.

Community

The fourth policy involves developing increased interaction among people through education. This policy is directed toward establishing a greater sense of community. If fulfillment of human needs and improvement of the environment and conservation of resources are to become realities, we must increase community involvement and cooperative participation at all levels from local to global. One of the first steps toward productive personal interaction is the elimination of prejudicial barriers to community. Specifically, educational programs should reduce prejudice, such as racism, sexism, ethnocentrism, and nationalism. As long as one individual, group, or nation has a need to dominate another, the opportunities for harmonious living are reduced and the possibilities for disastrous conflict increase. Establishing a greater sense of community is clearly a prerequisite related to achieving the other three policies.

Cooperation and mutual regard are values essential for effective implementation of this fourth policy. Inevitably, conflicts will arise in making the crucial choices inherent in managing sustainable growth. Societies can no longer afford to view military force as the major way of resolving conflicts, because force is ultimately divisive and results in destructive, not constructive, resolution of conflicts. Cooperative interaction is essential if all parties to a conflict are to achieve their goals and sustain a positive relationship. Finally, there is a need for a universal recognition of human rights and compassion for others. This is the value of mutual regard for one another now and consideration for future generations of humankind. Teachers can present these values as important considerations in the interaction of students in the classroom and of people at all levels of the local and global community.

Personal Freedom and Social Regulation

The educational policies form a coordinated system of ideas and values supporting sustainable development. These policies would facilitate sustainable growth while preserving personal freedom and minimizing authoritarian control. Public education based on these policies could simultaneously produce changes in the ideas and values of individuals and lead to different means of regulating social change. Regulation, however, would not necessarily mean the unilateral imposition of rules and laws by an authority on the majority. Regulation would involve, to use Garrett Hardin's phrase, "mutual coercion mutually agreed upon" (Hardin, 1968). Two factors justify this assertion. First, the ideas (needs, environment, resources, and community) and the values (justice, beneficence, stewardship, prudence, cooperation, and mutual regard) would be sources of personal obligation *as well as* sources of social regulation. Individuals with these ideas and values would be inclined to make informed decisions concerning their needs, the needs of others, the environment, and resources; practice self-restraint and self-reliance as necessary; and participate in the democratic development of rules based on the concept of sustainability. Second, a specific type of obligation is inherent in these ideas and values—obligation of reciprocity. The concern is not only for oneself but also for other people and their environments and resources.

Educational programs that emphasize a sense of reciprocal obligation would develop an individual's sense of duty to others and to the natural environment. Obligation alone can be engendered through social rules and laws; this type of obligation is unilateral and can easily become little more than obedience to authority. This tendency is reduced, but not eliminated, through reciprocity among people who respect one another and their environment. Since many individuals in social groups are reciprocally obligated to one another, this idea is neither uncommon nor unachievable. Reciprocal obligation is grounded in empathizing with other people, coordinating efforts to solve problems, recognizing different points of view, balancing good and bad, and cooperating in the resolution of conflict. Humankind must take this direction if it is to avoid human ecological catastrophes and develop patterns of sustainable growth.

Thus the educational policies proposed in this chapter converge on the goals of sustainability and preservation of personal freedom through development of reciprocal obligation. This view advocates a course of least restrictive regulation on the individual, based on the possibility of changing personal ideas and values through education. In other words, social regulation would increasingly influence the ideas and values—and hence the decisions—of those individuals whose ideas and values were once aligned with the old vision of industrial growth. An individual's freedom would be maintained to the degree that education achieves the goal of developing personal ideas and values that support sustainable growth. Public education would create a dynamic interaction between self-restraint and social restriction, and that interaction would maximize personal freedom while achieving sustainable growth.

SCIENCE EDUCATORS MUST IMPLEMENT PROGRAMS
AND PRACTICES

In the last half of the twentieth century, global changes such as ozone depletion, deforestation, the greenhouse effect, and acid rain have become sufficiently evident that we can talk of a planetary crisis. These frightening problems, which demonstrate the complexities and interrelationships of humans and natural systems, have become global in scope and have already produced some irreversible changes in population, resources, and environment. The reasons to change educational programs are compelling, and the justifications are clear. The situation is urgent; and there are scientific, technologic, and educational means available to prevent, avoid, or reduce the planetary crisis. The goal of increasing the number of individuals who recognize the need for sustainable development, who have internalized the ideas and values related to sustainable development and are willing to act on them, is gaining scientific, social, and educational acceptance.

Educators must implement programs and practices designed to introduce the knowledge, values, and skills required for sustainable development. Now is the time to initiate the process of changing educational programs and teaching practices. Following are four concrete suggestions for implementing the policies outlined earlier:

1. Begin with the realities of your present program.
2. Teach the underlying concepts of sustainable growth.
3. Encourage ethical reflection on local and global issues.
4. Accept the responsibility for changing your science program to reflect the ideas and values of sustainable growth.

Begin with the Realities of Your Present Program

Ask how the curriculum and instruction can be modified to incorporate concepts, values, and skills supporting the idea of sustainable development. Could you change a unit on ecology? Where could you introduce the ideas and values outlined in this chapter? The essential point is to find someplace in your current curriculum and initiate a change. The American Society of Zoologists (1985) publication *Science As a Way of Knowing II—Human Ecology* is an excellent resource for science teachers. John A. Moore's essay in that volume is especially insightful. There are also suggestions for teachers elsewhere in the literature (Bybee, 1984a, 1984b; Bybee, Hurd, Kahle, & Yager, 1981).

Teach the Underlying Concepts

Introduce students to the concepts underlying the planetary crisis—such as sustainability, carrying capacity, limits, systems, continuous low-level change, and exponential growth. For most students and many teachers, understanding problems such as global warming requires a great deal of background and sophistication. Understanding the concept of carrying capacity and "managing the commons"—oceans, space, and atmosphere, for example—is feasible for most students. These concepts should be introduced in a concrete context, not necessarily in the context of a more abstract issue such as global warming. We must teach students the fundamental ideas through experiences appropriate to their age and stage and extend the initial concepts to a global perspective. They can then understand more of the specific issues of deforestation, genetic diversity, and ozone depletion.

Encourage Ethical Reflection

Ethical debate is a process of thinking critically about moral decisions. Anchoring discussions with values (such as justice, beneficence, prudence, stewardship, cooperation, and mutual regard) or underlying principles (such as "Do unto others as you would have them do unto you" or "Act only as you would have others act in the same situation") is quite different from teaching what is right or wrong or presenting personal opinions. The latter is not what I am recommending. Having students construct ethical positions contributes to educational goals such as critical thinking and promotes values that are simultaneously central to American society (Bybee, 1990) and fundamental to sustainable development. Inclusion of ethical reflection contributes directly to one of the primary goals of education—citizenship (Bybee, 1982).

Accept the Responsibility for Change

Assume that other educators will not institute or mandate the changes suggested in this essay; in all probability, you will have to assume the leadership in doing so. If all educators assume some responsibility for implementing concepts, values, and skills related to sustainable development, there is hope for change.

DARE EDUCATORS BUILD A NEW SOCIAL ORDER?

George Counts (1932) asked a variation of this penetrating question in the 1930s, the era of progressive education, in *Dare the School Build a*

New Social Order? The question is as appropriate today as it was then. Essentially Counts concluded that the schools should build a new social order. How would I answer my variation on Counts's question today?

Education is only one among many public and private agencies. No one has argued that education *alone* will be sufficient to bring about a new social or global order based on sustainability. On the other hand, a social order based on sustainable growth will not come about without the support of major public and private institutions, including education. The public is educated in a variety of ways by a variety of institutions, including the media, family, church, museum, business and schools. What is needed is an ecological view of education, a perspective that incorporates the interrelationship among various educational institutions and their relationship to society in general and the individual in particular. Lawrence Cremin (1976) articulated such a view in *Public Education*.

According to Counts, John Dewey and the progressive education movement erred in their overemphasis on individualism, as evident in their child-centered approaches. Conversely, Dewey contended that Counts erred with an overemphasis on society. The educational policies defined in this chapter represent the interests of both society and the individual. This position incorporates the claims and criticisms of both Dewey and Counts. Educational policies should contribute to both the maintenance and change of society *and* to individual development in ways unique to education as a public institution.

Another theme in Counts's book is imposition—the nature and extent of the influence educators have on individual development. New policies imply the imposition of different ideas and values. Education has tacitly affirmed the ideas and values of industrial society, so whether educators do or do not impose a particular view is not really the central issue. Rather, the situation causes us to recall another educational question— "What knowledge is of most worth?"—asked by Herbert Spencer some 80 years before George Counts. My answer is—understandable ideas and acceptable values aligned with the idea of sustainable development. ·

CONCLUSION

In the last half of the twentieth century, environmental problems expanded from local to global prominence. Distant, early warnings such as Rachel Carson's *Silent Spring* have become clear and present alarms. Problems such as global warming, ozone depletion, and acid rain have yielded a planetary crisis. The indications for change are obvious, and the imperative for educators to respond is powerful.

In this chapter, I have argued that the lack of a crucial vision of sustainability is a serious omission in contemporary science education. Educators have responded to contemporary problems and have perceived the need to change; they have not, however, had a clear direction for change. Sustainable growth is the proposed direction. Concurrent with the goal of sustainable growth there must be policies with understandable ideas and acceptable values. Policies for curriculum and instruction that will enhance sustainable growth are based on the ideas of fulfilling basic human needs, improving the environment, conserving resources, and developing a sense of community. The values suggested for a sustainable society are justice and beneficence in the distribution of goods and services for basic needs; stewardship and prudence in the human use of the environment and resources; and cooperation and mutual regard in the development of a greater sense of community among people.

Public education has two responsibilities: one to society and the other to individuals within that society. The policies outlined in this chapter are directed toward sustainable growth for society and toward optimal personal development for individuals, while preserving, to the greatest degree possible, the individual integrity of choice. The development of a sense of reciprocal obligation is central to achieving and maintaining both sustainable growth and personal freedom.

At one time, the ideas and values of agricultural society guided education; then those of industrial society dominated. Now it is our responsibility to promote the ideas and values of sustainability. To proclaim the need for a new social vision is one thing; to present the vision is quite another. At best, this chapter outlines a vision of sustainability. The reality of ecological scarcity and the planetary crisis makes a vision of sustainability particularly compelling. Many discussions of a new vision often imply a technologic metaphor such as photography—the vision will emerge full blown in an instant. To the contrary, however, the vision will be constructed as a painter develops a painting: First there is the idea; then the rough sketch; and then color is added until the painting takes form. We are best served by not thinking of a new vision as something "out there" that will somehow emerge fully formed. To develop a new vision, we must construct it through educational policies and translate these policies into programs and practices. Science educators have an obligation to respond. The situation is urgent, the problems are clear, the means are available, and the role of education is critical.

Chapter 9

■ ■ ■ ■ ■ ■ ■ ■

THE STS THEME IN THE SCIENCE CURRICULUM

Revolutions in science and technology, public concerns about the environment and resources, and a general reform of the curriculum have contributed to a new educational theme, science–technology–society (STS) (Bybee, 1986a; Hurd, 1983/1984, 1987; Roy, 1985; Rubba, 1987b). Whether STS remains a fad or develops into an important organizing theme for the curriculum depends in large part on the translation of curriculum policies into classroom practices. This theme is developed here in three sections: the intended curriculum, the actual curriculum, and the learned curriculum (Murnane & Raizen, 1988). I selected the articles cited because they form a research base concerning the STS theme and complement another review on current research on STS (Rubba, 1987a). Research supporting STS constitutes a second theme of the chapter.

THE INTENDED CURRICULUM

STS and Contemporary Policies

Intended curriculum is defined as the curriculum represented by those persons and policies presenting a particular position or syllabus for curriculum. Note the important fact that, whether explicitly or implicitly, a proposed curriculum has an underlying philosophy, an orientation, and a particular emphasis (Roberts, 1982). In this case, the intended curriculum is STS and is characterized by the corpus of articles and policy statements recommending STS. Whether curriculum policies are used to develop curriculum programs is always a critical issue. It is in fact much

This chapter is adapted from an article originally published as "Science–Technology–Society in Science Curriculum: The Policy–Practice Gap," *Theory Into Practice, 30*(4), 294–302, 1991.

easier to make recommendations for reform than it is to change school programs and classroom practices.

In the late 1970s, a growing number of educators argued that science courses should include STS (Charles & Samples, 1978; Hurd, 1975; Zoller & Watson, 1974); by the 1980s, the National Science Teachers Association (NSTA) had published "Science–Technology–Society: Science Education for the 1980s," which directly promoted the STS theme. That NSTA (1982) statement proposes that students should:

> Use the skills and knowledge of science and technology as they apply to personal and social decisions; and, study the interaction among science–technology–society in the context of science-related societal issue. (p. 5)

The NSTA policy statement provided a rationale and general guidelines for incorporating the STS theme into the science curriculum and opened the door to implementing STS in school programs and to research on STS.

Research-Based Policies

In the early to middle 1980s, I and several colleagues completed a number of surveys related to the STS theme. We had three objectives: establishing the STS theme in the literature, incorporating a global perspective in science education, and providing answers to such practical questions as:

What STS topics are important to study?
How much time should be devoted to STS topics?
What were the trends in teaching STS?
What were the limitations in teaching about STS?

The populations sampled included scientists and engineers (Bybee, 1984a), citizens (Bybee, 1984b), college students (Bybee & Najafi, 1986), science teachers (Bybee & Bonnstetter, 1986), science educators in the United States (Bybee, 1987b), and an international population of science educators (Bybee & Mau, 1986).

The international survey (Bybee & Mau, 1986) was the most extensive, in that it included 262 science educators from 41 countries, with a response rate of 80%. Some results of that survey are reported here. Table 9.1 displays what science educators believe to be the most serious science- and technology-related problems. The results also indicate that a majority of science educators thought most of the global problems listed in Figure

TABLE 9.1 Science Educators' Ranking of Science and Technology-related
Global Problems

Global Problems	Rank	Mean
World Hunger and World Resources (food production, agriculture, cropland conservation)	1	3.92
Population Growth (world population, immigration, carrying capacity, foresight capability)	2	4.35
Air Quality and Atmosphere (acid rain, CO_2 accumulation and global warming, depletion of the ozone layer)	3	5.43
Water Resources (waste disposal, estuaries, supply, distribution, ground water contamination, fertilizer run-off and contamination)	4	5.53
War Technology (nerve gas, nuclear developments, nuclear arms threat)	5	5.80
Human Health and Disease (infectious and non-infectious disease, stress, noise, diet and nutrition, exercise, mental health)	6	5.82
Energy Shortages (synthetic fuels, solar power, fossil fuels, conservation, oil production)	7	6.30
Land Use (soil erosion, reclamation, urban development, wildlife, habitat loss, deforestation, desertification, salinization)	8	6.52
Hazardous Substances (waste dumps, toxic chemicals, lead paints)	9	7.49
Nuclear Reactors (nuclear waste management, breeder reactors, cost of construction, safety, terrorism)	10	8.38
Extinction of Plants and Animals (reducing genetic diversity, wildlife protection)	11	8.37
Mineral Resources (non-fuel minerals, metallic and non-metallic minerals, mining, technology, low-grade deposits, recycling, reuse)	12	9.40

9.1 would be worse by the year 2000. The majority felt that studying global problems in school was important, that an increased emphasis on science- and technology-related problems from lower to higher grade levels was necessary, and that science and social studies aspects of STS should be incorporated into one course (Bybee & Mau, 1986).

Rubba (1989) investigated the semantic meaning assigned to concepts associated with STS in a sample of exemplary secondary-level science teachers. The teachers had positive opinions of science and technology, their own understanding of science, and their ability to teach science. Relative to STS, the exemplary teachers also expressed positive opinions about students' understanding of STS concepts, students' need to understand STS, their own understanding of STS, and their ability to teach STS. However, the teachers did not allot much instructional time to STS. Thus Rubba found that science teachers are aware of, and support, implementing STS, but they do not translate policies to classroom practices. One of the first steps toward the development and implementation of a curriculum based on the STS theme is the identification of goals appropriate for STS. Several articles describe such goals (Bybee, 1986a, 1987b; Rubba & Weisenmayer, 1988).

The combination of policies statements by national organizations and research studies on STS suggests that this theme is important and widely supported. Although the review of literature and research supporting an intended STS curriculum is a first step in reform, policy statements and recommendations must not be confused with actual curriculum changes. In short, recommendations for change are not synonymous with actual changes in science curricula.

THE ACTUAL CURRICULUM

If STS is to be more than an accumulation of good ideas or a plethora of well-meaning policies, the theme must be actualized in school programs. That is, there must be a real and accurate representation of STS in curriculum materials and instructional strategies *that are used by science teachers*. Simply stated, the actual curriculum is defined as what science teachers use and what they do to portray STS to students.

Below I use textbook reviews and research on classroom practices to assess the degree to which STS has been implemented. That is, what changes have actually occurred in school science programs?

Textbook Reviews

Since the textbook dictates the curriculum in most science classes (Weiss, 1978, 1987), reviews of textbooks serve as indicators of the degree to which the STS theme is part of the actual curriculum. In the late 1970s, two separate studies analyzed biology textbooks for their inclusion of social issues (Boschmann, Hendrix, & Mertens, 1978; Levin & Lindbeck, 1979). The inclusion of STS issues in biology textbooks was neither quantitatively nor qualitatively significant.

An analysis of the STS content in high school biology textbooks (Rosenthal, 1984) produced no more promising results. In her study, Rosenthal clearly defined social issues, developed 12 categories of social issues based on an extensive review of the literature, and had the classification of social issues reviewed by experts. The study specifically evaluated the emerging STS theme by looking for evidence of STS issues in textbooks. Rosenthal summarized her finding:

> For 22 textbooks published between 1963 and 1983, the percentage of total textbooks dealing with social issues has declined. There is no evidence from this study that textbook authors and publishers have responded to the statements of numerous scientists and science educators' call for a greater emphasis on science and society in high school biology textbooks. . . . In general the treatment of science and society in high school biology textbooks minimizes the controversial aspects, avoids questions of ethics and values, lacks a global perspective, and neglects the interdisciplinary nature of problems. (p. 829)

Rosenthal's review of biology textbooks is particularly important for two reasons. First, more than 90% of high school biology teachers use one of the textbooks reviewed in this study. Second, for the majority of students, high school biology is the last science course they take (Hurd, Bybee, Kahle, & Yager, 1980).

Hamm and Adams (1987) reviewed and analyzed 4,393 pages in 10 sixth- and seventh-grade science textbooks for their treatment of global problems as identified by Bybee and Mau (1986). Less than 2% of the space was devoted to the global problems of population growth, world hunger, air quality and atmosphere, and water resources.

In sum, analysis of sixth- and seventh-grade science textbooks and tenth-grade biology textbooks in the mid-1980s indicated little STS content. Given that these levels include the upper elementary, middle level, and lower high school, I can only conclude that STS is minimally represented in the actual science curriculum for the majority of students.

The foregoing summary clarifies a critical issue, namely, that the STS theme has not been embraced by school personnel, textbook authors, and commercial publishers. Yet there is a variety of supplemental curriculum materials available to teachers wishing to include the STS theme in science (Jarcho, 1986; Penick, 1986). The important point here is that materials are available but they have not been implemented; that is, they are not used as the *actual* program. Several textbooks and curriculum materials incorporating the STS theme have been published for use in science courses. For example, *Global Science* (1984) and *ChemCom* (1988) are both textbooks for a full-year science course. *Science for Life and Living: Integrating Science, Technology, and Health* is a K–6 program (Bybee & Landes, 1988a, b; Bybee and Landes, 1990). *Design Technology: Children's Engineering* (Dunn & Larson, 1990) is another technology-oriented program for elementary school. Additional programs include *Science–Technology–Society: Preparing for Tomorrow's World* (Iozzi, 1987), *Exploring Technology* (Bame & Cummings, 1980), and *People Create Technology* (Heiner & Hendrix, 1980). It seems that the critical issue is not availability of materials; rather, it is the implementation of curriculum materials and development of new classroom practices.

Classroom Practices

Although little information exists about classroom practices and STS, a survey of science and social studies teachers (Barman, Harshman, & Rusch, 1982) indicated that the majority of teachers supported the integration of science and social studies and 90% of those surveyed supported teaching about STS topics. However, 68% were undecided about their level of commitment to initiating an STS program.

Probably the most insightful research on classroom practices was reported by Mitman, Mergendoller, Marchman, and Packer (1987):

> The instruction of 11 seventh-grade life science teachers was observed to determine the extent to which they made linkages between science content and its societal, reasoning, historical, or attitudinal implications. . . . Results showed that (a) teachers rarely or never addressed the non-content components of science in their presentations and academic work assignments, (b) students perceived content as the prominent focus of their teachers' instruction, and (c) teachers' references to the non-content components were unrelated to growth on all but one student outcome, where the association was negative. Altogether, the results indicate a large gap between scientific literacy as a normative goal of science instruction and current teaching practice. (p. 611)

This study provided a thorough and disturbing picture of what happens, or more appropriately what does not happen, relative to the STS theme in science classrooms.

Implementing STS

Why do teachers not implement programs based on the STS theme? What would contribute to incorporating STS topics in classrooms? In an effort to answer these questions, Bybee and Bonnstetter (1987) surveyed

317 science teachers. Results were similar to those found in earlier studies by Barman and colleagues (1982), Stubbs (1983), and Barrow and Germann (1987). A majority (89%) of the teachers surveyed had *considered* incorporating STS activities into some aspect of their program. More than 90% of the teachers said they *would* incorporate the STS theme *if* materials and instructional strategies were available. Seventy percent even suggested specific ways in which they would incorporate the STS theme. When asked about sources of information that might be useful in teaching STS topics, teachers mentioned such sources as journals and other professional publications, college courses, other teachers, and local specialists or coordinators. When the teachers were asked about the limitations on teaching about STS topics, top-ranked reasons were economical, personal, and pedagogical.

Carlson (1986) also conducted a survey focusing on factors that influenced implementation of STS in middle school science programs. Three factors influenced the adoption of STS topics by this sample of teachers: membership in professional organizations, amount of background knowledge, and administrative support. Actual implementation of STS topics was most influenced by time, resources, knowledge, and teaching experience.

Mitchener and Anderson (1989) reported a qualitative investigation of 14 secondary science teachers' perceptions of, and consequent decisions about, the implementation of a model STS program. Analysis of the data indicated that the teachers fell into one of three groups: those who accepted the STS program, those who accepted and altered the program, and those who rejected the program. Five themes were common to all three groups. These themes are helpful in locating reasons for accepting, altering, or rejecting the STS program. The themes, with clarifying questions, were the following:

1. Concerns over content, that is, is there enough science content?
2. Discomfort with student grouping, that is, how does one group students for STS activities?
3. Uncertainties about evaluation, that is, how does one evaluate STS outcomes?
4. Frustrations about the student population, that is, what about college-bound students?
5. Confusion about the teacher's role, that is, how does a science teacher teach about social issues?

This study reconfirmed the key place of the teacher in the implementation of a new program. Similar results were obtained in an investigation of STS education among secondary teachers in Tennessee (Rhoton, 1990).

Reviews of the actual curriculum reveal that the STS theme does not hold as significant a place as teachers believe it should. The disparity centers on the role of implementation, since there *are* curriculum materials available and surveys indicate that most teachers recognize the importance of the STS theme. The critical issue of the teacher's responsibility for implementing new ideas such as STS is raised by those findings. Who is responsible for closing the gap between the intended curriculum and the actual curriculum? Certainly, those who develop science curricula are partially responsible, but they seem to be responding by developing STS materials. However, review of major textbook programs and the actual practice of teachers reveals a significant disparity between the intended STS curriculum and the actual STS curriculum. I think there may be several explanations for teachers' failure to implement the STS theme. One reason has to do with the fact that the school environment does not encourage or support innovation; a second has to do with the reduction of budgets for new materials; and a third centers on the critical issue of assuming professional responsibility to update and improve science programs.

THE LEARNED CURRICULUM

Learned curriculum refers to the knowledge, attitudes, and skills that educators intend to influence via the curriculum. Regarding STS, the question is: "What are students learning about science- and technology-related social issues?" National assessments of science learning are reviewed and individual research is summarized below.

National Assessments

The National Assessment of Educational Progress (NAEP) reports on science have been available for 20 years. The 1976–1977 assessment was the first to include items on science and society and to assess students' awareness of the methods, assumptions, and values of science (NAEP, 1979). In 1976, students at ages 9, 13, and 17 were aware of science-related societal problems and were willing to contribute to the amelioration of the problems, but their reported participation in solving problems was low. Students lacked an overall understanding of scientific research methods and did not understand the difference between basic and applied research. In all, the 1976 results were disappointing and a basis for concern about students' understanding of and attitudes toward STS topics (Bybee, Harms, Ward, & Yager, 1980).

In the 1981–1982 national assessment of science, published in *Images of Science* (Hueftle et al., 1983; Rakow, Welsh, Hueftle, 1984), elementary students showed a statistically significant increase in their understanding of STS items. Middle and high school students' understanding generally increased, but the increase was not statistically significant. Hueftle and colleagues proposed a "media hypothesis" regarding students' awareness of STS issues. The increase in understanding occurred for topics that had received the greatest attention in the media, such as acid rain and food shortages.

STS topics were not prominent in the 1986 NAEP assessment items (Mullis & Jenkins, 1988), although several questions about the perceived applications of science were included. Students were more likely in 1986 than in 1977 to agree that the applications of science could help to preserve natural resources, reduce air and water pollution, and prevent birth defects. The largest changes across time were the decreases in the percentages of 13- and 17-year-olds who believed that science applications could help to resolve the problems of world starvation (p. 145).

The trend away from STS items in the NAEP assessments is disappointing. In the 1990 national assessment (NAEP, 1989), there were few STS items.

Research Studies

In 1986–1987, Robert Yager (1988a, 1988b) assessed the impact on student learning of science teachers who participated in STS workshops over a three-year period (1984–1986). In a follow-up study of the teachers, Yager, Blunck, Binadji, McComas, and Penick (1988) assessed student outcomes in five domains—connections and applications of science concepts, attitudes, creativity, understanding of scientific processes, and STS information. Assessment results were compared for the STS-trained and traditional science teachers in grades 4 through 9. Students of teachers in STS programs were better able to apply information to problems, to relate new information to other situations, to act independently, and to make decisions. They also had more favorable attitudes toward science, were more creative, had greater abilities with process skills, and learned at least as much scientific information as students in comparison classes.

Aikenhead, Fleming, and Ryan (1987) assessed Canadian high school graduates' beliefs about STS. Graduates were asked to write an argumentative paragraph on an STS topic. The researchers monitored the reasons that students gave to justify their opinions. An analysis of student responses was the basis for an assessment instrument entitled Views on Science–Technology–Society (VOSTS). Aikenhead subsequently validated the VOSTS instrument in a large-scale study and compared VOSTS with other means of assessing students' beliefs about STS topics (Aikenhead, 1988).

Analysis of the original data from the assessment of Canadian high school students' belief about STS was completed by Fleming (1987). He summarized students' understanding of STS interactions:

> In summary, one major interaction between science and society was viewed by students in a rather simplistic fashion: Science (techno-science) should inform society in order to resolve socioscientific issues, issues which students perceived as technical problems; our society should inform science in terms of science policy as it guides research programs. The formulation of policy for a research program was not perceived as a socioscientific issue. (p. 185)

The students did not differentiate between science and technology, and their view of STS interactions was that science should inform society about solutions to problems but that society should set policy for research.

Aikenhead (1987) summarized another portion of the results in this manner:

> In summary, high school graduates harbored diverse and contradictory beliefs about scientific knowledge. Students' paragraphs reflected a belief in certain aspects of authentic science; particularly, the nature of classification schemes, the tentative nature of knowledge, and the social dimensions of knowledge from within the scientific community. On other issues, however, students seemed to be uninformed; for instance, on the nature of scientific models, on the outside influences on scientific knowledge, on the motivations for generating knowledge, and on scientific method. Students generally viewed "the scientific method" as a vague rule of thumb—follow the procedure as given. (p. 485)

Ryan (1987) analyzed data from the Canadian study to determine the students' beliefs about the characteristics of scientists. The majority of students thought that scientists should be concerned with the potential effects of their discoveries and that scientists should be responsible in their actions.

In all, this line of research has provided insights concerning both methodology and findings. The VOSTS instrument supplied researchers with a valid and reliable means of probing students' understanding of STS issues. The findings suggest that there is need for education programs that introduce specific aspects of the STS theme.

Zoller and his colleagues (1990) used the VOSTS instrument in a study to assess goal attainment in STS education. The research team based their study on the question: "Do STS courses actually work?" The team compared students in an STS course with regular science students. The findings indicated that the STS course was effective in improving high school students' viewpoints concerning STS issues.

CONCLUSION

In the early 1980s, NSTA developed a policy statement supporting the implementation of STS. Several research surveys also showed support for including the STS theme in school programs and answered basic questions about the introduction of STS topics into the curriculum.

Based on this review of research, the actual curriculum does not appear to include as much about STS as the various policy statements might warrant. Textbooks do not typically include STS topics, and teaching practices reflect little or no recognition of STS themes, even though some curriculum materials and instructional strategies for teaching about STS themes do exist. Providing information that will help close the immense gap between policy recommendations and classroom practices seems to be the central issue. The efforts of teachers to implement the STS theme have lacked direction and have occurred infrequently. The need for greater understanding of systematic implementation—including administrative support, staff development programs, and techniques such as coaching of teachers in new strategies—poses important issues for translating policies to practices.

Evidence at both the national and local levels suggest that students *are* learning about STS issues. Although NAEP results indicate that students understand STS issues and have positive attitudes toward STS study, those findings are offset by other research indicating there is little being taught about STS in school programs. What students learn about STS is probably related to factors other than science instruction, namely, the media.

Sustaining the STS innovation requires the translation of policies to practices. Development of curriculum materials and changes in teacher education are essential. If we do not attend to the systematic translation of the STS theme from policies to practices, implementation will be insignificant and STS will be a passing fad.

REFLECTIONS

I remain convinced that the decisive component in reforming science education is the classroom teacher. We certainly need books, reports, and recommendations for new policies, and we need new materials, projects, and programs. However, unless classroom teachers move beyond the status quo in science teaching, the reform will falter and eventually fail. At the same time, teachers alone do not have sole responsibility for changing and improving science programs and science teaching. The school system is responsible for supporting innovative science teachers and teaching. We have to view this reform initiative from a systemic and evolutionary perspective.

In Chapter 7, "Contemporary School Science: The Evolution of Teachers and Teaching," I focused on several NSF science programs being developed at the national level as examples on which new curricula and instruction could be based. Even though many school districts are developing their own science programs, the basic theme of the chapter is still applicable—school personnel should concentrate on implementation of new programs.

The late 1980s were a period when the environmental movement took another scientific and social step forward. The scientific evidence continued to support the general predictions of earlier decades. Many problems related to the environment and natural resources were studied by notable scientists and scientific organizations; for example, the National Science Foundation began a global research initiative on a variety of problems. Many issues became increasingly socially relevant because increasing numbers of communities had environmental problems to resolve: wastewater management, hazardous chemicals, land use, and air pollution. Overpopulation, diminishing resources, and environmental degradation will continue to be problems in the 1990s.

Given my view that science educators have an obligation to contribute to the development of individuals and the aspirations of society and that we continue to change the planet's ecological systems in irreparable ways, I think there is a clear and compelling case for science educators to recognize and include environmental concerns in school science programs. In the 1960s, we had no trouble initiating a massive reform in science education in order to put men on the moon; and in the 1990s, we are engaged in a reform of education to improve our economic productivity. Why is it so difficult to incorporate an understanding of concepts, such as sustainable growth, continuous low-level change, limits, and systems? Why is it that every science educator makes choices about what to teach and not to teach based on scientific values (for example, objectivity, curiosity, appeal to data) and personal values, yet avoids values that are common to philosophy and theology, such as justice, beneficence, stewardship, prudence, cooperation, and mutual regard? Why is it so difficult to incorporate content and processes that will contribute to the improvement of our planet? What is the defensible position for not incorporating the position described in the Chapter 8, "Planet Earth in Crisis: How Should Science Educators Respond?"

The STS theme, which is significantly related to the ecological and environmental crisis, has the potential to be a significant organizing theme in science education. Yet it barely plays a role in our science classrooms. There are abundant policies and rationales for STS; we do not need further arguments in its favor. And although there are some materials on STS, we probably need more such materials. Most important, there is a need to implement the STS theme in classroom courses. As STS is implemented, there undoubtedly will be increasing research that will help support, correct, and refine our ways of presenting the theme.

Part IV

■ ■ ■ ■ ■ ■ ■ ■ ■

THE CONTEMPORARY REFORM
OF SCIENCE EDUCATION

We are in the midst of a great educational reform, and one of the most pressing questions has to be: "What should we do?" Everywhere there are recommendations, each set with the unique perspective of the group presenting the report. Yet we continue asking the same questions and seeking answers to the questions of what we should do and what we need. Perhaps we need national standards for science education. Perhaps we should improve assessment or promote new science curricula. Perhaps the answer is teacher education. Everyone realizes that there is not a single answer; everyone also realizes that we probably need all the aforementioned solutions. But how do all these components become a coordinated system?

Science education in the United States is a large and complex system with diverse constituents and dispersed power. Any successful reform of science education will have to account for this scale, diversity, and power.

In Chapter 10, I suggest what seems a reasonable answer. We must all become leaders and assume responsibility for our portion of the reform, which seems to be the only way to take into account the scale, diversity, and power of the science education system while also accommodating both the general demands on the national agenda and the unique needs of state and local systems. Thus distributed leadership among those within the science education community holds the greatest potential of improving science education by the year 2000.

Chapter 10

■ ■ ■ ■ ■ ■ ■ ■ ■

LEADERSHIP, RESPONSIBILITY, AND REFORM IN SCIENCE EDUCATION

Blinded by our search for larger-than-life leaders, we have not recognized the individuals or the forms and processes of leadership that will be most responsible for the contemporary reform of science education. We must realize that a majority, not a minority, of individuals in science education have leadership responsibilities. These include policy makers, curriculum developers, teacher educators, science supervisors, and classroom teachers.

Many individuals in society understand the general need for leadership. The literature of business and management, for example, is rich with references to leadership (Bennis, 1989; Covey, 1990; Drucker, 1990; Peters, 1987; Yukl, 1989). In education, however, we have not considered the issue of leadership in the same depth as other topics, although my literature review identified some exceptions (Barnett et al., 1992; Duke, 1987; Leithwood, 1992; Mitchell & Tucker, 1992; Sergiovanni, 1991). This general lack of attention to leadership in science education is curious, given the centrality of leadership to the success of the current reform movement.

Indeed, our search for solutions to the complicated problems of educational reform directs us toward the issue of leadership in science education. We certainly recognize the problems, because hundreds of reports document the reasons to reform science education. Doubtless, we also realize there are understandable and acceptable solutions to our problems, but science education needs widespread leadership to mobilize the available resources to achieve a new reform.

Because of the immense and diverse structure of science education and the scale and complicated nature of the contemporary reform, I am

---

This chapter is adapted from public lectures presented at the Edith Cowan University in Perth, Western Australia, April 1991; and at the annual luncheon of the Association for the Education of Teachers in Science and National Science Supervisors Association at the National Science Teachers Association convention, March 1992, Boston, MA. A portion of this chapter was previously published in *Science Educator,* 2 (1), 1993.

convinced that *distributed leadership* is one key to a successful reform. That is, all individuals associated with science education must contribute to the promotion of scientific literacy among all students.

In this chapter, I develop the themes of leadership and responsibility in reforming science education, and I consider the role of teacher educators, science supervisors, science education researchers, and science teachers. It is the science teachers who have the greatest burden and heaviest responsibility for reform. My stern judgment of science teachers should not be perceived as yet another round of teacher-bashing. Rather, my critical comments are grounded in a recognition of the essential position of teachers in this reform, the need for change, and compassion for their difficult task. I begin with an introduction to leadership in the context of science education. In the next sections, I introduce and elaborate on various definitions and dimensions of leadership, including the theme of empowerment. In subsequent sections, I turn to views of educational reform, and in the final section I present some paradoxes of leadership.

LEADERSHIP IN SCIENCE EDUCATION

What does one do to provide leadership in science education? A short poem provides some guidance.

The Leader

I wanna be the leader.
I wanna be the leader.
Can I be the leader?
Can I? Can I?
Promise? Promise?
Yippee, I'm the leader.
I'm the leader.
Okay, what shall we do?

—"Sky in the Pie," Penguin Publications

In a humorous way, this little poem expresses several key ideas: Leadership requires motivation, knowledge and skills, and, most importantly, a vision and a plan. The poem expresses the leader's motivation, but it is clear that the individual lacks a vision and a plan.

A Vision and a Plan

All leaders provide a vision. Providing leadership means constructing a vision; translating that vision for students, committees, organizations, and schools; and sustaining the vision while adapting it to science programs and teaching practices. Expression of each leader's vision must be in the context of that individual's own environment, organization, or institution. Although visions need not be complex or elaborate, they must be different from current programs and practices. Visions are not statements of the status quo; they are new, they are substantial, and they look to the future.

The countervailing force for any leader's vision of the future is the institutional or individual memory of the past. Variations on such statements as "We have tried that" and "We can change the curriculum, but what about tests?" and "Where is a particular topic in this new program?" are all examples of evaluations of the new in terms of the past. Many variations of memory can act as a force against vision. Teachers, parents, and even students have past experiences that are used to evaluate anything new. I cannot tell you what the unique examples will be, but I can tell you that your vision of science education will be compared to past and present programs. The effective leader has internalized his or her vision and conveys it at every opportunity. In most instances, providing leadership means persuading constituents of their potential to achieve new goals. A vision with substance meets the criticisms that will be offered; mere slogans do not.

After vision, leadership requires a plan. Following a leader's initial question—"What are we going to do to improve science education?"—the second question is: "How are we going to do it?" This seems a simple enough question, but some individuals have a plan but no vision—they are managers; others have a vision but no plan—they are utopians. Providing leadership requires both a plan of directed action and flexibility. One must give a sense of direction *and* be responsive to those with whom one is working. Being too rigid and authoritarian is ineffective; being too flexible and laissez-faire is equally ineffective. Providing leadership means continually reaffirming your vision while simultaneously adjusting your plans.

Consider developing a new Biological Sciences Curriculum Study (BSCS) program, an example I know well. There is no question about the need to clarify one's personal vision of the program, but you also have to communicate that vision to colleagues who will work on the project. Developing a proposal requires a plan for the design and development as well as the implementation of the new program. You have to have both—a vision and a plan. You also need personal qualities such as motivation and responsibility as well as the knowledge and skills relative to science, technology, education, and curriculum development to accomplish the project.

A LEADERSHIP MODEL

In *The Essence of Leadership,* Edwin Locke and his associates (1991) present a very succinct model of leadership. The model integrates many facets of the leadership literature and provides a synthesis for those providing leadership in science education. Figure 10.1 presents an adaptation of the leadership model originally developed by Locke and associates. My adaptation is for education, especially science education.

This model provides an overview of the essential qualities of leader-

FIGURE 10.1 A Leadership Model

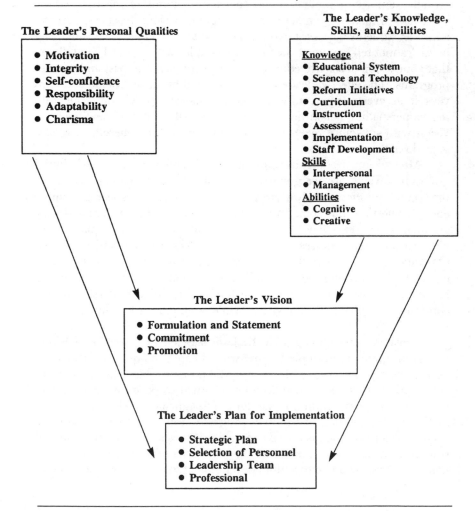

The Leader's Personal Qualities

- Motivation
- Integrity
- Self-confidence
- Responsibility
- Adaptability
- Charisma

The Leader's Knowledge, Skills, and Abilities

Knowledge
- Educational System
- Science and Technology
- Reform Initiatives
- Curriculum
- Instruction
- Assessment
- Implementation
- Staff Development

Skills
- Interpersonal
- Management

Abilities
- Cognitive
- Creative

The Leader's Vision

- Formulation and Statement
- Commitment
- Promotion

The Leader's Plan for Implementation

- Strategic Plan
- Selection of Personnel
- Leadership Team
- Professional

FIGURE 10.2   Definitions of Leadership

LEADERSHIP IS:

Making things happen, or not happen;

Getting others to do what they ought to do, and like it;

Making people think things are possible that they didn't think were possible;

Getting people to be better than they think they are or can be;

Inspiring hope and confidence in others to accomplish purposes they think are impossible;

Perceiving what is needed and right, and knowing how to mobilize people and resources to accomplish these goals;

Creating options and opportunities, clarifying problems and choices, building morale and coalitions, providing a vision and possibilities of something better than currently exists;

Empowering and liberating people to become leaders in their own right.

---

ship. The form and function of leadership in science education will vary with situations. The requisite qualities for effective leadership in science education—be it in science classrooms, colleges and universities, state departments of education, national organizations, or even nonprofit organizations—include personal qualities, knowledge, skills, a vision, and a plan for implementation.

DEFINING LEADERSHIP

Leadership defies easy definition. Figure 10.2 lists a number of definitions drawn from a variety of sources. Two common themes connect the definitions of leadership: The process involves relationships with people and achieving a group purpose. For this chapter, I define leadership as an individual's ability to work with others to improve science teaching and learning and to accomplish the goal of scientific literacy. Note that my definition implies the involvement of a majority of individuals within the science education community.

Status and power do not define leadership. A person who has the status may or may not be an effective leader. Status, however, certainly enhances the possibility of leadership. Being in a position with some status conveys expectations of leadership to others, and their expectations can contribute to one's ability to lead. Leadership is not only power, however. Individuals can have power for a variety of reasons, such as money, authority, or position. These can result in power, but they do not necessarily result in an individual's being able to lead a group toward a common purpose.

THE DIMENSIONS OF LEADERSHIP

At this point, you may ask: "What else should I know about leadership? What type of leadership is appropriate for my situation?" In this section, my discussion of leadership centers on three classic works, James MacGregor Burns's (1978) *Leadership,* Bernard Bass's (1985) *Leadership and Performance Beyond Expectations,* and John Gardner's (1990) *On Leadership.* I begin with a description of two different models of leadership, transactional and transformational.

Transactional Leadership

Burns has (1978) described transactional leadership as a relationship between leaders and followers based on the exchange of things such as jobs for votes and favors for campaign contributions. Transactional leaders let their followers know what is expected and what they will receive for meeting those expectations. This type of leadership focuses on services and rewards; according to Burns, such transactions represent the majority of relationships between leaders and followers. Burns primarily describes political relationships.

In a later work, Bass (1985) extended the definition to supervisory–subordinate relationships. In this relationship, the transactional leader first identifies what subordinates want from their work and sees that they get the rewards, if the performance warrants it, and then exchanges rewards for efforts.

In science education, the transactional approach requires the leader to identify outcomes and clarify the role of others. At the same time, the leader must identify what rewards will be bestowed when the outcomes are achieved. The subordinates have to have confidence that they can achieve the desired outcomes and believe that the reward is worth the effort.

Transformational Leadership

Burns (1978) also described a more complex and more potent type of leadership than transactional. Transformational leaders also have goals, but these goals focus on the personal needs or demands of their followers. Here, the leader identifies the motives and aspirations of followers and seeks to engage the individual follower on a personal level. Burns also suggests that transformational leadership may result in a relationship of mutual stimulation that elevates the follower to a leader and leaders to moral agents.

Burns based his conception of transformational leaders largely on Abraham Maslow's hierarchy of needs (1968, 1970, 1971), a theory that is important to the theme of leadership, particularly transformational leadership. The hierarchy of needs begins with the most basic physiological needs, such as food, water, air, and sleep, which have the greatest motivational force. When they are largely fulfilled, there emerges a need for order, structure, stability, and freedom from chaos and fear. The terms *safety* and *security* describe this level. Next, individuals need to belong, to give and receive affection, to have a friend, to belong to a group. The next level is the need for self-esteem—to have a stable, firmly based, positive perception of one's self. Finally, there is the need for self-actualization. When all other needs are largely met, there emerges the need to develop and use one's capabilities, talents, and potentials. The ways in which individuals actualize their potential vary, but having a mission such as purpose in science education is certainly one such way—and one that transformational leaders understand.

Again, Bass (1985) slightly modified Burns's (1978) original conception of transformational leadership. Bass suggested that transformational leaders influence followers first by raising their level of awareness about the goals or outcomes; second, by helping them transcend their self-interests for the sake of the larger mission; and third, by altering their level on Maslow's hierarchy vertically, from a lower to higher level, or horizontally, by expansion at the current level.

Burns (1978) originally characterized these two types of leadership as opposite ends of a continuum. Most leaders actually exhibit both types of leadership in varying amounts. Observation or review of leadership supports this refinement of the conceptually distinct types (Bass, 1985).

Moral Leadership

I cannot avoid mention of morals and ethics when discussing leadership because many of the characteristics of leaders are equally applicable to Adolf Hitler and Winston Churchill, Idi Amin and Martin Luther King, Jr. But real differences do exist among leaders when one considers the moral dimensions of the relationship between these leaders and their followers.

Burns (1978) clearly described the moral dimensions of leadership. He indicated first, that the leader and the led have mutual needs, aspirations, and values; second, that followers should have knowledge of alternative leaders and programs; and third, that leaders should take responsibility for their commitments. For Burns:

> Moral leadership emerges from and always returns to the fundamental wants and needs, aspirations and values, of the followers. I mean the kind of leadership that can produce social change that will satisfy followers' authentic needs. I mean less the Ten Commandments than the Golden Rule. But, even the Golden Rule is inadequate, for it measures the wants and needs of others simply by our own. (p. 4)

In discussing the moral dimension of leadership, John Gardner (1990) appealed to the categorical imperative when he stated: "We believe, with Immanuel Kant, that individuals should be treated as ends in themselves, not as a means to the leader's end, not as objects to be manipulated" (p. 73). Although leadership by science supervisors, teacher educators, and classroom teachers does not involve the influences and power that national or international leaders have, it is still important to have high and clear ethical standards and to assume responsibility for those standards.

Science educators can use the transactional and transformational models in understanding approaches to leadership. Teacher–student, supervisor–committee, and professor–graduate student relationships provide opportunities to apply both transactional and transformational leadership. The connection between these ideas about leadership and educational change can be discerned in the understanding of the concerns of beginning teachers and those experienced teachers implementing innovative programs as elaborated in the work of Frances Fuller (1969), Gene Hall and Shirley Hord (1987), and Michael Fullan (1982). These individuals take a perspective paralleling that of transformational leadership in that they focus on the needs and concerns of individuals in the process of educational change and personal development.

EMPOWERING PEOPLE

Bertrand Russell (1938) once said that "the fundamental concept in social sciences is power, in the same sense in which energy is the fundamental concept in physics" (p. 12). Providing leadership means giving energy, empowering the group or individuals (Ramey, 1991). Individuals require power to make decisions, develop ideas, and influence tasks as they relate to the overall vision. We have all been on committees that lacked either energy in the form of an enthusiastic leader or power in terms of a budget for implementing the recommendations. In either case, our participation was an empty exercise.

In *Power and Innocence,* the psychologist Rollo May (1972) described the human dimensions of power and defined power as the "ability to cause or prevent change" (p. 99). May reminds us that the ancient Greeks originally defined power as being, that is, the psychological essence of being human. Over the years, philosophers have conveyed this idea of power; for example, Henri Bergson's *élan vital,* Friedrich Nietzsche's "will to power," and Paul Tillich's "power to be." Such conceptions of power indicate the importance of leaders' empowering people and ties into the current educational theme of empowering teachers.

Rollo May (1972) described the types of power that are evident in human interactions and, by extension, in interactions between leaders and followers. Exploitive power is the destructive use of power to subject others to a leader's goals; slavery is an example. Manipulative power is the capacity to control another without the physical dimensions and force implied by exploitation. B. F. Skinner's operant conditioning is an example of manipulative power. Competitive power is power against another person or group; the obvious example is sports. The final two kinds of power are most relevant to this discussion of leadership. According to May, there is nutrient power, which is power on behalf of another person; parents' care for their children and teachers' concern for students are both examples. Most discussions of empowering teachers exemplify nutrient power. Finally, there is integrative power, the power that results from joining with another person; cooperative learning is an example of integrative power. In reflecting on the issue of empowering people and the types of power just described, it becomes clear that a leader's use of power is another area in which the moral dimensions of leadership are evident.

Leadership and Power

Although, as indicated above, power and leadership are not the same thing, effective leadership nonetheless requires power. The issue is not whether leaders have and use power—they do and they must—but rather the ethical uses of power. Is the leader using power to achieve morally sound and ethically defensible goals? We need to understand power for at least two reasons. First, effective leadership in science education entails empowering others, especially science teachers. Second, we need to understand the power relationship in school systems if we hope to achieve the purposes of this reform (Sarason, 1991). In short, if the leaders in science education do not understand and change the power relationships, the current system will not change and reform efforts will fail.

Empowering Science Teachers

Empowering science teachers is a prominent theme in the contemporary reform of science education (Nyberg, 1990; Spector, 1989). *Teacher empowerment* stands in interesting contrast with the phrase popular in the 1960s: *teacher-proof programs.* A teacher-proof curriculum was a set of materials designed to enhance student learning independent of, or in spite of, the science teacher. As early as 1965, in *The Genius of American Education,* Lawrence Cremin pointed out the misguided nature of a teacher-proof curriculum. He suggested that reformers had a legitimate concern about contemporary teachers and teaching, but he saw their solution of designing materials impervious to misuse as flawed. Cremin gave advice that is appropriate for any generation of leaders and reformers, especially those teacher educators and science supervisors who are directly responsible for the professional development of science teachers.

> But education is too significant and dynamic an enterprise to be left to mere technicians; and we might as well begin now the prodigious task of preparing men and women who understand not only the substance of what they are teaching but also the theories behind the particular strategies they employ to convey that substance. A society committed to the continuing intellectual, aesthetic, and moral growth of all its members can ill afford less on the part of those who undertake to teach. (1965, p. 57)

Note the disparity between the intention to make curriculum materials teacher-proof and the extent to which that goal was achieved. This approach to the curriculum did not work in large part because of the science teacher's power once the classroom door was closed. That it did not work demonstrates the power of classroom teachers.

After teacher-proof materials, there emerged teacher-dependent materials and programs. Essentially, teacher-dependent programs are sets of how-to activities on which the teacher depends and which can be used without understanding the subject, pedagogy, or context of the lesson. I use the term *dependent* here in two respects. First, in a reaction to attempts to teacher-proof the curriculum, there was a swing toward designing curriculum materials that were entirely contingent on the teacher. Second, and most important, in the decades since the teacher-proof programs, there has developed among many science teachers a dependence on short-term, quick-fix lessons and a general intolerance of curriculum programs with a fully articulated scope and sequence. Just as the pendulum swung too far in the 1960s, the corrective reaction was also too extreme in the 1970s, 1980s, and 1990s. Empowering science teachers to adapt science materials, be they local or national, will enhance the teaching and learning of science. Leaders should understand some of the qualities of empowerment.

Qualities of Empowerment

In a little book entitled *Leaders: The Strategies for Taking Change,* Warren Bennis and Burt Nanus (1985) described several dimensions of empowerment. One of the first dimensions is developing a sense of *significance* in others. Effective leaders create a vision that makes others feel as though they make a difference. To be significant, this vision must have substance and transcend the superficiality of slogans. Individuals are, for example, translating the vision into innovative science programs and sustaining the new programs through difficult situations. In so doing, they are really making a difference in the science education of students.

A second dimension of empowerment involves developing new *knowledge, skills,* and *attitudes.* This results in greater competence and a sense of mastery. Third, empowerment provides a sense of *community.* For example, when all the science teachers in a school system have the common purpose of improving K–12 science education, and they cooperate in achieving that purpose, they develop a sense of community and collegiality.

Empowering people results in their taking greater *enjoyment* in their work. This is a fourth dimension. Outdated theories of motivation and leadership suggested that only rewarding and punishing individuals could achieve desired results. These theories recognized only the lower levels of Maslow's hierarchy of needs. Contemporary theories of motivation and leadership recognize that individuals have higher needs, including needing to know and understand, engaging in meaningful work, and developing personal and professional efficacy.

My theme of *responsibility* suggests a final dimension of empowerment. A critical aspect of empowerment is assuming the responsibilities for achieving the tasks. So, with empowerment, science teachers have the responsibility to improve science teaching in their classrooms. Teachers also need to understand that every time they request how-to activities, require supplemental materials from publishers, refuse to understand the purposes or history of science education, and resist information because it is not relevant to their "real world," they are relinquishing power and avoiding the responsibilities they have for improving science education.

REFORMING SCIENCE EDUCATION

So far, I have only made reference to contemporary reform. In this section, I discuss issues related to reform leadership and explore answers to the question: "What are the prospects for reforming science education?"

Educational Reform

One of the abiding characteristics of American education is its *popularization,* the goal of making education widely available in forms appropriate to a diverse body of students (Cremin, 1990). In science education, popularization is represented in the vision of scientific and technologic literacy for *all* students; politicization, in the goal of maintaining America's economic productivity, national defense, social harmony, physical health, and ecological balance. During the 1980s, a decade of reports, there developed a crescendo of criticisms of American schools, all with a particular perspective and unique recommendations for improvement. These policy statements exemplify the third identifiable reform since World War II (Cremin, 1990), all of which have been characterized by a major change in educational policies and little change in classroom practices. So, what are the prospects for educational reform in the 1990s?

Seymour Sarason's (1991) *The Predictable Failure of Educational Reform* does not leave one with a sense of optimism. Sarason informs us that unless we confront social, political, and organizational dimensions of reform, contemporary reform will fail. The difference between Sarason's point and science educators' views is that teachers believe reform consists of changing curricula, instruction, assessment, and educational technologies. Sarason, however, believes we need a systemic approach to reform: "In education the mistakes in conception and action have been many, and almost all of them derive from an inability to comprehend the nature of school systems" (p. 27). He also believes that we will have to alter the power relationship within the system.

> There is . . . a ubiquitous feature of complex human systems that should inform thinking and action in regard to educational reform. It is a feature that, if not taken seriously, invites failure. This is the fact that any social system that can be described in terms of power relationships. Power is distributed unequally among members of the system, and there is always a rationale for this unequal distribution of power. (p. 27)

Reform Leadership

James MacGregor Burns (1978) devoted an entire chapter of *Leadership* to reform leadership. In that chapter, he argued that the leadership of a reform movement, as opposed to that of a revolution, is particularly difficult and exacting. Reform leaders usually work within extant institutions; the leader must coordinate a large number of individuals with reform and nonreform goals of their own; and reform leadership implies moral leadership because proper means must be used to achieve the goals. This is not encouraging news for educational leaders.

Regarding political reform, Burns points out the tendency of members of the aristocracy to assume leadership. This is essentially what happened in the 1980s and 1990s, when policymakers assumed leadership via their reports; classroom teachers have not been included in, nor have they assumed, leadership in the recent history of educational reform. Burns (1978) described another troublesome problem of reform leadership:

> Because reform leaders typically accept the political and social structures within which they act, their reform efforts are inevitably compromised, and usually inhibited, by the tenacious inertia of existing institutions. (p. 200)

He concluded with this insight about reform leadership: "Reform is ever poised between the transforming and transactional—transforming in spirit and posture, transactional in process and results" (p. 200).

Given this perspective on reform leadership and the history of educational change, is there hope of achieving any reform in science education? I believe there is. According to Bass (1985), in times of dissatisfaction, distress, and pressure, transformational leadership is more likely to emerge and be effective. I think the potential for real reform is high. *America 2000* has helped all of us set our sights on the turn of the century and, compared to other reforms since World War II, the present reform is widely supported and professionally systemic. That is, the social support for change is strong and the reform integrates all aspects of education. It is not solely a reform of science education. However, my optimistic view assumes that science educators, and especially science teachers, will provide their fair share of leadership.

In this section, I presented a larger, systems view of leadership. In the next section, I take a more personal perspective and discuss the paradoxes of leadership.

PERSONAL EXPERIENCES WITH PARADOXES

Recently, my work at BSCS has involved two major curriculum projects, one for elementary school, entitled *Science for Life and Living: Inte-*

grating Science, Technology, and Health, and one for middle school, entitled *Science and Technology: Investigating Human Dimensions.* I have given many presentations at professional meetings and had numerous discussions with colleagues during my work on these projects. Questions about the programs always emerge, and some of those questions are particularly troublesome. I use them as examples of problems associated with leadership and resolving paradoxes.

The Problem of Incomplete Programs

After I have described the curriculum, someone inevitably asks how BSCS will change teacher education, science supervision, or national assessments, since these are also essential to effecting change in science education. Although I agree that other components of the system need to change, BSCS has received funding only to develop curriculum materials, not to change teacher education, science supervision, or national assessments. The tone of the question implies that because BSCS has not changed other aspects of the educational system, our work is somehow incomplete. Still, the question about how other aspects of the educational system would change has stimulated my thinking about distributed leadership, because I know that teacher educators, science supervisors, and evaluation experts also are reforming science education. In addition, there are systemic initiatives that by design are working with the science education system within states.

The Problem of Inadequate Programs

A secondary category of questions involves the congruence of a BSCS program with other, often contradictory, criteria, such as national reports, state frameworks, and local syllabi. Almost without fail, someone would ask how the curriculum aligns with national reports, such as *Science for All Americans* (American Association for the Advancement of Science [AAAS], 1989). Then a state science supervisor would ask how the curriculum would meet the requirements for adoption in his or her state, or a district science supervisor would compare the curriculum to his or her local syllabus. And finally a science teacher would express concerns about the applicability of the curriculum in the classroom because of unique characteristics of the students, the teachers, or the school. How, I wondered, was BSCS supposed to develop materials that accommodated diverse and often contradictory situations? For example, some science teachers expressed concerns about gifted and talented students, while others expected the program to meet the needs of at-risk students. No matter what we did, there was the suggestion that we should have done something different and that what we did do was inadequate.

The Problem of Inappropriate Programs

A third category of teacher criticism was that an overview of the contemporary reform or an analysis of national reports on science education was inappropriate because it did not include how-to activities they could use on Monday. The criticisms confused me because there was nothing in the title of my presentation to indicate that how-to activities for classes would, or should, be included. The presentations generally had titles such as "Trends and Issues" or "Policies in Science Education." Yet the critical comments suggested that any presentation on science education ought to have how-to lessons.

After a while, I realized that such criticism about apparently incomplete, inadequate, and inappropriate programs was also leveled at presentations by other science educators. Certain similarities connected all such criticized presentations: The individuals making them were in leadership positions; the presentations suggested some form of change in science education, such as new programs or teaching practices; and there was the implication that because the presenter had not answered all questions and solved all the problems of science education from national to local levels, the questioner could not incorporate the recommendations.

The criticisms had other characteristics. The critics demonstrated tacit understanding of science education as a system consisting of components such as curriculum, assessment, and professional development. The comments also indicated that diverse individuals in a variety of contexts made decisions about science education. Finally, the criticisms focused on potentially contradictory goals, for example, how one could develop a curriculum that was appropriate for both a national agenda and local mandates. Yet the presentations had addressed real problems; we do, for example, need new curriculum materials. The reform movement is replete with difficulties, but resolution of difficulties is one of the qualities of effective leaders.

My personal reflection on these situations led me to the themes of leadership and responsibility. The situations clearly indicate a tacit understanding by the teachers of the diversity and hierarchy within the system of science education, which leads to my notion of distributed leadership. I have come to see the issue of leadership and responsibility as at the heart of the reform of science education—more important than all the policy reports and probably more important than new science programs.

RESOLVING THE PARADOXES OF LEADERSHIP

Science educators who assume the responsibilities of leadership will inevitably confront persons, situations, and actions that contain apparently contradictory aspects. My earlier discussion of personal experiences initiated my interest in paradox and its relationship to leadership. In *The State of the Presidency,* Tom Cronin (1980) presented the general idea that there are paradoxes associated with leadership. For example, Americans demand powerful, popular presidential leadership, yet we are suspicious of strong, centralized leadership and the abuse of power. Any person assuming responsibility for leadership will have to resolve paradoxes; indeed, the effectiveness of a leader can be assessed by the way he or she resolves paradoxes.

Thinking Abstractly and Acting Concretely

Virtually every discussion of leadership emphasizes the importance of a vision. Leaders must develop for themselves and convey to their followers a new and unique image of the future. The leader's vision by its very nature is abstract, complex, and elaborate. In science education, it must incorporate many ideas about science, students, schools, teachers, and society.

Every discussion of leadership also stresses the vision's implementation. The leader must translate the abstract qualities of the vision into concrete plans for action. The process includes such things as identifying policies and procedures, clarifying the process of reform, assembling teams, providing professional development, creating support for the plan, and revising the plan based on feedback.

I place this paradox first because having a vision and a plan is critical to resolving the other paradoxes. Consider, for example, the numerous workshops that school districts provide each year. The relationship of many such workshops to some larger vision for the school district is only tangential. Or consider the lofty ideas of the new superintendent who has no plan for implementing them. First and foremost, effective leadership in science education requires that individuals think abstractly but act concretely.

Having Direction and Retaining Flexibility

As mentioned above, effective leadership requires a vision and a plan. Still, the leader cannot ignore suggestions and feedback from those with whom he or she is working. This paradox is like science teaching. One has to have a goal for the lesson; yet one also has to be flexible in responding to the various unexpected situations that occur in classrooms. We have all seen beginning science teachers lock themselves into a lesson plan and continue teaching long after they have lost control of the students. On the other hand, there are the science teachers who are so flexible that learning does not occur. The effective leader simultaneously has a direction and demonstrates flexibility. A variation on this paradox is planning for the whole system or project while also handling each person's requests.

Initiating Change and Maintaining Continuity

Science educators must respond to the calls for reform and the accompanying demands for change. Yet a school system or a particular school also needs continuity with the past. The enduring purposes of science education—contributing to personal development and fulfilling social aspirations through the knowledge and processes of science—bring continuity to the changing nature of assessment, teacher education, curriculum, and science teaching. Some science educators will inevitably perceive innovation in science education as disruptive; protectors of the status quo usually articulate this position. We need only remind them that the status quo is the reason for a decade of reports recommending educational reform. Balancing change with continuity results in a successful transformation of science education. You cannot have progress without change, but you can have change without chaos.

Encouraging Innovation and Sustaining Tradition

This paradox is similar to the last one, except that it centers on innovative programs and practices. There is a need for bold, innovative curricula that also accommodate old policies, mandates, and obsolete syllabi. I alluded to this paradox in my earlier discussion of personal experiences. If you present a new curriculum framework, you can immediately expect a question grounded in an old topic. For example, if you present an integrated science program, someone will ask where the unit on rocks and minerals is. A variation on this paradox is promoting risk taking while providing security.

Fulfilling a National Agenda and Incorporating Local Mandates

Every leader in science education should be aware of the national agenda of reports such as *America 2000, Science for All Americans* (AAAS, 1989), and National Standards for Science Education. They also should be aware of new science programs developed by The Biological Sciences Curriculum Study (BSCS), the Education Development Center (EDC),

Technical Education Research Centers (TERC), Lawrence Hall of Science (LHS), Education Systems Corporation (ESC), National Science Resources Center (NSRC), Life Lab, Stanford University, Florida State University, University of Hawaii, University of Northern Iowa, and the National Science Teachers Association (NSTA) among others. At the same time, leaders at the local level must incorporate state requirements and local mandates into school science programs. Whether you are adopting a national program or developing materials locally, there is a need to balance these priorities.

Achieving Your Goals and Enduring Criticism

An irony exists in successful leadership: The more successful you are in achieving your vision and implementing your plan for better science education, the more you will be subject to criticism, some of which will be unjust. Whether it is from deans and colleagues in the school of education, superintendents and parents in school districts, or science teachers within the school, with success comes criticism. Recall that Abraham Lincoln, a great leader, was severely criticized throughout his presidency. Lincoln's words from the Cooper Institute Address of February 27, 1860, provide encouragement.

> Neither let us be slandered from our duty by false accusations against us, nor frightened from it by menaces of destruction to the government, nor of dungeons to ourselves. Let us have faith that right makes might, and in that faith let us to the end dare to do our duty as we understand it. (p. 174)

Science educators have neither the weight of fighting a civil war nor the power of a president, but we do have an important mission, and doubtless there will be judgments, reviews, and claims of catastrophe. Leadership requires self-confidence and fortitude and a style of dealing with this paradox. Perhaps we could use Lincoln's example—ignore most of the criticism and respond with vigor to the important attacks. Most important, have courage and maintain a sense of humor (Phillips, 1992).

CONCLUSION

In this chapter, I discussed the themes of leadership and reform in science education. In particular, I developed the idea that leadership has to be distributed across the community of science educators, including teacher educators, science supervisors, curriculum developers, policymakers, researchers, and, very importantly, classroom science teachers. I define leadership as an individual's ability to work with others to improve teaching and learning and to accomplish the goal of scientific literacy. This definition applies to the majority of individuals in science education; it is intentionally vague as to the "others" that educators are leading. The "others" may be students, colleagues, administrators, community groups, professional organizations, or national committees. The burden of leadership and reform must be carried by all of us if we are going to successfully accomplish the broad goals of scientific literacy or the specific goals of *America 2000*.

For the person willing to assume responsibilities of leadership, the first question is: *Where do you begin?* Begin with some introspection and clarification of your personal goals. If personal goals center on securing a salary, obtaining prestige, evading stress, and avoiding criticism, then perhaps the leadership role is not for you. But if you understand the problems of leadership and still see your mission as contributing to a cause that transcends material welfare and contributes to personal and professional growth for yourself and others and to society's aspirations for education, you have probably already assumed a role as leader.

The second question is: *Whom are you leading?* Obviously, you have a first answer: my students, the science teachers in my district or state, my colleagues in science education, my community, and so on. However, based on my descriptions of leadership in this chapter, there is another answer that may be more subtle and elusive. I refer to the motives, needs, aspirations, and goals of potential followers, as individuals and as a group. There should be some congruence between your motives and goals and those of your followers. As I pointed out earlier, leadership will probably be a combination of the transactional and transformational, but you should base it on an accurate view of your followers' motives and goals. In the beginning, you may have to use persuasion and rewards, but these should give way to mutuality of goals based on higher levels of motivation and values.

The third question is: *Where are you going?* Articulation of your personal vision is a prerequisite to all that follows. You should be able to describe your vision for the classroom, school, state, or nation in a paragraph of clear, ordinary language. Writing the statement may provide you opportunities to elaborate the details of your vision. Being able to articulate your vision and elaborate on its details defines the difference between having a vision and stating a slogan.

How will you achieve your vision? The fourth question returns to the need for a plan. You should consider immediate, short-term (six months to one year) and long-term (one to three years) objectives and specific actions. In the course of implementing your plan, these objectives and actions will undoubtedly change. This is acceptable. Remember that improving science education is your goal, and changing the system will result in modified plans and actions. In a sense, the more effective your leadership, the more you will have to modify your plans.

What about obstacles and barriers? This question is difficult to answer because you cannot anticipate all the various obstacles. Having a clear vision and plan and using a systems model should help overcome the barriers.

You may see these concluding questions and discussions as a process you already use. I hope so. In a very real sense, that observation confirms my point of distributed leadership and supports the widespread assumption of the responsibility for leadership by science educators. If this is the case, then reforming science education by the year 2000, although a tremendous challenge, is an achievable vision.

■ ■ ■ ■ ■ ■ ■ ■
REFLECTIONS

In this concluding reflection, I present a view that mentions the past but concentrates on the present reform and I maintain personal and social perspectives, the themes of this book. Reflections sometimes result in exact images and at other times distort the actual image. I doubt that my reflections on the reform of science education present an exact picture, clear in all details. They are informed, after all, by my personal and social perspectives. Still, I hope that this reflection provides some insights and a view of the contemporary reform that stimulates debate and leads to action. I begin with a brief historical reflection on reform in education.

Since World War II, there have been at least three identifiable periods of educational reform. The first was in the decades immediately following the war and are represented by the writings and leadership of Jerome Bruner (1960) and James B. Conant (1959, 1964). For Conant, the central issue of reform was how to enhance the quality of education, especially for the academically talented. He centered his recommendations on high schools with high academic standards and a strong basic curriculum, including science. Even though science educators usually refer to Jerome Bruner's (1960) *The Process of Education* and his recommendation to design science programs using the structure of the discipline as central to reform in the 1960s, Conant's policies also contributed to the 1960s curriculum movement and influenced the orientation of National Science Foundation programs, particularly the emphasis on developing talented students for scientific careers.

In the 1970s, a new set of policies and recommendations supported a second period of educational reform. Reports such as *Youth: Transition to Adulthood* (Coleman, 1974), *The Reform of Secondary Education* (F. Brown, 1973), and *The Education of Adolescents* (Martin, 1974) characterized this reform. That high schools had become too large and impersonal was seen as the central problem. The proposed solution was to make high schools smaller or create subschools within them and to design curriculum experiences that allowed students more options.

The 1980s witnessed a third reform that is best symbolized by a report from the National Commission on Excellence in Education announcing that we were *A Nation at Risk* (1983). More than 300 reports followed, each with a unique set of recommendations for reform; but most of these reports only elaborated on the themes outlined in *A Nation at Risk:* The schools needed to emphasize the basics and assure literacy for all students, the school system needed to be changed, and school personnel required better professional experiences.

I briefly recapitulate this history to make two points. First, despite all of these reports in the last 50 years, there has been little actual reform in American education. We have significantly changed educational policies and we have moderately changed science programs, but we have not changed classroom practices. The rhetoric and the reality of reform do not conform. If we do not confront this issue, the contemporary reform will be recorded only as one of reports and recommendations, with no response. Second, the American public has placed tremendous burdens of responsibility on the schools: fundamental skills, critical thinking, basic knowledge, creativity, vocational preparation, ethical and moral character, desegregation and integration, health education, lifelong learning, safe driving, safe sex, the dangers of drugs, career awareness—and the list goes on. We must ask: "What can we reasonably expect of science education in the schools given all the other forms of education students experience?"

National support exists for reform of the educational system. The president and governors have presented the goal of U.S. science education being number one in the world by the year 2000. The public and the science education community have supported this goal and embraced the theme of scientific literacy as the concrete measure of that goal. Scientific and technologic literacy is the major purpose of K–12 science education, and this goal is for *all* students, not just those destined for careers in science and engineering.

The present curriculum for science education is generally inadequate to the challenge of achieving nationwide scientific and technologic literacy by the year 2000. Many are urging a review of school personnel and science programs. Increasing the scientific and technologic literacy of students requires several fundamental changes in science curricula. First, the sheer amount of information presented must be decreased, to be replaced by fewer major concepts and skills that are learned in some depth. Second, the rigid disciplinary boundaries of earth science, biology, chemistry, and physics should be softened, with greater emphasis placed on connections among the disciplines themselves and with areas generally thought to be outside the domain of school science, such as technology, mathematics, ethics, and social studies. Third, the quality of science programs and science teaching must improve. We can no longer afford to use programs and teach lessons that lack conceptual and procedural integrity and unity. Finally, the appropriateness of science programs simply requires review and revision. If we claim that we are teaching science for *all,* then we have to develop programs with an appropriate orientation for all students. This requires a perspective that one could characterize as emphasizing general, rather than specialized, education. The design of science and technology programs appropriate for all citizens requires us to look from society to science instead of from science to society. That is, we have to assume the perspective of individuals in society and ask what knowledge, values, and skills they should develop as citizens rather than beginning with the structure and content of scientific disciplines and assuming that future citizens need to know all the concepts, facts, and information that constitute biology, chemistry, physics, and the earth sciences before a connection can be made to a social problem, such as environmental pollution, land use, or ozone depletion.

Scientific and technologic literacy means more than understanding major concepts and processes of science and technology. Indeed, there is some need for citizens to understand science and technology as an integral part of our society. That is, science and technology are enterprises that shape, and are shaped by, human thought and social actions. Science educators refer to this as the science–technology–society (STS) theme. But the prevailing approach to STS centers on science-related social problems. I recommend expanding the STS theme to include some understanding of the nature and history of science and technology. There is recent, and substantial, support for this recommendation, although few supporting curriculum materials. Including the nature and history of science and technology provides opportunities to focus on topics that highlight the development of scientific ideas and show connections between fields such as science and social studies. Such an expanded perspective introduces students to the strategies and processes of science and technology, the role of theories and laws in science, the difference between science and technology and nonscience or pseudoscience, and, very importantly, the cultural heritage of science and technology.

The substantial body of research on learning should be the basis for making instruction more effective. Research on learning suggests that students learn by constructing their own meaning of the experiences they have, including those in classrooms, museums, camps, and other formal and informal educational settings. A constructivist approach requires a variety of methods and strategies for science instruction, and it demands a careful structuring of experiences so students have opportunities and time to develop scientific concepts, skills, and habits of mind.

Directly related to the implications of research on learning theory is the recommendation that science teaching should consist of experiences that exemplify the spirit, character, and nature of science and technology.

Students should begin study with questions about the natural world (science) and problems about humans adapting the environment (technology). They should be actively involved with the process of inquiry and problem solving. They should have opportunities to present their explanations for phenomena and solutions to problems, and to compare their explanations and solutions to those given by science and technology. They should have a chance to apply their understandings in new situations and evaluate the adequacy of their explanations. In short, the laboratory is an infrequent experience for students, but we should expect it to be a central part of students' experience in science education. Extensive use of the laboratory is consistent with my other recommendations.

In the next decade, the issue of equity must be addressed in science programs and by school personnel. Calls for scientific and technologic literacy assume the inclusion of *all* Americans. For the last several decades, science educators at all levels have discussed the importance of changing science programs to enhance opportunities for historically underrepresented groups. Justifications—if any other than the fundamental idea of equality is needed—include the supply of future scientists and engineers, changing demographics, and prerequisites for work. Research results, curricula recommendations, and practical suggestions are available to those developing science curricula and teaching science.

Science education in middle schools presents a special concern. Numerous reports and commissions have addressed the need for the reform of elementary and high school science education, but few have specifically recognized the emergence of middle schools in the 1980s. Notable exceptions include the Carnegie Corporation report (1989), *Turning Points: Preparing American Youth for the 21st Century,* and the California report (1987), *Caught in the Middle.* The movement toward establishing middle schools and phasing out junior high schools is a significant trend in education. Yet, thus far, the middle school reform has not thoroughly addressed particular issues of the subject-matter disciplines, in this case, science and technology. The contemporary reform must not allow science education to be the responsibility only of elementary and high school science programs.

Improving curricula and instruction by the year 2000 will be a hollow gesture without concomitant changes in assessment at all levels, from the local classroom to the National Assessment of Educational Progress. In general, the changes in assessment practices must reflect the changes described earlier for curricula and instruction. Potential incongruities—such as teaching fewer concepts in greater depth and then testing for numerous facts in fine detail—would undermine the reform of science education. New forms of assessment are available and being recommended by researchers, policymakers, and practitioners.

Science educators must view the reform of science education as part of the general reform of education. Approaching the improvement of science education simply by changing textbooks, buying new computers, or adding a few new hands-on activities simply will not work. The improvement of science education must include reconstruction of all K–12 science programs for all students, a staff development program, reform of science teacher preparation, and support for new approaches to science teaching by school administrators. This comprehensive and systemic recommendation is based on the research literature on implementation and on school change and restructuring.

In conclusion, writing reports about reforming education and actually reforming education are two very different activities. The former requires that a small group agree on a set of ideas, express them clearly, and justify them adequately. The latter requires that thousands of autonomous school districts and millions of school personnel change. Changes in science education are smaller instances of this large-scale educational reform. In order for changes to occur in science education, school personnel must change; and the most important factors influencing the possibility of changing school personnel are the purposes, policies, programs, and practices that are currently in place and supported by the school system. Thus we come to the essential role of leadership at all levels within the science education community.

In science education, leadership occurs in the classroom, school, state, and national levels and through a variety of individuals and institutions at these levels. In a large-scale system such as science education, the system's vitality is maintained and changed through what I characterize as distributed, but coordinated, leadership. The possibility that one person or one organization will lead all of science education reform is remote. Individuals in diverse sectors and at different levels must assume responsibility for leadership. This distribution of leadership sustains democratic ideals, but it complicates reform unless the leadership is a coordinated effort. This is why leaders must have a clear purpose, such as promoting science literacy for all students.

Leadership in science education also varies with educational contexts. Leadership is different in schools, school districts, states, organizations, and national groups. It also varies with individuals and situations. Individual science teachers have responsibility for accommodating local needs and unique classroom situations. Leadership at this grass-roots level also provides feedback for others within the system and energizes leadership at all levels.

The forms of leadership vary. Leadership may take the form of instructing an undergraduate methods course, doing research on science teaching, conducting staff development workshops, constructing assessment instruments, developing curriculum materials, or teaching science in formal and informal settings. In most cases, leadership in science education has to do with teams and groups who are working on some aspect of the reform. The teams that accomplish these varied aspects of reforming science education all share the tasks and responsibilities of leadership.

As science educators, we usually direct our attention to subsystems of science education, such as curriculum, instruction, assessment, teacher education, supervision, and research. Seldom do we recognize science education as an organized system. Any person providing leadership must simultaneously realize the scale, forms, contexts, and complexity of science education regardless of his or her position within a local school district or on a national committee.

If all individuals within the science education community recognize and accept their responsibility for change and improvement, then reform can be accomplished. For each person who assumes the responsibility of leadership, the burden on others is reduced and we have taken a constructive step toward reforming science education.

REFERENCES

Adler, M. (1982). *The paideia proposal: An educational manifesto.* New York: Macmillan.

Aikenhead, G. S. (1987). High school graduates' beliefs about science–technology–society. III. Characteristics and limitations of scientific knowledge. *Science Education, 71*(4), 459–487.

Aikenhead, G. S. (1988). An analysis of four ways of assessing student beliefs about STS topics. *Journal of Research in Science Teaching, 25*(8), 607–629.

Aikenhead, G. S., Fleming, R. W., & Ryan, A. G. (1987). High school graduates' beliefs about science–technology–society. I. Methods and issues in monitoring students views. *Science Education, 71*(2), 145–510.

Aldridge, W. G. (1989). *Essential changes in secondary school science: Scope, sequence, and coordination.* Washington, DC: National Science Teachers Association.

America 2000: An educational strategy. (1991). Washington, DC: U.S. Department of Education.

American Association for the Advancement of Science. (1989). *Science for all Americans.* Washington, DC: Author.

American Chemical Society (1988). *ChemCom: Chemistry in the community.* Dubuque, IA: Kendall/Hunt.

American Society of Zoologists. (1985). Science as a way of knowing II—Human ecology. *American Zoologist, 25,* 277–637.

Anderson, C. W. (1987). *Incorporating recent research on learning into the process of science curriculum development.* Colorado Springs, CO: Biological Sciences Curriculum Study.

Anderson, W. (1976). *A place of power: The American episode in human evolution.* Santa Monica, CA: Goodyear.

Bailey, L. H. (1903). *The nature study idea.* New York: Doubleday.

Bame, E. A., & Cummings, P. (1980). *Exploring technology.* Worcester, MA: Davis.

Barbour, I. G. (1980). *Technology, environment, and human values.* New York: Praeger.

Barman, D., Harshman, R., & Rusch, J. (1982). Attitudes of science and social studies teachers toward interdisciplinary instruction. *The American Biology Teacher, 44*(7), 421–426.

Barnard, J. D. (1971). COPES, the new elementary science program. *Science and Children, 9,* 9–11.

Barnett, B., Caffarella, S., Daresh, J., King, R., Nicholson, T., & Whitaker, K. (1992). A new slant on leadership preparation. *Educational Leadership, 49*(5), 72–75.

Barney, G. (1980). *The global 2000 report to the president: Entering the twenty-first century.* Washington, DC: U.S. Government Printing Office.

Barrow, L. H., & Germann, P. (1987). Acid rain education and its implications for curricular development: A teacher survey. *Science Education, 71*(1), 15–30.

Bass, B. (1985). *Leadership and performance beyond expectations.* New York: The Free Press.

Bell, D. (1972). *The coming of post-industrial society.* New York: Basic Books.

Bell, D. (1974, March). *Science education in post-industrial society.* Damon Lecture presented at the NSTA National Convention, Chicago.

Bell, D. (1976). *The cultural contradictions of capitalism.* New York: Basic Books.

Bennett, W. J. (1986). *First lessons: A report on elementary education in America.* Washington, DC: U.S. Department of Education.

Bennis, W. (1989). *Why leaders can't lead: The unconscious conspiracy continues.* San Francisco: Jossey-Bass.

Bennis, W., & Nanus, B. (1985). *Leaders: The strategies for taking change.* New York: Harper & Row.

Berliner, D. C. (1984). The half-full glass: A review of research on teaching. In P. Hosford (Ed.), *Using what we know about teaching* (pp. 51–77). Alexandria, VA: Association for Supervision and Curriculum Development.

Bertalanfy, L. von. (1986). *General systems theory.* New York: Braziller.

Biological Sciences Curriculum Study. (1978). An update: The human sciences program. *Biological Sciences Curriculum Study Journal, 1*(2), 5.

Biological Sciences Curriculum Study (BSCS). (1989). *New designs for elementary school science and health.* Dubuque, IA: Kendall/Hunt.

Biological Sciences Curriculum Study (BSCS). (1993). *Developing biological literacy.* Colorado Springs, CO: Author.

Biological Sciences Curriculum Study & The NETWORK, Inc. (1989). *Getting started in science: A blueprint for elementary school science education.* Washington, DC: The National Center for Improving Science Education.

Boschmann, H., Hendrix, J., & Mertens, T. (1978). Six state-adopted biology textbooks: Do they raise bioethical issues? *Hoosier Science Teacher, 4*(1), 10–13.

Botkin, J., Elmandjra, M., & Malitza, M. (1979). *No limits to learning.* New York: Pergamon.

Boulding, K. (1964). *The meaning of the 20th century.* New York: Harper & Row.

Boyer, E. L. (1983). *High school: A report on secondary education in America.* New York: Harper & Row.

Brandt, W. (1980). *North–South: A program for survival.* Cambridge, MA: MIT Press.

Bredderman, T. (1983). Effects of activity-based elementary science on student outcomes: A quantitative synthesis. *Review of Educational Research, 53,* 499–518.

Bronowski, J. (1973). *The ascent of man.* Boston: Little, Brown.

Brook, M. (1986, December–1987, January). Curriculum development from the constructive perspective. *Educational Leadership,* pp. 63–67.

Brown, F. (1973). *The reform of secondary education.* New York: McGraw-Hill.

Brown, L. R. (1981). *Building a sustainable society.* New York: Norton.

Brown, L. R., Chandler, W. U., Durning, A., Flavin, C., Heise, L., Jacobson, J.,

Postel, S., Shea, C. P., Starke, L., & Wolf, E. C. (1988). *State of the world: 1988*. New York: Norton.

Brown, L. R., Chandler, W. U., Flavin, C., Jacobson, J., Pollock, C., Postel, S., Starke, L., & Wolf, E. C. (1987). *State of the world: 1987*. New York: Norton.

Brown, L. R., Chandler, W. U., Flavin, C., Pollock, C., Postel, S., Starke, L., & Wolf, E. C. (1985). *State of the world: 1985*. New York: Norton.

Brown, L. R., Chandler, W. U., Flavin, C., Pollock, C., Postel, S., Starke, L., & Wolf, E. C. (1986). *State of the world: 1986*. New York: Norton.

Brown, L. R., Chandler, W. U., Flavin, C., Postel, S., Starke, L., & Wolf, E. C. (1984). *State of the world: 1984*. New York: Norton.

Brown, L. R., Durning, A., Flavin, C., French, H., Jacobson, J., Lowe, M., Postel, S., Renner, M., Starke, L., & Young, J. (1989). *State of the world: 1989*. New York: Norton.

Brown, L. R., Durning, A., Flavin, C., French, H., Jacobson, J., Lowe, M., Postel, S., Renner, M., Starke, L., & Young, J. (1990). *State of the world: 1990*. New York: Norton.

Brownell, H. (1903). Science teaching preparatory for the high school. *School Science and Mathematics, 2*(2), 253.

Bruner, J. (1960). *The process of education*. New York: Vintage.

Bruner, J. (1961). The act of discovery. *Harvard Educational Review, 30,* 21–32.

Bruner, J. (1971). The process of education revisited. *Phi Delta Kappan, 5*(1), 17–21.

Brunkhorst, H. K., & Yager, R. E. (1986). A new rationale for science education—1985. *School Science and Mathematics, 86*(5), 364–374.

Buber, M. (original work published 1922, 1970). *I and thou*. New York: Scribner's.

Burke, M. (1980). Perceived needs of elementary science teachers. *Science and Children 18*(2), 15–17.

Burns, J. M. (1978). *Leadership*. New York: Harper & Row.

Bybee, R. W. (1974). *Personalizing science teaching*. Washington, DC: National Science Teachers Association.

Bybee, R. W. (1975). *Implications of the philosophy and psychology of Abraham H. Maslow for science education in the United States*. Unpublished doctoral dissertation, New York University, New York.

Bybee, R. W. (1977a). The new transformation of science education. *Science Education, 61*(1), 85–97.

Bybee, R. W. (1977b). Toward a third century of science education. *The American Biology Teacher, 39*(6), 338–341, 357–361.

Bybee, R. W. (1979a). Science education and the emerging ecological society. *Science Education, 63*(1), 95–109.

Bybee, R. W. (1979b). Science education for an ecological society. *The American Biology Teacher, 41*(3), 154–163.

Bybee, R. W. (1982). Citizenship and science education. *The American Biology Teacher, 44*(6), 337–345.

Bybee, R. W. (1984a). Global problems and science education policy. In R. W.

Bybee, J. Carlson, & A. J. McCormack (Eds.), *Redesigning science and technology education* (pp. 60–75). Washington, DC: National Science Teachers Association.

Bybee, R. W. (1984b). *Human ecology: A perspective for biology education.* Monograph Series II. Reston, VA: National Association of Biology Teachers.

Bybee, R. W. (1985). The restoration of confidence in science and technology education. *School Science and Mathematics, 85*(2), 95–108.

Bybee, R. W. (1986a). Science–technology–society: An essential theme for science education. In R. James (Ed.), *Science–Technology–Society* (pp. 3–16).

Bybee, R. W. (1986b). The Sisyphean question in science education: What should the scientifically and technologically literate person know, value, and do—As a citizen? In R. W. Bybee (Ed.), *Science–Technology–Society 1985 NSTA Yearbook* (pp. 79–93). Washington, DC: National Science Teachers Association.

Bybee, R. W. (1987a). Science education and the science–technology–society (STS) theme. *Science Education, 71*(5), 667–683.

Bybee, R. W. (1987b). Teaching about science–technology–society (STS): Views of science educators in the United States. *School Science and Mathematics, 87*(4), 274–285.

Bybee, R. W. (1990). Science education and the Constitution. *The American Biology Teacher, 52*(7), 397–400.

Bybee, R. W. (1991). Science–technology–society in science curriculum: The policy–practice gap. *Theory into Practice, 30*(4), 294–302.

Bybee, R. W. (1993). Leadership, responsibility, and reform in science education. *The Science Educator 2,* (1), 1–9.

Bybee, R. W., & Bonnstetter, R. J. (1986). STS: What do teachers think? In R. W. Bybee (Ed.), *Science–Technology–Society* (pp. 117–127). Washington, DC: National Science Teachers Association.

Bybee, R. W., & Bonnstetter, R. J. (1987). What research says: Implementing the science–technology–society theme in science education: Perceptions of science teachers. *School Science and Mathematics, 87*(2), 144–182.

Bybee, R. W., Champagne, A. B., Loucks-Horsley, S., Raizen, S., & Kuerbis, P. J. (1989a). *Getting started in science: A blueprint for elementary school science education.* Washington, DC: The National Center for Improving Science Education.

Bybee, R. W., Buchwald, C. E., Crissman, S., Heil, D., & Kuerbis, P. J., Matsumoto, C., McInerney, J. D. (1989b). *Science and technology education for the elementary years: Frameworks for curriculum and instruction.* Washington, DC: The National Center for Improving Science Education.

Bybee, R. W., Crissman, S., Heil, D., & Kuerbis, P. J. Matsomoto, C., McInerney, J. D. (1990a). *Getting started in science: A blueprint for science education in the middle years.* Washington, DC: The National Center for Improving Science Education.

Bybee, R. W., Buchwald, C. E., Crissman, S., Heil, D. R. & Kuerbis, P. J. Matsumoto, C., McInerney, J. D. (1990b). *Science and technology education for the middle years: Frameworks for curriculum and instruction.* Washington, DC: The National Center for Improving Science Education.

Bybee, R. W., & Ellis, J. D. (1989). Informational technologies and science education. In *1988 Yearbook of the Association for the Education of Teachers in Science (AETS)*. Washington, DC: ERIC Clearinghouse for Science, Mathematics and Environmental Education.

Bybee, R. W., Harms, N., Ward, B., & Yager, R. (1980). Science, society, and science education. *Science Education, 64*(3), 375–377.

Bybee, R. W., Hurd, P. D., Kahle, J. B., & Yager, R. (1981). Human ecology: An approach to the science laboratory. *The American Biology Teacher, 43*(6), 304–311, 326.

Bybee, R. W., & Landes, N. M. (1988a). The science–technology–society (STS) theme in elementary school science. *Bulletin of Science, Technology, and Society, 8,* 573–579.

Bybee, R. W., & Landes, N. M. (1988b, May). What research says about the new science curricula . . . The Biological Sciences Curriculum Study (BSCS). *Science and Children, 25*(8), 36–37.

Bybee, R. W., & Landes, N. M. (1990). Science for life and living: An elementary school science program from the Biological Sciences Curriculum Study (BSCS). *The American Biology Teacher, 52*(2), 92–98.

Bybee, R. W., & Mau, T. (1986). Science and technology-related global problems: An international survey of science educators. *Journal of Research in Science Teaching, 23*(7), 599–618.

Bybee, R. W., & Najafi, K. (1986). Global problems and college education. *Journal of College Science Teaching, 15*(5), 443–447.

Bybee, R. W., & Sund, R. (1982). *Piaget for educators.* Columbus, OH: Merrill.

Bybee, R. W., & Welch, I. D. (1972). The third force—Humanistic psychology and science education. *The Science Teacher, 39*(8), 18–22.

California State Department of Education. (1987). *Caught in the middle.* Sacramento, CA: Author.

California Department of Education. (1990). *The California science framework.* Sacramento, CA: Author.

Campbell, J. (1968). *The hero with a thousand faces.* Princeton, NJ: Princeton University Press.

Carey, S. (1986). Cognitive science and science education. *American Psychologist, 41*(10), 1123–1130.

Carlson, J. (1986). *Factors influencing the adoption and implementation of STS themes.* Unpublished masters thesis, Kansas State University, Manhattan, KS.

Carnegie Council on Early Adolescents. (1989). *Turning points: Preparing American youth for the 21st century.* New York, NY: Carnegie Corporation of New York.

Carnegie Foundation for the Advancement of Teaching. (1988). *Report card on school reform: The teachers speak.* Princeton, NJ: The Carnegie Foundation.

Carson, R. (1962). *Silent spring.* Boston: Houghton Mifflin.

Champagne, A. B. (1987). *The psychological basis for a model of science instruction.* Colorado Springs, CO: Biological Sciences Curriculum Study.

Champagne, A., & Hornig, L. E. (1987). (Eds.). *Students and science learning.* Washington, DC: American Association for the Advancement of Science.

Champagne, A., & Klopfer, L. (1984). The cognitive perspective in science education. In R. W. Bybee, J. Carlson, & A. McCormack (Eds.), *Redesigning science and technology education* (pp. 90–103). Washington, DC: National Science Teachers Association.

Charles, C., & Samples, R. (Eds.). (1978). *Science and society: Knowing, teaching, and learning.* Washington, DC: National Council of Social Studies.

Christensen, J. (1989). *Global science: Energy, resources, environment* (3rd ed.). Dubuque, IA: Kendall/Hunt.

Churchman, C. W. (1979). *The systems approach.* New York: Delta.

Cleveland, H. (1977). Growth values and the quality of life. Unpublished notes for an Aspen Institute Seminar.

Coleman, J. (1974). *Youth: Transition to adulthood.* Chicago: University of Chicago Press.

Commission on the Reorganization of Secondary Education. (1918). *The cardinal principles of secondary education* (U.S. Bureau of Education Bulletin No. 35). Washington, DC: U.S. Bureau of Education.

Committee for Economic Development. (1985). *Investment in our children.* New York: Author.

Commoner, B. (1974). *The closing circle.* New York: Bantam.

Commoner, B. (1990). *Making peace with the planet.* New York: Pantheon.

Conant, J. B. (1959). *The American high school today.* New York, NY: McGraw-Hill.

Conant, J. (1964). *Shaping educational policy.* New York, NY: McGraw-Hill.

Counts, G. S. (1932). *Dare the school build a new social order?* New York: John Day.

Covey, S. (1990). *Principle centered leadership.* New York: Summit.

Craig, G. S. (1927). *Certain techniques used in developing a course of study in science for the Horace Mann Elementary School* (Teachers College Contributions of Education, No. 236). New York: Teachers College Press.

Cremin, L. (1964). *The transformation of the school.* New York: Vintage

Cremin, L. (1965). *The genius of American education.* New York: Vintage.

Cremin, L. (1976). *Public education.* New York: Basic Books.

Cremin, L. (1990). *Popular education and its discontents.* New York: Harper & Row.

Cronin, T. (1980). *The state of the presidency.* Boston: Little, Brown.

Cuomo, M. (1990). *Lincoln on democracy.* New York, NY: HarperCollins.

Daly, H. 1977). *Steady-state economics.* San Francisco: Freeman.

Derr, T. (1975). *Ecology and human needs.* Philadelphia: Westminster.

Dewey, J. (1938). *Experience and education.* New York: Collier.

Dewey, J. (1944). *Democracy and education.* New York: The Free Press.

Dewey, J. (1945). Method in science teaching. *General Science Quarterly, 1*(1), 3.

Dobzhansky, T. (1956). *The biological basis of human freedom.* New York: Columbia University Press.

Drucker, P. (1990). *Managing the nonprofit organization: Practices and principles.* New York: HarperCollins.

Dubos, R. (1972). *The god within*. New York: Scribner's.

Dubos, R. (1980). *The wooing of earth*. New York: Charles Scribner & Sons.

Duke, D. (1987). *School leadership and instructional improvement*. New York: Random House.

Dunn, S., & Larson, R. (1990). *Design technology: Children's engineering*. Bristol, PA: Falmer.

Eckholm, E. (1982). *Down to earth: Environment and human needs*. New York: Norton.

Education Commission of the States. (1976). NAEP *Newsletter, 9*(5), 4–7.

Educational Policies Commission. (1961). *The central purpose of American education*. Washington, DC: National Education Association.

Ehrlich, P. R. (1968). *Population bomb*. New York: Ballantine.

Fleming, R. W. (1987). High school graduates' beliefs about science–technology–society. II. The interaction among science, technology and society. *Science Education, 71*(2), 163–186.

Forrester, J. (1973). *World dynamics*. Cambridge, MA: Wright Allen.

Foster, J., Julyan, C. L., & Mokros, J. (1988). What research says about the new science curricula . . . The National Geographic Kids Network, Technical Education Research Centers (TERC). *Science and Children, 25*(8), 38–39.

Fromm, E. (1968). *The revolution of hope*. New York: Harper & Row.

Fromm, E. (1976). *To have or to be*. New York: Harper & Row.

Fullan, M. (1982). *The meaning of educational change*. New York: Teachers College Press.

Fuller, F. (1969). Concerns of teachers: A developmental model. *American Educational Research Journal, 6*(2), 207–226.

Gagne, R. M. (1967). *Science—A process approach: Purposes, accomplishments, expectations* (pp. 67–72). Washington, DC: American Association for the Advancement of Sciences (AAAS) Miscellaneous Publication.

Galbraith, J. (1977). *The age of uncertainty*. Boston: Houghton Mifflin.

Gardner, J. (1990). *On leadership*. New York: The Free Press.

Good, R., Herron, J. D., Lawson, A., & Renner, J. (1985a). The domain of science education. *Science Education, 69*(2), 139–141.

Good, R., Kromhout, R., Lawson, A., & Renner, J. (1985b, April). *Science education: Definitions and implications for research*. Paper presented at the annual meeting of the National Association for Research in Science Teaching, French Lick, IN.

Good, R., Renner, J., Lawson, A., & Herron, J. D. (1985c). Two views on science education. *Journal of College Science Teaching, 14*(3), 155.

Goodlad, J. (1979). *What schools are for*. Bloomington, IN: Phi Delta Kappa Educational Foundation.

Gould, J. (1987). *On the teaching of elementary science*. Brattleboro, VT: The Teachers Laboratory.

Hall, G., & Hord, S. (1987). *Change in schools: Facilitating the process*. Albany, NY: State University of New York Press.

Hamm, M., & Adams, D. (1987). *An analysis of global problems and issues in sixth and seventh grade science textbooks*. Columbus, OH: ERIC Clearinghouse.

Hardin, G. (1968). The tragedy of the commons. *Science, 162*(13), 1243–1248.

Harms, N. C., & Yager, R. E. (1981). (Eds.). *What research says to the science teacher,* (Vol. 3). Washington, DC: National Science Teachers Association.

Harte, J. (1989). Literacy, numeracy, and global ecology. In W. G. Rosen (Ed.), *High school biology: Today and tomorrow* (pp. 17–20). Washington, DC: National Academy Press.

Harvard Committee. (1945). *General education in a free society.* Cambridge, MA: Harvard University Press.

Heilbroner, R. (1974). *An inquiry into the human prospect.* New York: Norton.

Heiner, C. W., & Hendrix, W. R. (1980). *People create technology.* Worcester, MA: Davis.

Hines, L. (1973). *Environmental issues.* New York: Norton.

Hirsh, F. (1976). *Social limits to growth.* Cambridge, MA: Harvard University Press.

Hofstein, A., & Yager, R. (1982). Societal issues as organizers for science education in the 80s. *School Science and Mathematics, 82*(7), 539–547.

Howe, E. G. (1894). *Systematic science teaching.* New York: D. Appleton.

Hueftle, S., Rakow, S., & Welsh, W. (1983). *Images of science: A summary of results from the 1981–82 national assessment in science.* Minneapolis: Minnesota Research and Evaluation Center.

Hunter, G. W., & Knapp, R. (1932). Science objectives at the junior and senior high school level. *Science Education, 16*(5), 414.

Hurd, P. D. (1961). *Biology education in American schools 1890–1960* (Biological Sciences Curriculum Study Bulletin No. 1). Washington, DC: American Institute of Biological Scientists.

Hurd, P. D. (1969). *New directions in teaching secondary school science.* Chicago: Rand McNally.

Hurd, P. D. (1970). Scientific enlightenment for an age of science. *The Science Teacher, 37*(1), 13–14.

Hurd, P. D. (1972). Emerging perspectives in science teaching for the 1970's. *School Science and Mathematics, 72*(3), 22–28.

Hurd, P. D. (1975). Science, technology, and society: New goals for interdisciplinary science teaching. *The Science Teacher, 42,* 27–30.

Hurd, P. D. (1983, December/1984, January). Science education: The search for a new vision. *Educational Leadership,* pp. 20–22.

Hurd, P. D. (1984). *Reforming science education: The search for a new vision.* Washington, DC: Council for Basic Education.

Hurd, P. D. (1986). Perspectives for the reform of science education. *Phi Delta Kappan, 67*(5), 353–358.

Hurd, P. D. (1987). A nation reflects: The modernization of science education. *Bulletin of Science, Technology, and Society, 7,* 9–13.

Hurd, P. D. (1989). Problems and issues in science curriculum reform and implementation. In W. G. Rosen (Ed.), *High school biology: Today and tomorrow* (pp. 291–297). Washington, DC: National Academy Press.

Hurd, P. D., Bybee, R. W., Kahle, J., & Yager, R. (1980). Biology education in secondary schools of the United States. *The American Biology Teacher, 42*(7), 388–410.

Huxley, A. (1932). *Brave new world*. Garden City, NY: Doubleday.

Independent Commission on International Development Issues (ICIDI). (1983). *Common crisis, North-South: Cooperation for world recovery*. London: Pan Books.

International Union for the Conservation of Nature and Natural Resources (IUCN), World Wildlife Federation (WWF), and United Nations Environment Programme (UNEP). (1980). *World conservation strategy*. Gland, Switzerland.

Iozzi, L. A. (1987). *Science–technology–society: Preparing for tomorrow's world. A multidisciplinary approach to problem solving and critical thinking* (Teacher's guide). Longmont, CO: Sopris West.

Jackman, W. (1891). *Nature study for the common schools*. New York: Holt, Rinehart.

James, R., & Hord, S. (1988). Implementing elementary school science programs. *School Science and Mathematics, 88*(4), 315–334.

Jantsch, E. (1975). *Design for evolution*. New York: Braziller.

Jarcho, I. (1986). Curriculum approaches to teaching STS: A report on units, modules, and courses. In R. W. Bybee (Ed.), *Science-Technology-Society* (pp. 163–173). Washington, D.C.: National Science Teachers Association.

Jaus, H. (1981). Students tell teachers what they want from school. *Science and Children, 18*(6), 23.

Johnson, R. T., & Johnson, D. W. (1987). *Cooperative learning and the achievement and socialization crises in science and mathematics classrooms: Students and science learning*. Washington, DC: American Association for the Advancement of Science.

Johnson, R. T., Johnson, D. W., & Holubec, E. J. (1986a, June). *Circles of learning: Cooperation in the classroom* (rev. ed.). Edina, MN: Interaction Book Company.

Johnson, R. T., Johnson, D. W., & Stanne, M. B. (1986b). Comparison of computer-assisted cooperative, competitive, and individualistic learning. *American Educational Research Journal, 23*(3), 382–392.

Joyce, B., & Showers, B. (1988). *Student achievement through staff development*. New York: Longman.

Kennedy, J. F. (1961). Special message to a joint session of Congress, May 25, 1961. In *The Public Papers of the Presidents of U.S.* (pp. 404–405). Washington, DC: Superintendent of Documents.

Kluckhohn, F., & Strodtbeck, F. (1961). *Variations in value orientation*. Evanston, IL: Row Peterson.

Kohlberg, L. (1975). Moral education for a society in moral transition. *Educational Leadership, 30,* 46–54.

Kohlberg, L., & Turiel, E. (1971). Moral development and moral education. In G. Lesser (Ed.), *Psychology and educational practice* (pp. 46–54). Chicago: Scott, Foresman.

Kromhout, R., & Good, R. (1983). Beware of societal issues as organizers for science education. *School Science and Mathematics, 83*(8), 647–650.

Kuerbis, P. J. (1987). *Learning styles and elementary science*. Colorado Springs, CO: Biological Sciences Curriculum Study.

Kuhn, T. (1970). *The structure of scientific revolutions*. Chicago: University of Chicago Press.

Laszlo, E. (1972a). (Ed.). *The relevance of general systems theory*. New York: Braziller.

Laszlo, E. (1972b). *The systems view of the world*. New York: Braziller.

Laszlo, E. (1974). *A strategy for the future*. New York: Braziller.

Laszlo, E. (1977). *Goals for mankind*. New York: Dutton.

Leithwood, K. (1992). The move toward transformational leadership. *Educational Leadership, 49*(5), 8–12.

Leonard, G. (1973). *The transformation*. New York: Delta.

Leonard, G. (1974, June). How we will change. *Intellectual Digest*, pp. 50–58.

Levin, F. S., & Lindbeck, J. S. (1979). An analysis of selected biology textbooks for the treatment of controversial issues and biosocial problems. *Journal of Research in Science Teaching, 16*(3), 199–203.

Linn, M. C. (1987). *Designing science curricula for the information age*. Colorado Springs, CO: Biological Sciences Curriculum Study.

Locke, E., et al. (1991). *The essence of leadership*. New York: Lexington Books.

MacLeish, A. (1965, June 7). The revolt of the diminished man. *Saturday Review*, pp. 16–19, 61.

MacNeill, J. (1989). Strategies for sustainable economic development. *Scientific American, 261*(3), 154–165.

Managing planet earth [Special issue]. (1989). *Scientific American, 261*(3).

Markley, O. W. (1974). *Changing images of man*. Menlo Park, CA: Stanford Research Institute.

Martin, J. (1974). *The education of adolescents*. Washington, DC: U.S. Office of Education.

Maslow, A. H. (1959). (Ed.). *New knowledge in human values*. Chicago: Regnery.

Maslow, A. H. (1968). *Toward a psychology of being*. New York: Van Nostrand Reinhold.

Maslow, A. H. (1970). *Motivation and personality*. New York: Harper & Row.

Maslow, A. H. (1971). *The farther reaches of human nature*. New York: Harper & Row.

Matson, F. (1966). *The broken image: Man, science and society*. Garden City, NY: Anchor.

May, R. (1972). *Power and innocence*. New York: Norton.

May, R. (1977). *The meaning of anxiety*. New York: Norton.

McHale, J., & McHale, M. C. (1977). *Basic human needs: A framework for action*. Houston: The University of Houston Center for Integrative Studies.

McInerney, J. D. (1989). Human ecology: Restoring life to the biology curriculum. In W. G. Rosen (Ed.), *High school biology: Today and tomorrow* (pp. 117–130). Washington, DC: National Academy Press.

McKibben, B. (1989). *The end of nature*. New York: Random House.

Meadows, D. (1977). (Ed.). *Alternatives to growth*. Cambridge, MA: Ballinger.

Meadows, D., Meadows, D., Randers, J., & Behrens, W. (1972). *The limits to growth*. New York: The American Library.

Mesarovic, M., & Pestel, E. (1974). *Mankind at the turning point*. New York: Dutton.

Mitchell, D., & Tucker, S. (1992). Leadership as a way of thinking. *Educational Leadership, 49*(5), 30–35.

Mitchener, C. P., & Anderson, R. O. (1989). Teachers perspective: Developing and implementing an STS curriculum. *Journal of Research in Science Teaching, 26*(4), 351–369.

Mitman, A. L., Mergendoller, J. R., Marchman, V. A., & Packer, M. J. (1987). Instruction addressing the components of scientific literacy and its relation to student outcomes. *American Educational Research Journal, 24*(4), 611–633.

Moore, J. A. (1985). Science as a way of knowing—Human ecology II. *American Zoologist, 25,* 483–637.

Mullis, I., & Jenkins, L. (1988). *The science report card: Properties of failure . . . Elements of recovery.* Princeton, NJ: National Assessment of Educational Progress, Educational Testing Service.

Murnane, R., & Raizen, S. (1988). *Improving indicators of the quality of science and mathematics education in grades K–12.* Washington, DC: National Academy Press.

National Assessment of Educational Progress. (1978). *Science achievement in the schools: A summary of results from the 1976–77 national assessment of science.* Denver, CO: Education Commission of the States.

National Assessment of Educational Progress. (1979). *Attitudes toward science.* Denver, CO: Education Commission of the States.

National Assessment of Educational Progress. (1989). *Science objectives: 1990 assessment.* Princeton, NJ: Educational Testing Service.

National Commission on Excellence in Education. (1983). *A nation at risk: The imperative for educational reform.* Washington, DC: U.S. Department of Education.

National Research Council. (1990). *Fulfilling the promise: Biology education in the nation's schools.* Washington, DC: National Academy Press.

National Science Board. (1983). *Educating Americans for the twenty-first century.* Washington, DC: National Science Foundation.

National Science Foundation. (1965). *Science education in the schools of the United States* (Report to the House Subcommittee on Science Research and Development). Washington, DC: U.S. Government Printing Office.

National Science Teachers Association. (1982). *Science–technology–society: Science education for the 1980s.* Washington, DC: National Science Teachers Association.

National Society for the Study of Education. (1932). *A program for teaching science. 31st yearbook of the National Society for the Study of Education, part 1.* Bloomington, IN: Public School Publishing Company.

National Society for the Study of Education. (1960). *Rethinking science education. The 59th yearbook of the National Society for the Study of Education, part 1.* Chicago: University of Chicago Press.

Neuman, D. (1981). Elementary science for all children: An impossible dream or a reasonable goal? *Science and Children, 18*(6), 4–6.

Newmann, F. M. (1988). Can depth replace coverage in the high school curriculum? *Phi Delta Kappan, 69*(5), 345–348.

NSTA Curriculum Committee. (1964). *Theory into action*. Washington, DC: National Science Teachers Association.

NSTA Curriculum Committee. (1971). School science education for the 70s. *The Science Teacher, 38*(8),

Nyberg, D. (1990). Power, empowerment, and educational authority. In S. Jacobson & J. Conway (Eds.), *Educational leadership in an age of reform* (pp. 47–64). New York: Longman.

Odum, E. (1959). *Fundamentals of ecology*. Philadelphia: Saunders.

On the place of science in education. (1928). *School Science and Mathematics, 28,* 640–664.

Ophuls, E. (1977). *Ecology and the politics of scarcity*. San Francisco: Freeman.

Orwell, G. (1949). *1984*. New York: Harcourt Brace.

Passow, A. H. (1975). Once again: Reforming secondary education. *Teachers College Record, 77*(2), 161–187.

Penick, J. (1986). A brief look at some outstanding science, technology, and society programs. In R. W. Bybee (Ed.), *Science–technology–society* (pp. 159–161). Washington, DC: National Science Teachers Association.

Perelman, L. J. (1976). *The global mind: Beyond the limits to growth*. New York: Mason/Charter.

Peters, T. (1987). *Thriving on chaos*. New York: Harper & Row.

Phillips, D. T. (1992). *Lincoln on leadership*. New York: Warner.

Piaget, J. (1973). *To understand is to invent*. New York: Grossman.

Piaget, J., & Inhelder, B. (1969). *The psychology of the child*. New York: Basic Books.

Piel, E. J. (1981). Interaction of science, technology, and society in secondary schools. In N. Harms & R. E. Yager (Eds.), *What research says to the science teacher, 3* (94–112). Washington, DC: National Science Teachers Association.

Pirages, D. C. (1977a). (Ed.). *The sustainable society: Implications for limited growth*. New York: Praeger.

Pirages, D. C. (1977b, October). "Social Paradigms." Paper presented at Alternatives to Growth Conference, The Woodlands, Texas.

Pirages, D. C. (1978). *Global ecopolitics: The new context for international relations*. North Scituate, MA: Duxbury Press.

Pirages, D. C., & Ehrlich, P. R. (1974). *Ark II*. New York: Viking.

Platt, J. (1974, June). World transformation: Changes in belief systems. *The Futurist*, pp. 124–125.

Porter, A., & Brophy, J. (1988, May). Synthesis of research on good teaching: Insights from the work of the Institute for Research on Teaching. *Educational Leadership, 45*(8), 74–85.

Progressive Education Association. (1938). *Science in general education*. New York: Appleton–Century–Crofts.

Pugh, G. E. (1977). *The biological origin of human values*. New York: Basic Books.

Rakow, S., Welsh, W., & Hueftle, S. (1984). Student achievement in science: A comparison of national assessment results. *Science Education, 68*(5), 571–578.

Ramey, D. (1991). *Empowering leaders*. Kansas City: Sheed & Ward.

Rapoport, A. (1968). Foreword in W. F. Buckley (Ed.), *Modern systems research for the behavioral scientist*. Chicago: Aldine.

Ravitch, D. (1976). Education and economic depression. *New York University Education Quarterly, 7*(2), 9–15.

Renner, J. (1982). The power of purpose. *Science Education, 66*(5), 709–716.

Renshaw, E. (1976). *The end of progress*. North Scituate, MA: Duxbury Press.

Report of the Committee on Secondary School Science of the National Association for Research in Science Teaching. (1938). *Science Education, 22*(5), 223–233.

Rhoton, J. (1990). An investigation of science–technology–society education perceptions of secondary science teachers in Tennessee. *School Science and Mathematics, 90*(5), 383–395.

Roberts, D. A. (1982). Developing the concept of curriculum emphases in science education. *Science Education, 66*(2), 243–260.

Rogers, C. (1961). *On becoming a person*. Boston, MA: Houghton Mifflin.

Rokesch, M. (1973). *The nature of human values*. New York: The Free Press.

Rokesch, M. (1974). Change and stability of American value systems 1968–1971. *Public Opinion Quarterly, 38*(2), 222–238.

Rosen, W. G. (Ed.). (1989). *High school biology: Today and tomorrow*. Washington, DC: National Academy Press.

Rosenthal, D. (1984). Social issues in high school biology textbooks: 1963–1983. *Journal of Research in Science Teaching, 21*(8), 819–831.

Roy, R. (1985). The science/technology/society connection. *Curriculum Review, 24*(3), 12–16.

Rubba, P. (1987a). The current state of research in precollege STS education: A position paper. *Bulletin of Science, Technology, and Society, 7*, 248–252.

Rubba, P. (1987b). Perspectives on science–technology–society instruction. *School Science and Mathematics, 87*(3), 181–186.

Rubba, P. (1989). An investigation of the semantic meaning assigned to concepts affiliated with STS education and of STS instructional practices among a sample of exemplary science teachers. *Journal of Research in Science Teaching, 26*(8), 687–702.

Rubba, P., & Weisenmayer, R. L. (1988). Goals and competencies for precollege STS education: Recommendations based upon recent literature in environmental education. *Journal of Environmental Education, 19*(4), 38–44.

Ruckelshaus, W. D. (1989). Toward a sustainable world. *Scientific American, 261*(3), 166–174.

Russell, B. (1938). *Power: A new social analysis*. New York: Norton.

Rutherford, F. J. (1964). The role of inquiry in science teaching. *Journal of Research in Science Teaching, 2*, 80–84.

Rutherford, F. J. (1971). Preparing teachers for curriculum reform. *Science Education, 55*(4), 555–568.

Rutherford, F. J. (1972). A humanistic approach to science teaching. *NASSP Bulletin, 53*(361), 53–63.

Ryan, A. G. (1987). High school graduates' beliefs about science–technology–society. IV. The characteristics of scientists. *Science Education, 71*(4), 489–510.

Salk, J. (1973). *The survival of the wisest*. New York: Harper & Row.

Salk, J., & Salk, J. (1981). *World population and human values.* New York: Harper & Row.

Sandler, J. O., Worth, K., & Matsumoto, C. (1988). What research says about the new science curricula . . . The Education Development Center's (EDC) improving urban elementary science: A collaborative approach. *Science and Children, 25*(8), 37–38.

Sarason, S. (1991). *The predictable failure of educational reform.* San Francisco: Jossey-Bass.

Schneider, S. (1989). *Global warming.* San Francisco: Sierra Club Books.

Schwab, J. (1975, May/June). Learning community. *The Center Magazine,* pp. 30–44.

Scientific literacy [Special issue]. (1983, Spring). *Daedalus, 112*(2).

Sergiovanni, T. (1991). *Value-added leadership: How to get extraordinary performance in schools.* New York: Harcourt Brace Jovanovich.

Shen, B. (1975). Science literacy: The public need. *The Sciences, 24*(6), 27–28.

Shulman, L. (1986). Those who understand: Knowledge growth in teaching. *Educational Researcher, 15*(2), 4–14.

Shulman, L. (1987). Knowledge and teaching: Foundations of the new reform. *Harvard Educational Review, 57*(1), 1–22.

Shymansky, J., Kyle, W., Jr., & Alport, J. (1982). How effective were the hands-on science programs of yesterday? *Science and Children, 20*(3), 14–15.

Shymansky, J., Kyle, W., Jr., & Alport, J. (1983). The effects of new science curricula on student performance. *Journal of Research in Science Teaching, 20,* 387–404.

Simon, S., et al. (1972). *Value clarification: A handbook of practical strategies for teacher and student.* New York: Hart.

Spector, B. (1989). *Empowering teachers: Survival and development.* Dubuque, IA: Kendall/Hunt.

Starr, C., & Rudman, R. (1973). Parameters of technological growth. *Science, 182*(4), 358–364.

Staver, J., & Bay, M. (1987). Analysis of the project synthesis goal cluster orientation and inquiry emphasis of elementary science textbooks. *Journal of Research in Science Teaching, 24*(7), 629–641.

Stivers, R. (1976). *The sustainable society: Ethics and economic growth.* Philadelphia: Westminster Press.

Stubbs, H. (1983). Factors influencing introduction of a current environmental topic into the curriculum. *Dissertation Abstracts International, 43,* 3503-A. (Order No. DA8308131)

Task Force for Economic Growth. (1983). *Action for excellence.* Denver, CO: Education Commission of the States.

Thibodeau, F. R., & Field, H. H. (1984). (Eds.). *Sustaining tomorrow: A strategy for world conservation and development.* Hanover, NH: University Press of New England.

Thorsheim, H. (1986). Systems thinking: The positive influence of STS on educational motivation. In R. W. Bybee (Ed), *Science–technology–society.* Washington, DC: National Science Teachers Association.

Tinbergen, J. (1976). *Reshaping the international order.* New York: Dutton.

Tyler, R. (1962). Forces redirecting science teaching. In A. DeGrazin & D. Sohn (Eds.), *Revolution in teaching: New theory technology and curricula* (pp. 187–193). New York: Bantam.

Underhill, O. E. (1941). *The origins and development of elementary school science.* Chicago: Scott, Foresman.

U.S. Department of the Interior, Office of Education. (1932). *Instruction in science* (Bulletin No. 17, Monograph No. 22). Washington, DC: Author.

Wallace, A. F. C. (1956). Revitalization movements. *American Anthropologist, 58*(2), 264–281.

Wallace, A. F. C. (1972). Paradigmatic processes in cultural change. *American Anthropologist, 74*(3), 467–478.

Ward, B. (1979). *Progress for a small planet.* New York: Norton.

Ward, B., & Dubos, R. (1972). *Only one earth: The care and maintenance of a small planet.* New York: Norton.

Watson, R. G. (1983). Science education: A discipline? *Journal of Research in Science Teaching, 20*(3), 263–264.

Weiss, I. R. (1977). *Report of the 1977 national survey of science, mathematics, and social studies education.* Research Triangle Park, NC: Center for Educational Research and Evaluation.

Weiss, I. (1978). *Report of the 1977 national survey of science, mathematics, and social studies education.* Washington, DC: U.S. Government Printing Office.

Weiss, I. (1987). *Report of the 1985–86 national survey of science and mathematics education.* Research Triangle Park, NC: Research Triangle Institute.

Westmeyer, P. (1983). The nature of disciplines. *Journal of Research in Science Teaching, 20*(3), 265–270.

White, L. (1967). The historical roots of our ecological crisis. *Science, 155*(10), 1203–1207.

World Commission on Environment and Development. (1987). *Our common future.* New York: Oxford University Press.

Yager, R. (1983a). Defining science education as a discipline. *Journal of Research in Science Teaching, 20*(3), 261–262.

Yager, R. (1983b, December/1984, January). Toward new meaning for school science. *Educational Leadership, 41*(4), 12–18.

Yager, R. (1984). Defining the discipline of science education. *Science Education, 68*(1), 35–37.

Yager, R. (1985a). An alternate view. *Journal of College Science Teaching, 14*(3), 223–224.

Yager, R. (1985b). In defense of defining science education as the science/society interface. *Science Education, 69*(2), 143–144.

Yager, R. (1988a). *Assessing the impact of the Iowa Honors Workshop on science teachers and students: A final report for NSF.* Iowa City: University of Iowa, Science Education Center.

Yager, R. (1988b, February), s/T/s produced superior student performance. *Chautauqua Notes, 3*(5), 1–3.

Yager, R., Blunck, S., Binadji, A., McComas, W., & Penick, J. (1988). Assessing impact of s/T/s instruction in 4–9 science in five domains. Unpublished manuscript. Iowa City: University of Iowa, Science Education Center.

Yager, R., & Hofstein, A. (1984). Enlarging the boundaries of school science. *Curriculum Review, 23*(2), 144–146.

Yukl, G. (1989). *Leadership in organizations.* Englewood Cliffs, NJ: Prentice-Hall.

Zoller, U., Ebenezer, J., Morely, K., Paras, S., Sandberg, V., West, C., Wolthers, T., & Tan, S. (1990). Goal attainment in science–technology–society (s/t/s) education and reality: The case of British Columbia. *Science Education, 74*(1), 19–36.

Zoller, U., & Watson, F. (1974). Technology education for the non-science students in secondary school. *Science Education, 58*(1), 105–116.

INDEX

Adams, D., 137
Adler, Mortimer, 56, 66–67, 74
Aikenhead, Glen S., 56, 141–142
Alport, J., 105, 108
American Association for the Advancement
of Science (AAAS), 53, 101, 162, 165
American Chemical Society (ACS), 53, 122
American Society of Zoologists, 129
Anderson, C. W., 110
Anderson, R. O., 139
Anderson, W., 31

Bailey, Liberty Hyde, 9
Bame, E. A., 138
Barbour, Ian G., xiv, 2, 124
Barman, D., 138–139
Barnard, J. D., 12
Barnett, B., 149
Barney, G., 62, 121
Barrow, L. H., 139
Bass, Bernard, 154–155, 161
Bay, M., 106
Behrens, W., 18, 27, 39, 120, 123
Bell, Daniel, 17–18, 28, 32
Bennett, W. J., 104
Bennis, Warren, 149, 159
Berliner, D. C., 109
Bertalanfy, L. von, 113
Binadji, A., 141
Biological Sciences Curriculum Study
(BSCS), xiv, 13, 16, 45, 53, 61, 98,
101, 106–111, 113, 122, 151, 161–
162, 165–166
Blunck, S., 141
Bonnstetter, R. J., 95, 134, 138–139
Boschmann, H., 137
Botkin, J., 122
Boulding, Kenneth E., vii, 32
Boyer, Ernest L., 74, 106
Brandt, W., 121
Bredderman, T., 105, 108
Bronowski, Jacob, 31

Brook, M., 107
Brophy, J., 109
Brown, F., 169
Brown, Lester R., 120, 123–125
Brownell, H., 10
Bruner, Jerome, 12–13, 15, 169
Brunkhorst, H. K., 104
Buber, Martin, 50
Burke, M., 106
Burns, James MacGregor, 154–156, 160–
161
Bybee, Rodger W., x–xi, xiv, 13, 40, 53,
71n, 76, 84, 93–95, 104, 106, 119,
129–130, 133–140

California Science Framework, The, 53
Campbell, J., 22
Carey, S., 107, 110
Carlson, J., 139
Carnegie Council on Early Adolescents,
172
Carnegie Foundation for the Advancement
of Teaching, 112
Carson, Rachel, 25, 60–61, 119–120, 131
Champagne, Audrey B., xiv, 101, 103n,
107, 110
Charles, C., 134
Christensen, J., 122
Churchman, C. W., 113
Club of Rome, 27, 29, 39
Coleman, J., 169
Commission on the Reorganization of Sec-
ondary Education, 91, 93
Committee for Economic Development,
104
Commoner, Barry, 119, 121
Community, 127
educational goals of, 49–50
and reform of science education, 113–
114
Conant, James B., 169
Counts, George S., 17, 130–131

ABOUT THE AUTHOR

Rodger W. Bybee is associate director of the Biological Sciences Curriculum Study (BSCS), The Colorado College, Colorado Springs. He is also principal investigator for three new National Science Foundation programs: an elementary school program entitled *Science for Life and Living: Integrating Science, Technology, and Health,* a middle school program entitled *Middle School Science and Technology,* and a high school program entitled *Biological Sciences: A Human Approach.* He also chaired the curriculum and instruction study panels for the National Center for Improving Science Education. Prior to joining BSCS staff in 1985, Dr. Bybee was professor of education at Carleton College in Northfield, Minnesota. He received his Ph.D. degree in science education and psychology from New York University. He received his B.A. and M.A. from the University of Northern Colorado. He has taught science at the elementary, junior, and senior high school levels. Dr. Bybee has been active in education for more than 25 years. He is a member of the National Science Teachers Association, National Association of Biology Teachers, National Association of Research in Science Teaching, and the American Association for the Advancement of Science, among other organizations. Throughout his career, Dr. Bybee has written widely, publishing in both education and psychology. He is co-author of a leading textbook entitled *Becoming a Secondary School Science Teacher.* Over the years, he has received awards for Leader of American Education and Outstanding Educator in America, and in 1979 was Outstanding Science Educator of the year. In 1989, he was recognized as one of the 100 outstanding alumni in the history of the University of Northern Colorado.